THE DISCOUNT HOUSES IN LONDON

THE DISCOUNT HOUSES IN LONDON

Principles, Operations and Change

G. A. FLETCHER, B.A., M.Sc. (Econ.)

Lecturer in Economics
University of Liverpool

Macmillan of Canada/Maclean-Hunter Press

© G. A. Fletcher 1976

First published 1976 by
THE MACMILLAN PRESS LTD
London and Basingstoke

First published in North America 1976 by
THE MACMILLAN COMPANY OF CANADA LIMITED
70 Bond Street
Toronto M5B 1X3

ISBN : 0–7705–1502–9

Printed in Great Britain

To Kay

Contents

Preface

The most remarkable fact about the discount houses is that they have survived recognisably intact since their emergence in the early nineteenth century among the brokers and jobbers of the London bill market. The houses have changed in number, name and legal status but the principles upon which they have operated provide an unbroken link. Two powerful influences have combined to produce this result. First, the houses themselves have repeatedly demonstrated a tremendous capacity for changing their main line of business whenever events have threatened a familiar and settled way of life. Second, very potent forces working for the preservation of the discount houses have been in operation in the form of the Bank of England and the clearing banks. The policy goals of the authorities and their chosen methods of pursuing them and the resulting lack of competition which has characterised the later development of the British banking system, have provided interests in defence of which the Bank and the clearing banks have been prepared to ensure the maintenance of a stable, well-defined and regulated discount market based on the discount houses.

The pattern continued even when, in 1971, the degree of competition was radically increased and the techniques of control became more broadly based and therefore less discriminatory. Though the familiar guidelines of convention and direct regulation were swept away, the discount houses re-emerged undiminished. The apparent volte-face on the desirability of competition, however, once again represented a recognition by the central bank and the clearing banks of the new direction in which their interests lay. Rather than making the houses redundant the new scheme of Competition and Credit Control guaranteed them renewed importance, as the vital growth point at which the 'traditional' discount market and the newer 'parallel' or 'complementary' markets could the more readily fuse. For the purposes both of monetary control and of banking business, the two sets of markets which had been forced to grow apart had to be reunited.

Previous writers have attempted to provide justification for the continued existence of the discount houses on the grounds that they perform their functions cheaply and efficiently and that in their absence the functions would have to be performed by other institutions. In the present volume however it is argued that over the years the position occupied by the discount houses in the financial system, their business and the manner in which they have performed it, have all to a large extent been determined by the cartelised nature of the British banking system. There would, for example, have been no 'parallel' or 'complementary' system, separate from the 'traditional' money market, if the clearing banks and the discount houses had not been subject to such close regulation and restriction. The discount market would instead have developed and grown freely, as the discount houses sought new business and adapted their services to meet changing needs and to encompass innovation. Doubtless the pressures of competition would have caused houses to amalgamate more readily or even to withdraw from business but it is arguable that the discount market as a whole would have been a more dynamic, responsive and efficient institution. The advent of Competition and Credit Control in 1971 was important not only because it speeded the reunification of traditional and complementary markets but also because it dispelled the idea that the discount houses were inherently cosy and traditionalist institutions the existence of which commentators felt the need to justify.

The subject chosen for this book was the London discount houses, that is the member houses of the London Discount Market Association (L.D.M.A.), rather than the discount market or the money market. While the discount houses have always been at the centre of the bill market and the discount market, they have not comprised the whole of those markets (the houses are, however, the biggest constituents and the terms are often used synonymously). Similarly, although the houses have traditionally provided the most important part of a key money market in London, namely the call-money market, the London money market has always been – and especially so in recent years – a much broader and disaggregated system.

The British financial system has grown yearly more complex and, as the system has developed, definitions and classifications applied at a particular stage of development have rapidly become first strained and then out-dated by the march of events. However, the crucial distinction that has continued to identify the members of the L.D.M.A. and to separate them from those institutions carrying on an essentially similar type of business – the 'Silver Ring' of discount or running brokers – and from other banks and institutions is that the discount houses have from the early days of their development enjoyed the unique privilege of being able to obtain cash from the Bank of

England, in the Bank's role as 'lender of last resort' to the British banking system.

The chapters which follow provide a comprehensive and detailed examination of the operations and role of the discount houses and show how these have changed over time. The emphasis is very much on the period 1951–75, but prominence is also given to the principal features of the houses' earlier development and in particular to the forces and events which have been influential in shaping the character of the modern discount houses. Because of their long involvement in the implementation of monetary policy, the part played by the discount houses in the mechanism of monetary control forms a major theme of Parts Two and Three.

I have received the assistance of a number of people in the preparation of this volume and wish to record my gratitude to the following : Professor J. S. G. Wilson of Hull University, who first suggested a study of the London discount houses and who arranged some fruitful introductions; his colleague Mr P. S. Milne, for advice and encouragement in the early days; Messrs G. H. Bullard (Gillett Brothers Discount Co. Ltd), D. G. Campion (Seccombe, Marshall and Campion Ltd), M. J. B. Todhunter (Jessel, Toynbee and Co. Ltd), R. J. Petherbridge (Union Discount Company of London Ltd) and the staff of Clive Discount Co. Ltd, all of whom gave of their time to answer my questions and who kindly arranged for me to see the discount houses at work.

Professor J. S. G. Wilson and Professor J. E. Wadsworth (City University) commented on an earlier version of Parts Two and Three. Detailed criticisms of individual chapters were provided by Mr M. J. B. Todhunter (Chapters 13 and 14), Mr D. G. Campion (Chapter 14) and Mr G. H. Bullard (Chapter 7). Mr R. J. Petherbridge read and commented on the majority of the manuscript in an earlier draft. All have saved me from numerous errors and have improved the book at many points. I have also benefited from discussion with my colleague Dr W. A. Thomas. For the final version, the views expressed and the errors that remain, however, I alone am responsible.

For her skill in typing successive drafts of the manuscript my thanks go to Mrs P. Coster. My final debt is to my wife, for her patience and encouragement throughout. To her the book is dedicated.

University of Liverpool
July 1975

G. A. FLETCHER

Part One

THE EVOLUTION OF THE LONDON DISCOUNT HOUSES

1 The Origins of the Discount Houses in the Early Nineteenth Century

CHARACTERISTICS OF DISCOUNT HOUSES

There are certain features inherent in the business of present day discount houses that have characterised their operations throughout their history. In the first place, although some of them operate as brokers through subsidiaries, acting to bring together buyers and sellers, discount houses carry on their main business as principals, by the purchase and sale of financial claims on account of their own portfolios, deriving a profit from the difference between the price at which they buy and the price at which they sell. Secondly, to finance their portfolios, which will contain a variety of short and longer-term assets – for example, certificates of deposit, bills and bonds – discount houses borrow funds at very short term from a wide range of banks, non-bank financial intermediaries and other institutions. All but a very small fraction of funds are borrowed on a secured basis which means, in effect, that the institutions which have provided the funds hold as collateral the assets in which the houses have invested the borrowed money. For the lenders the discount houses provide a very important adjustment mechanism through which banks and other institutions can regulate their liquidity position on a daily basis.

Wilfred King, in his classic definition, clearly had these criteria in mind when he wrote in 1935 :

> The term [discount market] is usually restricted to the operations of certain specialised financial intermediaries which act as the connecting link between the ultimate borrowers and the ultimate lenders . . . Of these intermediaries, by far the most important are the London discount houses. These houses, unlike the few firms known as 'running brokers,' are not, however, pure agents. Their function is to make available for borrowers the funds of lenders, but

in so doing they interpose their own credit and responsibility between the ultimate parties. Instead of merely bringing together lenders and borrowers – the buyers and sellers of bills – and then leaving the parties to strike a bargain, as the true bill 'broker' would do, they take upon themselves the risk of the loans which they grant in buying bills. Moreover, they procure the funds which they lend by themselves borrowing, as principals and not as agents, from the banks and other houses which constitute the remaining part of the London Money Market. In other words they are *intermediary discounters* or dealers, who utilise borrowed money to finance the bills which they buy and hold.[1]

Although it captures the essential aspects of the discount houses' business, King's definition speaks only of operations in bills, whereas at the time he wrote the houses were sustaining themselves to a large extent on a diet of short-term bonds. The variety of assets to be found in portfolio broadened further after the Second World War and during the 1960s it came to include certificates of deposit denominated both in dollars and sterling, the bills and bonds of local authorities and foreign bills. In addition there were the longer-established bank acceptances and trade bills, British government Treasury bills and gilt-edged securities. On this basis, the discount houses could be categorised, in terms of a modern scheme of classification, as financial intermediaries which act partly as second degree intermediaries (i.e. taking funds from other financial intermediaries) in the deposit banking system and the secondary banking system, and held as assets a range of public and private sector direct debt.

The picture, however, is still incomplete until we add the unique feature which distinguishes the discount houses (the members of the London Discount Market Association) from the rest of the discount market, namely that they have the right to borrow at last resort from the Bank of England in amounts limited only by the price at which the Bank chooses to lend. The grant of the privilege *ipso facto* made the discount houses the linking mechanism through which the Bank should exercise its support and regulatory functions in relation to the banking system.

It was during the course of the nineteenth century that the key elements of the present system took on their modern form and the discount houses assumed their buffer role between the central bank and the rest of the banking system : (1) banking changed from its 'unit' form of organisation, dichotomised between London and country banks, into a branch-banking system, organised on joint stock principles, with nationwide coverage; (2) the market in which bills of exchange were discounted, which was originally composed of pure intermediary brokers and of bill jobbers, came increasingly to be dominated by bill dealers who carried portfolios of bills financed with funds borrowed from banks and others and who enjoyed rediscount facilities at the Bank; (3) London became an international rather than a merely domestic money market; (4) the Bank of England's position developed from that of competitive commercial banker with special roles (sole London note-issuer and banker to the government) and responsibilities (rough forms of credit management) to that of central bank with conscious mastery over the other elements of the financial system, adjusting credit conditions at home and managing the gold-payments position abroad.

THE ROOTS OF THE BUSINESS

Although the discount houses as we know them today only came into being in the nineteenth century their pedigree stretches back to the infancy of money dealing in England. In describing the modern discount house as an intermediary discounter, financing its book with surplus funds borrowed from the banks, Wilfred King stressed that in tracing its evolution it is to the 'agency' (financial intermediary) function that we must look rather than to the 'discounting' function. This conclusion is based on the arguments first that money dealers acting as pure intermediaries probably preceded the function of discounting in this country though not the bill of exchange itself; and secondly discounting tended to be financed from private or commercial rather than banking sources. It is not certain that the early money brokers actually carried on operations in bills of exchange but they did function in a manner essentially similar to that of the bill brokers of the early nineteenth century from which the discount houses developed.[2]

Financial intermediaries, called 'procurers' or 'inducers', were in business to arrange loans between merchants or between merchants and gentry in pre-Tudor times, and were subject to regulation by statute. One type of intermediary, the 'money scrivener' or 'scrivener', was originally in business to prepare the documents required by merchants and others in the course of trade. From the knowledge thus gained of his clients' needs and resources he was eventually able to provide an intermediary service, bringing together deficit and surplus units in return for commission or 'brokerage'.

The origins of the bill of exchange lay outside England and at first the supply of bills flowed from overseas trade. Because the money scriveners were concerned primarily with transactions that were domestic in origin it is probable that their bill business was not important until early in the seventeenth century when inland bills became more common. Thereafter the importance of their operations in arranging bill finance increased as the domestic use of bills grew. By the mid-eighteenth century the use of bills was 'really general' and finance was more easily raised by discounting such bills than by any other means. Money scriveners were well on the way to becoming bill brokers except that their business was largely limited to the arrangement of finance between individuals. The process of transformation was completed by the entry of financial institutions as lenders and borrowers in the bill market : these financial institutions were the country banks.

COUNTRY BANKING AND THE EMERGENCE OF BILL BROKERS

While banking was confined to London, surplus funds could usually be placed without the intermediation of a bill broker, but with the establishment of banks in the regions away from London the situation began to change fundamentally.[3] Because of the circumstances of economic life peculiar to each region in which the country banks became localised, bankers tended to find that they had either an excess of supply of deposits over demand for loans or excess of demand for loans over supply of deposits. The first country bankers tended to find themselves with surpluses and generally placed these funds in London through their agents (bankers) or with a bill broker. Later, the development of industry and the expansion of trade brought about the introduction of banking services in growth regions in which the perennial problem was that of a net shortage of funds for investment. Conditions were now conducive to the full development of the bill broking function, with brokers collecting bills from bankers in deficit (industrial) areas and arranging for their discount with bankers in surplus (London and agricultural) areas, in return for a commission.

It is important to notice that these institutions, from which the discount houses were to develop, would not have come into being on any scale if the country banks had not remained localised but had instead developed into larger institutions with networks of branches – as they were to do much later. The crucial factor that inhibited the amalgamation of unit banks and so encouraged the development of bill broking was the monopolistic position of the Bank of England deriving from Acts of 1708 and 1742. Banks having more than six partners were prohibited from issuing notes. Because prior to the 1830s note-issuing was practically synonymous with banking the country banks had either to remain small and therefore localised or to carry on banking as a supplement to some other form of business.

It was not until the late 1780s, 'perhaps a dozen years before the date (1800) suggested by Clapham', that the term bill broker came into use.[4] It was at this time that the rapid growth of country banking was accompanied by expansion in the number of bill brokers acting as intermediaries. In arranging bill finance between London and the country banks they worked alongside banker agents in the capital who were no longer adequate to handle all the (much increased) business.[5] Particularly rapid growth of bill broking came in the period of credit expansion which followed the Suspension of Cash Payments by the Bank in 1797 and continued until the end of the war. If evidence submitted to the Select Committee on the High Price of Bullion (1810) is taken as an indicator then by 1810 the bill-broker agency system was well established and widespread.[6] For a number of reasons, however, the importance of bill brokers in the London money market at this time can be over emphasised.[7] In the first place, London bankers made no decisive move away from bill transactions until after the 1825 crisis : during the Suspension they merely restricted the scope of their operations. When they chose to discount country bills they were better placed than the bill brokers, for in addition to their ordinary banking funds they might have discount accounts at the Bank – a facility not enjoyed by the bill brokers until after 1830. Secondly, the bill brokers were still only acting as agents and the call money that was taken was largely employed on the Stock Exchange, not in the bill market.[8] Thirdly, the bill agency system may not have been as widespread as the evidence of Thomas Richardson, the 'outstanding pioneer' of bill broking, might suggest, for his contacts were mainly in the north and east whereas there were large numbers of banks in the agricultural south and west. Furthermore, because his firm was probably a 'giant among the pigmies' the large size of his business cannot be taken as typical of contemporary bill broking. A further important point is that the preponderance of the bill brokers' business did not consist of forwarding for discount bills from the country banks but rather of bills from London merchants for discount at London banks. Finally, there was still no standard form for transacting business among the brokers, although by this time the practice had probably disappeared whereby country bankers (the lenders) might pay a commission to brokers to procure them bills (a practice usual among the banker agents). It was never followed by Thomas Richardson, who developed his business considerably by charging commission to the *borrower* for discounting his bills. Although at this time brokerage charges were variable the discount rates were fixed at the maximum possible under the Usury Laws.

Between 1810 and the crisis in 1825 bill broking grew steadily, with the increasing number of country banks on one hand and the merchants on the other. It was evidently a hazardous occupation that attracted many who had been unsuccessful in more established forms of financial business. While nineteen firms were listed in the 1813 directory, that for 1822–3 listed twenty-five firms. However, between 1811 and 1826 thirty-seven bill brokers failed – thirty-six of them after the war, of which the crisis period of 1825–6 claimed twelve.[9]

THE CRISIS OF 1825 AND ITS EFFECTS

(a) The crisis of 1825
Whereas in banking history the year 1844 was a climacteric, with the Bank Charter Act opening a new epoch, this was not the case for the London discount market. Influences of far greater consequence had emerged in the wake of the crisis of 1825. It has been argued that, discussed *in vacuo*, the history of discount business can be treated as a single narrative from 1825 to about 1858.[10] The results of the events of 1825 were important not only for the evolution of the discount houses but also for the way in which the constituent parts of the British financial system – London and country banks, bill brokers and the Bank of England – were made aware of their interdependence. There was recognition by the Bank of its duty towards the market in a supportive role. Discount houses recognisable in modern form appeared and took up their position between the Bank on the one side and the banks on the other.

The crisis itself was chiefly the result of widespread speculation brought on by a number of factors including, of crucial importance, 'improvident finance on the part of the country banks'.[11] As a background to this factor lay action by the central authorities. The issue of country bank notes of a denomination lower than five pounds was to have been forbidden as from 1823 but in 1822 it was decided that their issue would be allowed for a further ten years. In addition, the Bank had built up very large reserves against the expected reduction of the country circulation and in attempting to employ them it had (in December 1821) extended the currency of bills which it was prepared to discount from sixty-five to ninety-five days and (in June 1822) reduced its discount rate to 4 per cent. Consequently, credit was freely available for the finance of speculation in commodities, company formations and investment projects in South American republics. With the boom came rising prices and an unfavourable trend of the foreign exchanges, for against her imports Britain was exporting capital and exporting goods on credit. By the end of 1824 the gold reserves had fallen significantly and early in 1825 the Bank belatedly sought to bring about a contraction. During 1825 there was growing unease and alarm in the money market and towards the end of the the year country banks began to fail. Increasing strain was placed on London banks with the collapse of overseas trade and the demands of country correspondent banks. At the beginning of December Pole, Thornton and Co., agent for over forty banks, failed. In the panic that followed the Bank averted total breakdown by a reversal of policy that involved lending against all sorts of security deemed 'eventually' secure.[12] The panic was stopped, but many banks failed and confidence was badly shaken.

In framing the reforming legislation that soon followed, two considerations applied. First, the vulnerability of the banking system was seen to stem largely from the fact that outside London most banks were small, had only local experience and tended to have inadequate reserves. This situation, it was contended, was directly due to the Bank's monopoly of joint stock banking. Secondly, it was argued that the freedom granted to issue one pound notes was an inducement for country banks to over-issue. That similar difficulties had not arisen from the issue of one pound notes in Scotland was put down to the greater banking acumen of Scottish bankers.

In the first of two Acts of 1826 the issue of notes below five pounds denomination was forbidden. The second Act aimed to strengthen the organisation of the banking system and contained the following provisions. First, banks with any number of partners were to be allowed to operate outside a radius of sixty-five miles from London provided that they had no London office and that partners' liability was unlimited. Since restrictions on joint stock enterprises had been lifted by an Act of the previous year the way was clear for the establishment of joint stock banks outside London. Secondly, the Bank was to be allowed to open branches outside London.

(b) The end of rediscounting by London private banks
Apart from these two new lines of banking development produced by the second Act of 1826 the crisis itself stimulated a third line : a more immediate change which was to have a profound and lasting effect on the nature of bill market operations. This was the ending of rediscounting at the Bank of England by the London private banks.[18] Previously, their practice had been to employ resources to the full and to discount bills freely at the Bank whenever they had urgent need of cash. The pressures put upon them during the crisis had emphasised very strongly their dependence upon the policy and resources of the Bank, which had shown an unnerving hesitancy in giving aid. In place of the practice of rediscounting the London bankers began to

maintain liquid reserves of their own. These they held in Bank of England notes, balances at the Bank and, as a second line of defence, bills of exchange and money at call. The bill brokers benefited from the increased demand for bills but in the long run the greater benefit stemmed from the desire of the bankers to put out balances with them, at a rate of interest slightly below the yield on bills, which the brokers would guarantee to repay at call and could secure on bills of undoubted quality.

In the earliest years of the new system its scope was limited by the small number of suitable houses to which the bankers might lend. Already in the 1820s there were houses of influence and standing which were beginning to combine with their bill-broker intermediation function new business as bill dealers, financing a portfolio of bills on their own account with funds borrowed from bankers. In the years after 1825 bill dealing was encouraged by a steadily declining level of the market rate of interest, which after the crisis fell below the maximum permitted under the Usury Laws – 5 per cent. By June 1826 it was 4½ per cent and one year later 3 per cent. The differential permitted a profitable margin between the rate on borrowed funds and bill rate. In 1833 bills and notes with less than three months to run were made exempt from restrictions under the Usury Laws. By the end of the decade the largest brokers were held in sufficient regard for them to be accorded the right to discount bills at the Bank. The largest and most influential house in the market was Overend, Gurney and Co., which was doubtless the first broker to be favoured by London bankers with their call money and the first to possess discount facilities at the Bank (in November 1830). Gurneys were followed by Sanderson and Co., Alexander and James Bruce.

(c) Bill market rediscount facilities at the Bank
On the supply side of the call-money market bankers were encouraged to put out money in 'brokers' loans' by the guarantee of liquidity implicit in the right to borrow at 'last resort'. In this way the granting of discount accounts satisfied a vital prerequisite for bill dealing on any scale. In practical terms, the recognition by the Bank of its support role when financial stability was threatened by a failure of confidence meant that the Bank had to be ready to relieve a critical shortage of funds. When the London bankers ceased to rediscount, the Bank saw that the bill dealers, in providing a market for surplus funds from the bankers, would tend to be the point at which a general stringency would first show itself. This was the rationale on the Bank's side for the opening of discount facilities : the fourth major line of development produced by the crisis of 1825. In addition, the Bank had resolved, in

June of the previous year, that it would give help to all comers on approved security during the 'shuttings', that is the periods of one month prior to the quarterly payments of interest during which the Bank's stock registers were closed for the preparation of interest warrants, when a stringency generally developed. These arrangements proved to be of direct practical help to the banks and bill dealers.

Although these innovations made a formal beginning the Bank's last-resort function did not operate along modern lines until after 1890. It was only then finally made clear that the volume of central bank lending to the financial system via the discount houses would be limited only by the price at which it was offered. Indeed, between 1858 and 1890 the practice of rediscounting as a method of giving help in the last resort was suspended and the Bank was prepared only to make advances quarterly during the shuttings and special advances at its own discretion in times of need. The discontinuation of last-resort facilities to the discount houses was intended to encourage them to carry more funds of their own and to become less dependent on the Bank – though in fact the authorities continued to provide support in time of crisis. After 1890 there was clear recognition of the Bank's obligation to stand ready to give support by rediscounting or by making advances on approved security.

(d) The rise of joint stock banking

Because the Act of 1826 left the Bank of England with its London monopoly, joint stock banking began in the provinces (in the north of England), but after the Bank Charter Act of 1833 the banks were permitted in London provided they did not issue notes. The relative importance of the movement increased, as in addition to new joint stock enterprises, private banks were reduced in number through amalgamation with joint stock banks, or by reconstitution as joint stock banks, or through failure. Concomitantly with the development of joint stock banking there was rapid growth of bill broking, much of the new business being due to the practice of rediscounting by the provincial joint stock banks.[14] Wilfred King described joint stock banking as 'for close upon fifty years the most important single buttress of the original form of the bill market'. Later, however, it was to make the bill-broker agency system redundant. The reason is that whereas after 1825 banking was increasingly conducted on joint stock lines, it remained localised in unit banks which had continuing need of the agency services of the bill brokers. When at the century's end banking became more integrated through amalgamation and the growth of branch networks, the equalisation of the supply of credit could be undertaken by banks themselves and did not require the intermediation of the brokers.

Prior to 1825 the bill brokers had essentially acted as a supplement to the London agent bankers for the private country banks. The nature of joint stock banking made the brokers' functions indispensable. Private banking was based upon the issue of notes whereas joint stock banking was primarily deposit banking.[15] Therefore the new banks had to attract depositors from among individuals and institutions previously 'unbanked' or to bid the business away from the private banks by offering sufficiently attractive rates of interest on deposits. Competition between joint stock banks forced interest rates to high levels. Consequently, for business to remain profitable resources had to be kept fully employed. This meant that, apart from till money, virtually no cash reserves were kept and country joint stock bankers managed their liquidity positions by discounting bills through the London bill brokers, who benefited accordingly.

Moreover, whereas the country private bankers had discounted only at times of pressure, the joint stock bankers regarded rediscounting as an integral part of their operations – to be undertaken continuously. As competition for deposits pared profit margins there was a dangerous tendency for the joint stock banker to restore his income by increasing the volume of local bills discounted and correspondingly increasing his rediscounts through London. In such circumstances bankers were tempted to guarantee by their endorsement rather dubious paper.

In addition to the greater volume of rediscounts the bill brokers also benefited from the increasing popularity of the bill of exchange as a form of investment. Even before the exemption of bills of exchange from the provisions of the Usury Laws in 1835 there was a preference among the joint stock bankers for commercial bills over government securities because of their superior liquidity. Surplus balances, which in the case of banks in agricultural areas could be very substantial, were therefore held in the form of bills of exchange. For the brokers this meant that the demand for bills was increasing at the same time as the supply.

The rise of joint stock banking brought in its train another influence, of great importance for the emergence of a discount market dominated by bill dealers. This was the practice of leaving money at call with the brokers, a practice which was carried on by both London and provincial joint stock bankers, whereas rediscounting was an almost exclusively provincial phenomenon. By 1836 it was quite well developed, but until the 1850s it was of less importance to the joint stock banks than their rediscounting operations. Most probably it developed out of rediscounting, for provincial banks had arrangements with London brokers whereby the latter would undertake to accept agreed amounts of bills each week. When the banks' demand for cash fell below the value of bills discounted the surplus balances thus produced were left with the brokers at interest to be 'called' for when required. As the practice became established bankers were encouraged to lend all their surplus funds to the brokers, for they could get no return on deposits left with their London banker agents. In addition, call loans were seen as a viable alternative outlet at a time when Exchequer bills were becoming increasingly less attractive as investments after about 1835. Because they were exclusively deposit banks the London joint stock banks had lent call money from their beginning, but this source of loans was not of great importance in the early years, due to the small number of banks involved and the lack of serious competition for deposits.

(*a*) *Bank of England branches*

As compensation for the introduction of joint stock banking in the provinces the 1826 Act gave the Bank powers to open branches. Concentrating on centres conducive to the development of banking business, twelve branches had been established by 1834. Not only was the movement not injurious to the bill brokers' business, it proved to be positively beneficial. It was intended that the branches should improve the provision of banking facilities in the provinces and, of great importance, to extend the availability of Bank of England notes as the medium of exchange. Because of restrictions imposed on their mode of operation the latter was to be achieved by discounting bills. The branches' competitive rediscounting operations did not harm the brokers' business because of the fastidiously 'sound' rules by which the operations were governed: these had the effect of excluding most of the paper available for discount. Consequently, in order to strengthen their hand in the face of competitive private and joint stock note-issues, the Bank branches offered the relevant banks preferentially low terms for discount accommodation on condition that they substituted Bank of England notes for their own and replaced the issues by rediscounting at the branches. The net effect was to depress local rates in general, especially so as the branches did not impose a commission on discounts. There was, therefore, a tendency for paper to be diverted from the market in London, though the loss of business was probably not great because the note-issuing banks had not been large discounters.

While the brokers' agency business does not appear to have been harmed, the transmission of funds service that the branches set up gave great assistance to the London bill brokers. Previously, because of the cost and difficulty of arranging remittances many smaller traders and industrialists were cut off from the London market and had to make as good a bargain as they could with the local bankers. The Bank branches arranged at very small cost for the remittance of bills direct to the London bill brokers, who benefited from the extra business. The proceeds of the discount would be paid by the broker into the Bank for credit to the drawer at a particular branch. For the brokers the new links established with manufacturers were of lasting value.

THE ROLE OF THE BANK OF ENGLAND

In summary, the bill market as an agent for the domestic distribution of credit reached its zenith in terms of size and economic importance during the period of localised joint stock banking, between about 1830 and the 1860s or 1870s. Nevertheless, even in the early days of this period there appeared the bill dealers, who derived great stimulus from the bankers' need for a short-term loan market and who were eventually to replace the bill brokers as the characteristic constituent of the discount market. A vitally important factor that allowed the bill dealers to continue to exist and to supersede the brokers after the end of localised joint stock banking was the assumption by the Bank of its last-resort role, mentioned above.

The Bank's first step in the direction of money market control and regulation as central bank came with the recognition of its responsibility to 'equalise' the market during the shuttings. The second step was the provision of discount accounts for the principal operators in the discount market. The Bank reasoned that the position the brokers and dealers had assumed in the financial system would enable them to act as a channel through which the Bank could smoothly and almost automatically supply the necessary cash to the system – by the repayment of call loans and by fresh discounts. Consequently, it was not because of concern for the bill brokers as such that the Bank took this action but rather as a convenient facility for the exercise of last-resort functions. The Bank cannot have been aware that its action would promote the development of a call-money market that would ensure the continued existence of the discount market as a separate entity. Some members of the bill market, the brokers proper, did not need rediscount facilities, while others began to shape their whole mode of operations around them. One, certainly unlooked for, effect was that the rapidly growing discount houses contributed to the abuse of bill credit that became widespread over the following thirty years.

Another landmark in the development of the Bank's central banking role lay in the implementation of the Bank Charter Act of 1844, framed in the light of the excesses of bill finance and consequent crisis of the period 1836–9. Victory for the 'currency school' view meant that the problem of credit control by the Bank was to be viewed solely as a problem of currency control, that is control of the note issue.[16] Private note issues were limited and new banks of issue forbidden. The Bank's credit control operations became a much more mechanical process, as note issues were to fluctuate automatically with the size of the bullion holding. In dividing the Bank's ordinary banking business off from the function of note issue the Act gave the Bank freedom to carry on competitive banking like any private bank. The Bank immediately introduced a policy of aggressive discounting with a view to employing fully the resources of the Banking Department.

Despite the Bank's new policy – which had serious consequences in that it was a major cause of the crisis of 1847 – the discount market experienced a period of steady growth and prosperity. The main influences were those which had arisen earlier, namely the rapid expansion of joint stock banking coupled with an increase in domestic and overseas trade. Branch banking was in its infancy and remained localised so that what was essentially still a unit banking system had to handle a much greater amount of commercial transactions. Therefore, there was still a need for the equalising function of the bill market and the business of its members grew with the expansion of trade and a widening of the use of banking facilities. The Bank's new policy did not disadvantage the bill *brokers* for whether bills were to be discounted eventually with an ordinary commercial bank or with the Bank of England, the intermediation of a broker was still required. On the other hand the Bank's new operations were virtually the same as those of the discount houses and would have affected them severely had the total volume of business not increased at the same time. In a market in which many bankers did not wish their endorsements to be available for scrutiny by competitors the Bank could offer confidentiality, whereas discount houses had either to rediscount the paper they bought or to put it out as security on borrowed funds. Consequently, the Bank's discount rates, although higher, were still competitive.

Nevertheless, bill dealers prospered not only from the increase in discounts but also from the more and more popular practice of putting out money at call with them. Call loans became increasingly popular with bankers for the employment of surplus funds after investors' preferences had moved massively in favour of railway securities and away from the Exchequer bill market, leaving it 'thin' and consequently highly unstable and therefore unsuitable for short-term 'in-and-out' operations. In addition to these longer-term influences of bill market growth the immediate effect, paradoxically, of the Bank's commercial discounting business was directly and indirectly to stimulate a general increase in the demand for bill credit, which 'far surpassed the volume of actual bills withdrawn from the outside market into the Bank's own portfolio'.[17]

The Bank's policy of competitive discounting came to an end with the crisis of 1847. In the light of the official inquiries of 1848, it became clear that for the future the proper function of the Bank should be that of regulator of the market rather than competitive element within it. In turn, this meant that the Bank's discount rate would have to be kept not only in touch with market conditions as they developed but also effective as well—that is above market rate. In fact in normal times Bank rate was kept above the market rate, but at times of cash shortage when applications at the Bank to meet the deficiency increased, Bank rate was often below market rate. At such times, however, the eligibility rules for bills discountable at the Bank were stiffened. Furthermore, the Bank would no longer grant temporary loans at competitive rates. Instead the principle was established that the Bank would always be willing to give accommodation at a price (the published minimum), against approved security. However, in order to help the hard-pressed discount market and others during the shuttings the Bank introduced the practice of lending at a fixed margin below minimum rate.

Finally, on the state of development of the bill market at the mid-century, there were four large bill-dealing houses—Overend, Gurney and Co., Alexander and Company, Bruce, Buxton and Company and Sanderson and Company. Overend, Gurney was still the giant, the extent of whose business probably equalled that of the other houses combined. The deposits of the four houses at this time have been estimated at about £11 million. There were twenty-five other firms in the market classified as bill brokers, discount agents and discount brokers.[18]

2 Emergence of the Modern Framework, 1850-1913

INTRODUCTION

In the second half of the nineteenth century the financial sector of the British economy became subject to forces of change which were to alter it almost beyond recognition. The growth of international trade, in which Britain took full part, meant that banking and other financial institutions had to become responsive to and be involved in the conduct and finance of foreign trade and in the international movement of capital.

The business of the discount market, no longer confined to the broking and discounting of domestic bills, became increasingly involved with transactions in paper that arose from trade between Britain and foreign countries and between third-party countries alone. There grew up in London an 'acceptance business' whereby for a commission merchant banks would 'accept' (give their guarantee to) bills drawn for the finance of foreign trade. The bills would then be eligible for discount in the market at 'fine' (low) rates. At the repayment date the bills would be presented for payment to the acceptor who would then seek reimbursement from the client. By means of this mechanism the 'bill on London' rose to the status of an internationally accepted means of payment. However, not all of the foreign, as distinct from domestic, paper handled by the discount market arose from trade. As a parallel to the new means of payment that appeared for use in domestic transactions – the cheque coupled with the bank overdraft – the increasing use of the telegraph made possible the communication of interest rate differentials between financial centres and hence to a growing supply of foreign 'finance' bills drawn to effect the international movement of short-term capital. By the end of the century such bills had become the characteristic constituent of discount market business.

The organisation of financial business was transformed. The bank amalgamation movement which produced joint stock banks of large size with extensive branch networks was eventually able to perform the 'equalising of credit' function that had been the mainstay and justification of the bill brokers and dealers from the time of the widespread establishment of country banking. In the discount market, bill dealing based on call loans and with last-resort facilities freely enjoyed came to predominate and bill broking continued only as a function of secondary importance. In imitation of the banks, discount houses appeared organised as joint stock companies and having limited liability.

The second half of the century was also the period of the Bank of England's increasing recognition of its central banking role and of its struggle for mastery of the British monetary system, a mastery not finally secure until the decade before the First World War. The Bank's operations were increasingly of international importance. With the growth of the international economy gold became the medium of exchange and store of value in settlement of international transactions. In principle, by linking movements in each country's money supply to inflows and outflows of gold it was intended that a persistent imbalance between a country's imports and exports would be automatically adjusted via movements in the domestic price level. As central bank of the world's most advanced financial centre the Bank of England assumed a position of key importance in the control of the international gold standard.

For present purposes the evolution of the discount market down to 1914 can be dealt with by focusing attention on three topics: the withdrawal and subsequent reinstatement of rediscount facilities by the Bank; the formation of joint stock discount companies; the decline in the importance of inland bills of exchange as discount house assets.

BILL MARKET OVERCOMMITMENT AND THE WITHDRAWAL OF
REDISCOUNT FACILITIES

The 1850s were remarkable both as a period of enormous expansion of business in the bill market and of 'one of the most grave cycles of credit abuse which are to be found in the entire history of the market'.[1] Externally, free trade policies and improved means of communication and, internally, the spread of the railway system, stimulated industry and commerce. At the same time there were important gold discoveries in California and Australia. Partly as a result and partly as a cause of the growth of economic activity there was a concomitant increase in banking resources. For the members of the bill market the impact of these developments was felt in the form of an enormous expansion of their operations.

They benefited not only from the increase in the demand for and supply of bill credit but also from the fact that banking expansion was most pronounced among those banks which relied most upon the system of call money, that is the joint stock banks. There was also increasing use of the system by the private country banks. Because of the high rates that bankers were paying on their deposits there was a tendency to put out at call a higher proportion of total deposits with the discount houses and to demand from them a larger quantity of bills as investments. The transition of the discount market from bill broking to bill dealing was accelerated as bill brokers took advantage of the plentiful supply of funds to launch into bill dealing, taking a 'quick turn' on the difference between buying and selling prices. In this situation of expanding business there was a move by the larger houses to stimulate direct contacts in the provinces, so as to tap sources of supply of funds and demand for bill credit not mobilised by country bankers for remittance to the London market. In terms of the paper dealt in, there was more widespread use of the acceptance credit in the 1850s than ever before. Increasingly the transactions they financed were overseas rather than domestic in nature.

A measure of the strength of a discount house was the 'soundness' of the bills it carried in portfolio, i.e. the likelihood that they would be honoured when presented at maturity. The traditional skill of a bill dealer lay in his ability to judge the soundness of bills coming forward for discount, and the degree of soundness he would require would to some extent depend upon conditions in the money market. At times when money was cheap and relatively easy to obtain the increased demand for bills would cause the dealer to lower his standards somewhat. As soon as conditions tightened, however, all but the best bills would tend to be excluded. In addition, the demand for bill credit (supply of bills) would tend to be affected by the fluctuating rate of discount on bills. In the early 1850s the arrival of gold from the finds in California and Australia had the effect of expanding the supply of credit autonomously and of enforcing a severe depression of interest rates. In this situation, the confidence born of economic prosperity and general optimism produced an unprecedented tendency towards overcommitment and a readiness to countenance dubious paper. Finance bills proliferated and circumstances caused the discount houses to become over-reliant on loans that had to be repaid at call.

Discount houses of all types found themselves taking a far higher proportion of money at call than ever before and in circumstances that put them in a precarious state. On the one hand, because of their conventional business relationship they were forced to take massive sums from bankers whose deposits were increasing rapidly. Competi-

B

tion between the banks forced up the cost of deposits for which the
bankers expected a high rate at call and a good return on the bills that
they demanded as investments. At the same time there was an ever-
increasing outlet for funds with provincial bankers who were rediscounting excessively. As reliance on call money grew it would have
been proper for the discount houses to have increased their reserves
in the form of highly liquid bills and cash balances. Unfortunately,
competition between the banks for deposits and bills had the effect
of raising the cost of call money at the same time as it reduced the
yield on bills. Consequently, the gross profit on the houses' bill business
was too small to enable them to maintain adequate reserves. Thus they
were driven to meet temporary stringencies by rediscounting at the
Bank.

A higher frequency of resort to the Bank of England during the
early 1850s than previously was not in itself proof of commercial in-
discretion on the houses' part. Rather it flowed from the new dependence on call loans, disruption to liquidity flows engendered by external
influences and the imperfections of the London money market. Nevertheless overtrading did take place in the bill market. Because
Bank rate was at this time above market rate, it was not profitable to
finance bills on money borrowed from the Bank but it was considered
a speculative manœuvre to take on a volume of business in the form
of call loans and rediscounts out of all proportion to the extent of
capital resources and to gamble that if it became necessary to rediscount
at the Bank, the profits from overtrading would more than offset any
losses incurred through having to sell bills at a loss. Moreover, the
laxity of the Bank's eligibility rules for rediscounts was such as to
encourage overcommitment. However, it is possible to misjudge the
extent of credit abuse in the discount market if the yardstick employed
is the amount of rediscounting at the Bank. There had been growth in
total banking resources relative to those of the Bank, and even without
overtrading by the discount market rediscount applications would
have involved growing strain on the Bank's reserves. The Bank's judgement of bill market behaviour was based only on the absolute increase
in the amount of rediscount demands rather than their increase relative
to the growth of market turnover and underlying economic variables.
The consequences of this judgement for the discount houses were to
be serious.

Certainly the Bank was in an unfamiliar position. In the past it had
exercised a control based on vastly superior resources : now there
loomed the new problem of acting as a central bank with resources
which had by no means grown in proportion to its greatly extended
responsibilities. (The decline of the Bank's resources relative to those

of the banking system as a whole is examined below, pp. 30–1. If the crisis of 1857 had not occurred the Bank would no doubt have accommodated itself to the changed circumstances and developed more subtle techniques of control over the banking system. The crisis, however, forced the pace and the Bank struck at those institutions that had seemed *most immediately* to threaten its own security – namely the discount houses.

The course of the crisis need not be described here but it involved the Bank in giving assistance to the market on a massive scale, through loans and rediscounts, with consequent strain on the Bank's resources. Even before the 1858 Select Committee on the Operation of the Bank Act of 1844 had finished sitting the Bank announced that the right of bill brokers and discount houses to rediscounts and temporary advances would be discontinued, apart from quarterly advances during the shuttings which would be granted on the same conditions as applied to everyone else. The decision was controversial.

Certainly a case could be made for action to restrict the right of access to rediscounts of the discount houses and brokers on the grounds that without their active participation severe overtrading could not have occurred. There is support for the view, however, that the Bank acted only to safeguard what it saw at the time to be its own interest.[2] Moreover the rule contained a possible weakness that was recognised at the time : that while it was imposed in order to protect the Bank in times of crisis, it was at such times that the Bank would be duty bound to give aid to the system. Nevertheless, it could be argued that although in normal times the frequency of rediscounting was relatively low, restraint *prior* to the onset of a crisis would moderate the extent of discount market overtrading and so reduce the ultimate impact on the Bank's reserves. On the other hand, there was a danger that if the discount houses did not take bills offered they would be discounted direct by the banks.

The Bank's new rule seemed to envisage the discount houses providing their own liquidity through pursuit of a reserves policy analogous to that of the banks. It was pointed out, however, that discount houses were in principle intermediaries that gave security for all their borrowings and so could not both discharge their true functions and follow the same reserve policy as a bank. One final but most important point is that there were fears that if members of the discount market, whose money position merely reflected that of the market as a whole, were refused discounts, then that efficient and sensitive buffer mechanism would be destroyed, and in times of great pressure the banking and commercial world would discount direct at the Bank and the public would suffer.

One small source of comfort for the discount houses was that they were given time to readjust to the new conditions by the continuance of trade depression and consequent excess of supply over demand for loanable funds. The larger houses took asset 'reserves' in the form of consols and Exchequer bills and attempted to reduce their dependence on money at call by offering interest differentials so as to induce bankers to increase funds repayable at notice.[3] Houses large and small, in a course of action that has a very modern ring, sought to reduce the overall maturity of their portfolio by larger and more frequent sales to the banks.

Nevertheless, in pressures of 1859 and 1860 the full ramifications of the operation of the new rule were seen. Because it was widely known that the discount houses had been deprived of their discount accounts, direct commercial demands on the Bank increased out of all proportion. As soon as there was a hint of danger, market institutions sought to protect their own positions, which had the effect of raising short-term rates, immobilising funds and causing a loss of liquidity (in terms of marketability) of 'reserve assets' such as Exchequer bills and consols. The lesson was that, in fear of an impending pressure, the absence of normal last-resort facilities would cause vulnerable financial institutions to take action which would have most disruptive and costly effects on the commercial community at large.

Ultimately the Bank was to accept that if a strong discount market was necessary as a buffer in the monetary system and that discount market strength derived primarily from the soundness of the paper that it carried, then the Bank's efforts should be directed towards improving the quality of paper discounted. In this way control would be *qualitative*, that is the Bank would itself only discount bills of good standing and refuse to rediscount inferior paper presented by discount houses. The consequent improvement of the houses' portfolios would in turn influence the quality of paper demanded and supplied by the banks. In the meantime the severance of the discount houses from free day-to-day contact with the Bank was to have serious repercussions in the period after 1858.

JOINT STOCK DISCOUNT COMPANIES

Until 1856 the discount houses and bill brokers were organised on the legal basis of private partnerships with unlimited liability. That year, however, saw the formation of the National Discount Company Ltd, the first joint-stock discount house and one of the first limited liability companies. The National was followed in the next ten years by similar joint stock flotations, either of new foundation or of the incorporation of existing firms or reconstruction of failed companies. Overall, it was a decade that saw 'more important discount formations than any other' : the formations coming in two waves, of which the second began in late 1863.[4] Most disappeared within a period of between one to four years of incorporation. The most notorious failure was that of the old-established and market-dominating firm of Overend, Gurney and Co., which finally became a limited liability company in July 1865 only to collapse spectacularly amid scenes of 'wildest panic' ten months later (see below, p. 24). In the 1870s only the National and two other companies, both 'reconstruction' flotations of 1867, were still in existence.

Whereas the crises of 1847 and 1857 had led to important changes in the relationship between the Bank and the discount houses, the crisis of 1866 did not fundamentally alter the structure of the market. It did, however, bring about great changes in its membership. The decade prior to 1866 is of interest not so much because it led up to the destruction of the most famous discount house but because of the influences that brought about the introduction of discount companies and because it saw the beginnings of an increasing preoccupation of the discount market with the finance of overseas business.

The first stimulus towards the formation of discount companies was the demonstration effect stemming from the success of the joint stock banking movement, in the form of rapid increases in bank profits and the dividends paid on bank shares in the early fifties. The expansion of banking had been accompanied by the growth of bill dealing. It was perceived that a form of business that had provided the partners of the larger discount houses with huge personal fortunes could be an attractive form of investment for a public eager to pursue high dividends. An added inducement was provided by the fact that joint stock companies, apart from banks, could now enjoy limited liability status. The success with which the first companies got on to their feet in unpropitious circumstances and came intact through the crisis of 1857 encouraged further flotations, including some of an unsound and speculative character. However, the heavy losses incurred in the bill market in the leather trade crisis of 1860 led to the winding up of three companies leaving only the original company, the National, by the end of 1861. The confidence of the public and of company promoters was shaken. The inherent riskiness of the business and the Bank's no-rediscounting rule led to the belief that this form of enterprise was best left to the private firms and, indeed, no new promotions were seen until the second phase of discount company formations began in 1863.[5]

In the early 1860s, especially after 1862, the desire of the public for high dividends produced a boom in company flotations in commerce,

banking and finance, an exploitable situation for unscrupulous promoters, and an unprecedented wave of reckless speculation and financial
abuse. In order to produce the high dividends demanded, any form
of business was countenanced – however unsound – so long as it contained the promise of high profits. In the discount market, the managers
of the new discount companies, as a class of men, have been described
as 'incompetent, reckless, or actually fraudulent'.[6] Finding that conventional bill dealing was not as profitable as had been expected they
readily accepted high-yielding but unsound paper in large quantities
and began to combine profitable 'finance' business with their ordinary
discounting.[7]

In spite of a crop of company failures in late 1864 following months
of very high money rates (due to the effects of competition and an
external gold drain) the boom continued. In July 1865 Gurneys became
a public limited liability company, at a time when informed observers
had more than an inkling that the business of this firm, the name of
which had become a byword for strength and integrity, involved a
proportion of 'finance' paper that was too large for its safety. In fact,
Gurneys had become heavily committed in speculative and 'lock-up'
(illiquid) business of many kinds. Public confidence in the company
was undermined when enterprises with which Gurneys were known
to be involved – including one of a very similar name – began to fail.
As the value of the company's shares crashed, a massive 'run' by
depositors caused the firm to suspend payments. The crisis that followed
brought widespread failure in the financial system, a Bank rate of ten
per cent and suspension of the Bank Act.

Gurneys suffered the greatest disaster but of the five companies in
existence at the beginning of 1866 all, apart from the National, suffered
heavy loss. In 1867 only three companies remained – the National and
two 'reconstructions' of that year, the United Discount Corporation
and the General Credit and Discount Company of London. In 1885
the latter two companies merged to form the Union Discount Company
of London. In addition, many new private firms had been formed in
1866, 1867 and 1868 from the remains of failed 'boom' companies.
Consequently, by the mid-1880s there were about twenty private firms.
Increasingly the public's preference was for firms that published
accounts, so that in 1891 the biggest private firm, Alexanders, became
a limited liability company, although it did not become a public
company until 1911. With the incorporation of Alexanders the discount market took the general form – of three large limited companies
and twenty or so private firms – that existed until the First World
War. In 1894 the deposits of Union Discount exceeded those of National
and so made it the largest house in the market: a distinction held down

to the present day. Although the market's structure remained stable until 1914, its operations expanded greatly over the period. In the twenty-three years after 1890 the aggregate deposits of the three largest houses more than doubled.[8]

INTERNATIONAL FINANCE AND THE DECLINE OF THE INLAND BILL

The influence of the international economy had long been felt in the London money market through the links forged by individuals and institutions in the finance of foreign trade, investment in foreign enterprises and dealings in foreign securities. Because of the state of communications, however, external pressures generally made themselves felt only in times of crisis or when a particularly large discrepancy developed between conditions in different centres. There was no rapid and smooth adjustment to international interest-rate differentials. With the great expansion of world trade and finance in the 1860s, the concomitant increase in interdependence between countries soon made the leading money markets part of a larger international market. London's international connections were strengthened and widened, particularly in the 1860s and early 1870s when the City became the leading market for loans to foreign governments and also with the influx of foreign bankers, who took advantage of the native institutions' preoccupation with self-rehabilitation, following the crisis of 1866, to provide services which were in demand.[9] Foreign exchange rates began to be advised by cable regularly from about the time of the 1866 crisis. By 1877 commentators observed that the bill of exchange was being superseded as a means of remittance by telegraphic transfer and international coupons. Under the influence of these various factors London had by 1875 been made into a truly international market.

The growth of London's international operations and prestige brought costs in the shape of fluctuations in rates, sometimes sudden and violent, induced by events abroad. The operations of the discount houses had the effect of reinforcing this tendency. Because they paid interest on virtually the whole of their resources the houses had to keep them fully employed. In times of monetary ease they were not afraid to bid down yields on bills, so long as money rates moved down in step : in times of stringency they forced up the price of scarce money with equanimity, so long as bill yields rose in sympathy. The overall effect was to make the cost of money very elastic in response to small changes in the supply.

The increasingly international character of finance in general and the London market in particular had effects of fundamental importance on the nature of the discount houses' business. Gradually, the houses became engaged in the discount of paper that originated in external rather than internal transactions, so that Wilfred King could argue that 'by the close of the century, the market had become primarily an instrument of external finance and only secondarily one of domestic finance'. He further argued that whereas this change was in the first place brought about by the growth of the international economy in general and the expansion of world trade in primary products in particular, foreign trade '. . . would not have led to such a marked preponderance of "external" paper in Lombard Street had there not been a simultaneous decline in the importance of the internal bill'.

Following this line of thought it became customary to argue that at the same time as internal bills were on the wane the supply of foreign bills increased to fill the gap, so that the chief function of the London discount market became one of financing international trade. Recently, however, the whole question has been investigated afresh and the results obtained cast serious doubt on some of King's key propositions.[10]

The causal sequence advanced by King was relatively straightforward. The decline in the importance of the inland bill for the discount houses may have begun shortly after the crisis of 1857, although it did not become pronounced until the 1870s. At first it was brought about by a fall in country bank rediscounting, a practice that had been discredited in the 1857 crisis. In its place country banks were sustained by the growth of the banking habit and by their action to make bank deposit accounts a viable alternative form of personal investment. Reduced rediscounting by the banks did not necessarily mean that the total internal bill supply was reduced but it did reduce the amount sold in the discount market. The discount houses responded by establishing agencies in the provinces to compete for bills. This action provided some offset for a time but in the 1860s and 1870s new influences were at work to reduce the total quantity of internal bills in circulation. Of these new influences,

> By far the most important . . . was the bank amalgamation movement, bringing with it a great expansion of branch banking, and enabling many banks each to perform within its own organisation the 'equalising' function for which the bill market had previously been indispensable . . . After 1878 . . . the era of really large-scale banking began . . . Thus the spread of branch banks was accompanied in many trades by a gradual displacement of the internal bill by the 'open credit' system as the standard means of finance.[11]

Other factors that were simultaneously working to displace the internal bill included : the improved communications that moved goods to customers more quickly and so shortened credit terms; the increasing size of industrial undertakings that produced difficulties in checking the quality and ensuring the payment of customers' bills and so brought about a shift in favour of cash settlement or credit transfer (in any case payment by bill became unprofitable as business competition brought the introduction of a cash rebate scheme); the spread of banking facilities and of the banking habit that made bills redundant as a form of local currency.

It should be noted that King saw the decline of the internal bill, both in total use and in importance as a discount house asset, as taking the form of a 'comparatively slow tendency' until about 1890. It was then given a fillip by the repercussions of the Baring crisis, which accelerated the absorption of private banks, and by a prolonged easiness of monetary conditions in London that encouraged London banks to extend their operations into the provinces in order to take advantage of the more attractive interest rate conditions there. Although the fall-off in the use of domestic bills was widely recognised by 1900, neither the structure nor the prosperity of the discount market suffered severely. There were compensating factors at work, including the great expansion of external discounts, the continued demand from banks for tailored portfolios of bills and the growing availability to the market of British government Treasury bills, which had been introduced in 1877. Of these factors the external business was the most important, while Treasury bills provided only a partial offset to the decline in internal trade paper.

In the face of the accepted explanation S. Nishimura has revealed that what superficially appears as a simple transition of function and consequent substitution of one asset for another, all brought about by a straightforward main cause and several subsidiary causes, was in fact the outcome of a more complex interplay of several developments. His attack centred first upon the timing relationship between cause and effect in King's thesis.

The development of large-scale banks with balanced nationwide branch networks was largely the result of the bank amalgamation movement, which accelerated particularly in the 1890s. Prior to this decade there was no bank, apart from the National Provincial Bank, that was sufficiently developed to be 'capable of performing such functions as the transference of liquid funds from "agricultural" areas to industrial counties'. On the other hand, the estimated amount of bills drawn began to decline in 1873 and continued until 1894. Therefore, on the evidence, King was attempting to explain an 'effect' of the 1870s by a 'cause' that appeared twenty years later, in the 1890s.

With regard to movements in the supply of bills, Nishimura estimated that the heyday of inland bills lay in the decade up to 1873, after which date the amount declined until 1894 and never again reached its former peak. Moreover, foreign bills, which were strongly on the increase prior to 1873, *declined* after that date, hand in hand with inland bills though to a smaller extent. Consequently, a shortage developed in the market of both inland bills and foreign bills. After 1894 foreign bills recovered far more strongly than inland bills and reached their apogee in the first decade after 1900.[12]

Within the total of inland bills drawn, the decline in the volume of bills supplied to the London market was argued to have been a function of several variables. First, there was a decline in the average usance of inland bills. Secondly, the increase in the number of bank offices and the spread of the banking habit among the public caused the banks' (longer-term) deposits to increase more rapidly than discounts and advances. Prior to 1873 the ratio of discounts plus advances to deposits had been extremely high in industrial districts, indicating a level of demand for money which the local banks could not satisfy without relying on the London money market. Because they were in a dominant position *vis-à-vis* borrowers in industrial districts the banks could choose to lend on bills of exchange, which at the same time would serve them as liquid assets. With the decline in the ratio of discounts plus advances to deposits the banks could afford to hold more liquid assets other than bills and so were not bound to employ bills of exchange as their main lending medium. They were now able to hold their bills to maturity instead of rediscounting them in London, so reducing the supply to the brokers. Third, there was a general preference among the public for cash payment on the grounds of the greater flexibility in repayment of advances and the possibility of rebates.

Because the ratio of discounts plus advances to deposits had fallen there was a relative shift as between demand and supply in the money market, with a parallel shift of market strength in favour of borrowers. Consequently banks, in order to maintain profit margins, had to become more willing to lend by means of overdrafts. As overdraft lending became more widespread the need to resort to bill finance – and therefore the supply of bills – declined.

The influence of these developments extended to the way in which international trade was financed. As banks, including those abroad, became more liquid they were better able to provide their customers with overdraft facilities so that payment might be effected by cheque or telegraphic transfer. A comparison of the values of foreign trade and of foreign bills drawn gives support for this view, in that after the 1870s the amount of foreign bills drawn came to represent a declining proportion of foreign trade, despite a large increase in the amount of foreign bills.[13]

So far, the shift in the banks' portfolio from bills to overdrafts has been dealt with in terms of an increase in the supply of deposits. There were, in addition, important changes on the demand side of the money market. Prior to the 1870s the lack of speedy communications meant that the conduct of production and trade was subject to great uncertainty. Consequently, the merchant occupied a key position between producer and consumer in smoothing irregularities of supply and demand. This he did by maintaining inventories, which had to be financed by discounting large amounts of bills in the market. The technological revolution in communications and transport, by reducing the need to finance large inventories, also reduced the pressure of demand in the money market. This, in conjunction with the increase in the supply of deposits, enabled banks to lend in the form of overdrafts and so caused the supply of bills to decline.

After 1894 foreign bills recovered to a much greater extent than inland bills and came to dominate the market. In part, the increase can be attributed to the growth of the acceptance business in London as a centre for the finance of international trade. More importantly, however, as the world's money markets came to be connected by telegraph a large proportion of foreign bills were finance bills, drawn to take advantage of international interest-rate differentials.

EXPERIMENTS IN MONEY MARKET REGULATION

The formal exclusion of the discount houses from the privilege of re-discounting at the Bank was maintained from 1858 until 1890, though during this period the Bank in practice continued to provide last-resort facilities in time of pressure by means of advances.[14]

It has been said that the essence of central banking lies in the 'discretionary control of the monetary system'.[15] This had been precluded for the Bank of England by the Bank Charter Act of 1844 (the 'Bank Act'), which had provided a framework for monetary stability in terms of a currency based on gold, progressive restriction of private note issues leading to an eventual monopoly of issue by the Bank, with the role of the Bank made automatic by the observance of explicit rules. The strict separation of the Bank's functions into those of note issue and banking fostered the view that in its banking functions the Bank should be no different from any other bank. In general, the conditions created had the effect of precluding innovation in Bank rate technique and methods of credit control until the 1870s. Such changes as did take place seemed to be made on an *ad hoc* basis rather than as part of a conscious development policy. In day-to-day operations the Bank kept to the rule that Bank rate should follow market rate rather than lead it.

During the second half of the nineteenth century two developments were of particular importance for the Bank in its role as central bank, namely the continued growth of joint stock (deposit) banking and the increasingly international character of London as a financial centre. They had the effect of concentrating attention on the question of the nature and proper function of the Bank reserve both as regards regulation and support of the banking system and in the protection of sterling. There was one major crisis of interest, apart from that of 1866 (dealt with above) : the Baring crisis of 1890, in which the authorities were forced to take action to bolster confidence and prevent a potentially disastrous run on sterling. Unfortunately, the opening for reform thus presented was allowed to pass 'by a miserable conjunction of confusion over the problems involved, uncertain handling of the proposals, poor co-operation between bankers and the Bank of England, and political tensions'.[16]

The operations of the joint stock banks in 'banking' an ever-wider public had the effect of raising the popularity of bank accounts as substitutes for currency so that the mechanism by which the Bank Act sought to impose automatic checks on the money supply was increasingly undermined. Furthermore, as was mentioned above, the Bank was suffering a relative quantitative decline *vis-à-vis* the rest of the banking system.[17] Between 1844 and the mid-1870s the ratio of bank deposits to national money income, which had increased by about twenty per cent, probably rose from 1 : 6 to 1 : 2·5. Bank deposits rose from about nine times the Bank's non-bank private deposits and about twelve times its government deposits to thirty-three and seventy times respectively. Also the level of bankers' balances at the Bank often rose close to the level of the Banking Department's holdings of notes and gold coin. In the macro-economy the private sector gained at the expense of the public sector and correspondingly private-sector assets came increasingly to dominate the monetary system. With the reduction of the national debt after the Crimean War the proportion of the Bank's money market dealings involving public sector assets fell : to continue open market operations was therefore to appear to compete on an increasing scale in ordinary bill business and consequently to alienate the bankers.

Both the relative growth in size of the private sector banking system and the banking practices pursued within it posed serious problems for the Bank reserve. Because joint stock banking was deposit banking, intense competition for deposits meant that resources had to be kept fully employed. Therefore, cash holdings were kept to a minimum and bankers relied upon their cash balances at the Bank to meet an increased need for cash. In this way the Bank reserve was subject to potential pressure from an internal drain – of cash into circulation. The effect could be compounded by the adverse effect of competition on the balance of payments, bringing a possible outflow of gold. Moreover, in competing for bills of exchange, either directly or by increased lending to the discount houses, the banks could bring about a relative fall in London rates. Internationally this would reduce the demand for sterling to hold, while internally London assets would become less attractive for funds from the provinces, so that country banks would either suffer a loss of profitability or would be more prepared to accept higher yielding but more risky business.

Thus a many-branched threat to the Bank reserve would continue, because Bank rate followed market rate, until an excess demand for cash pushed up market rates and gave the opportunity for an increase in Bank rate. This, by increasing the demand for London bills, would work to restore the reserve by bringing gold to London while the reinforced rise in interest rates would act as a check to the expansion of banks' business.

Given this system, the most fruitful approach to the problem of control of banking activity seemed to lie in interest rate policy. From about 1860 a Bank rate policy was adopted that involved raising Bank rate in large steps and reducing it in small ones – so as to enforce a more powerful effect on the gold flow through influence on the demand for London bills. There was also, however, increasing preoccupation with the question of the proper size of reserves that should be held by banks and at the Bank of England. As time went by the reserves question came more and more to be concerned with the maintenance by the Bank of a gold hoard as a safeguard against massive panics, which might be brought on through the instability of the banking system at home or through runs of confidence against sterling abroad, or against the demands for gold in time of war.

Such a hoard would constitute excess reserves rather than function as part of the Bank's working portfolio, for bankers feared that because the Bank's attitude towards its central banking role appeared uncertain, the authorities might not be prepared to give support during a crisis in time to prevent a large-scale failure of banks. Indeed, in order to satisfy its shareholders the Bank might be led to neglect reserves in the pursuit of profit and in so doing contribute to a monetary pressure. Then, in its role as bankers' bank it would be free to exploit the conditions so created by giving assistance to the market on very profitable terms. On a more technical level, support for a policy of maintaining excess reserves stemmed from doubts about the efficacy of an interest rate policy by which a high Bank rate was supposed to rectify an external drain and a low one to stop a drain into circulation.

Throughout, there was confusion on the reserves question between the *external* problem of the need to protect sterling, which required international means of payment, and the *internal* problem of a panic demand for cash, which could be stopped by making sufficient supplies of legal tender available. Walter Bagehot, who continued to argue for the maintenance of substantial reserves, was both subject to and helped to prolong this confusion. However, he did see that so long as Bank rate merely followed market rate, the latter would be more important because it was the rate at which foreign bills could be discounted and therefore the rate that influenced money flows to and from London. Under these arrangements the Bank had not got command of the rate that had such great influence on the size of the Bank reserve. Therefore, Bank rate policy should work positively to influence market rates. In this respect innovation was hampered by the continuance of the 1858 rule, which had of course been introduced as a way of protecting the reserve by a policy of withdrawal from the market – just at a time when new avenues of influence were opening, in the form of deposit banking and the reserves bankers kept at the Bank.

In fact, by the mid-1870s the Bank had worked out a policy towards Bank rate and the Bank reserve which, though it was the Bank's, owed a great debt to the work of Bagehot. The 'Greene–Gibbs' policy (named after the Governor and Deputy Governor of the Bank) held that the size of the reserve kept by the Bank should be related to the nature of its liabilities and not (as argued by Bagehot) be fixed at some arbitrary level. In fulfilling its duty simply defined as being ready to meet its liabilities, the Bank would act to counter any weakness in the reserve by means of open market sales or by raising Bank rate. While it was accepted that the reserve could be exhausted in a crisis through internal or external drain the problem could be overcome by the combined tactics of lending freely at a suitably high level of Bank rate.

In 1874 a potential outflow of gold was dealt with by a rise in Bank rate at a time when the policy of following market rate would have indicated a fall. However, the new policy did little to endear the Bank to the market. Frequent fluctuations in Bank rate were not liked and because it was often above and in poor contact with market rate bankers and discount houses made little profit, for their deposit rates were rigidly linked to Bank rate while their earnings were based on market rate. Houses were tempted into risky paper and there was a culmination in the accommodation bill frauds of June 1875.[18] In

1878 it became known that in discounting for its own customers the Bank would in future not keep to its published rate but would choose a rate at or near market rate. This was interpreted by bankers as a move to return to cut-throat competition but in fact unless the Bank was to cease its discounting business altogether the only alternative would have been to make Bank rate itself a competitive rate. The real significance of the change was that the Bank recognised the continuing ineffectiveness of its published rate.

The Greene–Gibbs policy was continued in the 1880s together with some relaxation of the 1858 rule, but no real progress was achieved until 1890. In the early 1880s the Bank's command over the market was increased by the greater frequency of stringencies that derived from the increased activity of the Treasury in the market. In response to demand, the Bank began to grant advances outside the shuttings. In turn the bill market gradually came, as in the 1850s, to depend upon the Bank for help whenever a stringency made itself felt, and this reliance again led to overtrading. The rules were tightened in 1883 in the hope of urging moderation of competition so that Bank rate might be made more effective.

For a time the policy worked but aggressive competition among the banks soon drove rates down again. The Governor, William Lidderdale, attempted to strengthen the Bank's control of the market by regulating the availability of funds from sources over which it could attain influence.[19] In addition, steps were taken to increase the influence of the Bank in the money market. The first, in June 1890, was the reinstatement of the discount market's discount accounts and facilities for regular borrowing. The second was more controversial and involved increasing the Bank's contact with local bankers by means of transacting more business with them – either through co-operation or, if necessary, through competition.

With regard to the first, the new policy took effect in July 1890 when the Bank began to discount for its own customers at a rate below market rate. The discount market was allowed to discount bills (fifteen-day bills at not less than Bank rate) at the Bank later in the same month. Rules as to the eligibility of paper soon followed. From fifteen days, the tenor of bills was increased to thirty days in 1894, to three months in 1897 and to four months in 1910. In this way the Bank's influence in the money market was reinforced.

The year 1890 was also remarkable for the occurrence of the sort of (financial) crisis that had been foreseen as possible – even likely – for many years. The crisis occurred in November when Baring Brothers, leaders in merchant banking – particularly for Latin America – were threatened by a disastrous collapse in the value of securities they held as underwriters for Argentinian loans. The importance of the crisis lies in the way in which it was handled : for the first time the banks drew together under the acknowledged leadership of the Bank of England to meet a common danger posed by the virtual certainty of domestic panic if Barings' weakness were exposed. Rejecting the possibility of suspension of the Bank Act the Bank of England offered to support Barings, subject to an indemnity guarantee from leading City banks. The banks would collectively make good any loss incurred by the Bank in liquidating Barings' liabilities within a time limit of three years.

The experience of the crisis cannot be said to have fostered 'central banking', in the sense of discretionary control of the banking system, and the important plan for reform put forward by the Chancellor of the Exchequer (G. J. Goschen) was first mutilated and finally dropped altogether. Nevertheless, the crisis did emphasise the central problems to be solved. It also demonstrated dramatically the dependence of the monetary system on the central reserve and so promoted the eventual recognition of the Bank of England as central bank. Indirectly the crisis also contributed to the development of central banking through courses of action taken by bankers : first, the desire of the banks to strengthen themselves through amalgamation and branching concentrated control of the banks in London and so made any future co-operation a more simple business; secondly, the leading banks seemed to have increased their cash reserves and to have kept them stable.

3   The Effects of War and Depression, 1914-38

The four years of war from 1914 to 1918 provided a further important phase of development for the discount houses, because of the very marked and lasting effect that the circumstances of war had on their business and therefore on the functions they performed. International trade and finance, which had come to dominate the life of the market by 1913, were so disrupted and reduced in volume during the period of hostilities that they ceased to provide a sufficient livelihood for bill dealers and brokers. Through pure necessity the houses substituted on an increasing scale in their portfolios the public sector debt that was an indispensable product of war finance.

The war, for the London bill market, began with a crisis. It was caused by the inability of foreign debtors to remit payment in discharge of their liability on bills, mostly accepted by London acceptance houses and joint stock banks, which were outstanding in London. Immediately, the interdependent bill and money markets were threatened by the possibility of breakdown and heavy loss : acceptance houses and banks by default on their acceptances, banks and discount houses by sudden depreciation in value on their bill portfolios, and banks by the amount of money they had out at call with the discount houses. Then, the closure of the Stock Exchange increased the illiquid position of the banks, which were unable to sell bonds or call in loans from brokers, making them vulnerable to loss of confidence and a consequent 'run'. The banks continued to call from the discount houses, which resorted to the Bank and discounted heavily. High rates of discount were enforced with Bank rate rising from 3 per cent to 10 per cent. The Bank's reserve was quickly depleted and on 1 August the Bank Act was suspended. The next day a moratorium for bills of exchange was proclaimed that on the 6 August was made applicable to financial obligations in general. This had the effect of relieving pressure on the discount houses, both as regards the bills they had discounted and the call money outstanding from the banks.

Although the authorities' action had the effect of staving off the immediate danger, the problem of widespread default on foreign bills and the threat posed by the breakdown of the international payments system remained. It was decided that the government should accept liability for the bills and that the Bank of England would discount all approved bills accepted before 4 August at Bank rate, with any loss to the Bank on bills not eventually honoured to be met by the Exchequer. Subsequently a system of advances, repayable after the war, was introduced to enable acceptors to meet bills as they matured. Parallel government intervention in regard to loans outstanding on the Stock Exchange brought a new firmness in government security prices that enabled the market to be reopened at the beginning of 1915. Also, successful action in the foreign exchange market brought a more normal rate of exchange for sterling.

Although these measures did much to restore confidence at home and abroad, the problems posed by the natural wariness of acceptors in conditions of war and the physical difficulties of remittance remained. The overall effect of the crisis was to depress discount houses' business severely for some time. One estimate put the level of business in October 1914 at less than 5 per cent of the pre-crisis average.[1]

In terms of the scale of government borrowing the First World War was unprecedented.[2] For the year 1914–15 more than half of government expenditure had to be financed from sources other than revenue; for 1915–16 the proportion was more than 70 per cent. To help finance the massive borrowing requirement the government expanded the Treasury bill issue, so that the amount outstanding rose from around £15½ million in July 1914 to a staggering £1098 million in January 1919. Although for short periods, at the beginning and towards the end of the war, the bills were offered at the tender, they were mainly tap issues made available in limited amounts to banks and discount houses only, at fixed rates.

Bank rate was changed five times during the war but it had ceased to be effective as a regulatory device, with government expenditure being financed by Ways and Means advances whenever the market was unable to absorb more Treasury bills. The key rates now were the tap rate on Treasury bills, which the authorities kept stable for very long periods, and the closely regulated rate at which the clearing banks lent to the discount market. The government's rescue operation in 1914 had left the market highly liquid and this coupled with the shortage of bills produced a very low bill rate. Government policy on the other hand was to push up short-term rates, both to help the foreign balance and also to bring short-term rates into line with rates currently being offered to maximise the marketability of longer-term government debt. Consequently, the tap rate was raised during 1915 and 1916 to a peak of 5½ per cent, when Bank rate was at 6 per cent. During 1916 a system of financing was begun whereby clearing banks were required to make Special Deposits with the Bank, which on-lent them as Ways and Means advances to the government. The rate on Special Deposits was set at ½ per cent below, and was moved in step with, tap bill rate.

Once the initial crisis was over discount market business during the war was 'an easy life, and, in some ways, a profitable one'.[3] Not only was the rate at which the houses took money from the banks regulated by the authorities but so also was the rate at which they took up Treasury bills; the margin being sufficient for the houses to make a wholly acceptable level of profit. Bond business was less safe and pre-dictable. The pre-war tendency for bond yields to rise continued and houses were forced successively to reduce their holdings, taking losses in the process. In sum, the discount houses survived the disruption caused to their normal business by the effects of war, by becoming part of the government's machinery for war finance and dealing in public sector debt.[4]

For analytical convenience the period between the wars can be divided into two parts. The decade after 1919 was characterised by the prevalence of a belief, that became increasingly strained in the later years, that with the war safely over disruption and deprivation would have only temporarily to be endured before economic and social conditions returned to the 'normality' of pre-1914. Only with the great slump after 1929 and the final departure from gold in 1931 was the discount market forced fundamentally to reassess its position.

In the 1930s, economic and financial circumstances combined to subject the houses to a squeeze of unprecedented severity from which they were delivered only by the self-interested intervention of the Bank of England and the clearing banks. It was in this latter phase that the structure of the discount and money markets and the relationships between their constituent parts were moulded into the form familiar for a quarter of a century after 1945. As regards the direction followed by discount houses' business, throughout the inter-war period the houses' portfolios became increasingly dependent upon the supply of public sector debt.

THE RETURN TO THE GOLD STANDARD

The general longer-term goals of official post-war economic policy were provided by the recommendations contained in the *First Interim*

Report of the Cunliffe Committee in August 1918.⁵ The Committee
had been required to 'consider the various problems which will arise
in connexion with currency and the foreign exchanges during the
period of reconstruction and report upon the steps required to bring
about the restoration of normal conditions in due course.'

Following advice given by witnesses the Committee recommended
that 'the conditions necessary to the maintenance of an effective gold
standard should be restored without delay'. This conclusion was based
on the belief that the gold standard machinery was the only effective
remedy for an 'adverse balance of trade and an undue growth of
credit' and that in its absence an unchecked credit expansion would
bring about an external drain of gold which would threaten the
convertibility of the note issue and jeopardise the country's international
trade position. The conditions thought necessary for restoration included : budgetary policy which would obviate the need for government borrowing; the reinstatement of an effective Bank rate which
would operate to check a foreign drain of gold and the speculative expansion of credit; the limitation by law of the issue of fiduciary notes
and an end to the arrangement whereby deposits at the Bank
could be exchanged for legal tender currency without affecting the
reserve of the Banking Department.

The Report's recommendations evidently accorded with sentiment
generally and although there was no specific guidance on short-term
policy formation, the main implication of the Report was clear. If
an effective gold standard was to be restored at the old parity, with a
free market for gold, there would have to be some degree of general
deflation – the amount to be determined by economic conditions
abroad and particularly in the United States, which had already
returned to gold. The American exchange thus became the crucial
pointer for policy measures.⁶

It was necessary for the implementation of this policy that control
be restored over the financial situation at home. The government
deficit in the financial year 1918–19 stood at 65·5 per cent of total
expenditure and both the banking system and the public were in a
highly liquid state. Furthermore, with almost one-third of the national
debt due to mature in under five years, there was need for an active
debt policy. Finally, as described above, the structure of market
interest rates followed not Bank rate but the rate fixed by the government on tap Treasury bills.

During the next three years the government successfully converted
the budget deficit into a series of budget surpluses and the proportion
of short-term gilts was reduced from one-third to one-fifth. Banks'
cash and liquidity ratios were tightened and there was some reduction

in the money supply. The degree of deflation achieved by the end of 1922 is shown by the Board of Trade wholesale price index and the Ministry of Labour cost of living index, which stood at 64·5 per cent and 79·1 per cent respectively of their November 1918 levels and 48·0 per cent and 64·4 per cent respectively of the 1920 peak levels.

Restoration of Bank of England control over the domestic monetary system was also achieved in 1922. The fiduciary issue of currency notes had been limited in December 1919 and through a policy of adding Bank of England notes to the currency note reserve the actions of the Bank were made more responsive to the needs of the domestic credit situation which were thus transmitted via movements in the Bank's reserve.[7] In April 1922 the authorities again began to issue Treasury bills through the tender and with the virtual cessation of tap issues in July market forces were once more the prime determinants of money and bill market rates. This action also freed Bank rate, for previously an increase in Bank rate brought about a reduced demand for Treasury bills at the old tap rate, a shift in demand to commercial bills and a resort to inflationary Ways and Means advances from the Bank. In the summer of 1922, in a much strengthened position, the Bank began actively to regulate the market by means of open market operations in Treasury bills and by the year's end the authorities were able to begin to plan in detail for the implementation of Cunliffe's main recommendation.

Nevertheless 1923 was a year of waiting, for domestic considerations took priority and internationally uncertainty over war debts and reparations adversely affected the exchanges. The authorities resolved to delay until the expected inflation in the United States should decisively alter the exchanges in Britain's favour. By 1924 recovery from the 1920–2 slump was well advanced but the external position was still weak. On top of the effects of wartime inflation and fundamental weakening of the capital position both trade and invisible accounts of the current balance had deteriorated markedly in real terms. Also, in the domestic money and bill markets there were major changes compared with 1913 which had an important bearing on the international position. In 1913 the 'bill on London' was the prime source of finance for international trade and the value of Treasury bills outstanding represented only about 1 per cent of the value of commercial bills outstanding. The wartime interruption of trade allowed innovation in technically superior methods of finance so that, even taking into account price increases, the value of commercial bills outstanding was rarely above the pre-war level of £500 million. Moreover, the finance bill, which before the war had accounted for 60 per cent of the prime acceptances outstanding, ceased to predominate as the Bank of England tightened eligibility rules for rediscounting. On the other hand, the value of Treasury bills outstanding was between £425 million and £575 million.[8]

The decline of commercial bills both absolutely and as compared with Treasury bills had important implications for the conduct of monetary policy. Whereas before the war the total volume of bills in the market was largely a function of the level of business activity and the level of prices, after the war it became strongly influenced by the authorities' budgetary and debt management policies. Furthermore, commercial bills gave rise to a roughly proportionate volume of sterling deposits in London – both because acceptors had to carry working balances with their London acceptance houses and because those houses had to hold funds in anticipation of the maturity of their acceptances. The amount of the balances was reduced in line with the decline of the commercial bill.

Also, because the volume of finance bills drawn on London was highly interest-elastic compared with ordinary commercial acceptances (which were relatively interest-inelastic in supply) the decline of the finance bill carried implications for the transmission mechanism of monetary control. Previously it had been possible to ease pressure on the exchange rate by raising Bank rate, which worked partly by reducing the volume of finance bills drawn relative to maturities and partly by attracting funds from abroad. In the new conditions Bank rate policy had to be more vigorously employed, for in the absence of an appropriate fall in the demand for bill finance the mechanism had to rely more heavily on the attraction of funds to London.

The Bank of England had established greater moral control over the market through the close relationship forged in wartime and now had the additional weapon of open market operations in Treasury bills to make Bank rate effective. Nevertheless, in the face of the changes described above and given the large size of the floating debt and the active management it required, the Bank's freedom to operate was significantly restrained. Furthermore, the control of events in London was made increasingly difficult by the rise to importance of New York as an international financial centre. The authorities were constrained to impose credit policies to deal with situations induced primarily by the day-to-day financing operations of, or changes in the relative attraction for deposits of, the New York money markets.

The debate over the issue of a return to gold and the circumstances leading to the decision to go ahead at the pre-war parity are matters beyond the scope of this book though they have been most competently dealt with elsewhere.[9] Suffice it to say that from a level of $4.43 in March 1922 the sterling–dollar exchange rose to $4.78 at the beginning of 1925, interim fluctuations being determined primarily by the relative movements of interest rates in London and New York. Between July 1923 when Bank Rate was raised to 4 per cent and the return to gold on 28 April 1925, the Bank operated to force market rates closer to Bank rate, which was raised again to 5 per cent in March 1925. Increasing sensitiveness to the problem of unemployment at home made the authorities reluctant to raise Bank rate too far in support of the pound, the exchanges being strengthened rather by pushing up the market rate of discount.[10]

BILL BUSINESS IN THE POST-WAR WORLD

As the authorities strove to return the economy to 'normality' the discount houses carried on a species of business very similar to that of wartime, waiting hopefully for a restoration of international trade and with it a new flowering of the 'bill on London'. This was the expectation that characterised the 1920s: it was only in the 1930s that the houses sought for an alternative in a revival of the inland bill.[11]

A reduced supply of bills after the war coincided with conditions of increased demand. The trend among foreign central banks in the twenties was towards holding international reserves in the form of 'gold exchange' rather than gold itself. It was for their 'gold exchange' or interest-bearing assets convertible into gold that these banks chose to hold the internationally recognised prime London acceptance. The increased demand pushed down the fine rate very close to and sometimes below the Treasury bill rate so that for the discount houses good-quality bank bills became a less important part of the portfolio in terms of profitability as well as total volume.

The reduced availability of commercial bills in the market, due to factors of both supply and demand, emphasised the importance of the Treasury bill for discount houses' bill business in the post-war world. Conditions after 1918 did not allow the authorities to achieve their goal of reducing issues to pre-war levels, and as a proportion of all bills in the market Treasury bills never accounted for less than two-thirds and often for three-quarters or more.[12] The discount houses found, as they took on increasing amounts of this plentiful and relatively profitable business, that they were driving head on into competition with the clearing banks – an interesting parallel to the foreign-based competition they were meeting on bank bills.

There were considerable changes too on the borrowed funds side of the houses' business and specifically in the conditions of supply in the call-money market. The London money market was now dominated by the 'Big Five' clearing banks which had emerged from the final phase of the bank amalgamation movement. Concentration of power in this way enabled collusion on matters affecting, among others, the discount houses.[13] Not only did the banks agree on rates for call money but also on the rates at which they would tender directly for Treasury bills for their own portfolios. It was thus possible on occasion for the houses' profit margins to be squeezed from both the borrowing side and the lending side. In defensive measures taken by houses about 1924 to meet the dangerously severe competition at the tender can be detected the first steps towards syndicated tendering. At that stage the aim seems simply to have been to reduce uncertainty by exchanging information and by putting in collective bids, but there was no reduction of competition at the tender to the degree common in later times.[14]

During the seven years preceding the return to gold the new influences at work in the money market, including the conditioning operations of the Bank, were to provide the discount houses with a variety of monetary regimes. In the post-war boom years of 1919–21 the houses experienced profitably wide margins between the cost of money and the high rates on bills. In pursuit of the longer-term Cunliffe goals and the immediate need to control the boom the Bank had imposed dear money conditions, and when slump came these conditions were continued. As the demand for bill finance fell so did bill rates, but the cost of borrowing from the banks was maintained in line with the high Bank rate. The houses thus suffered on their bill business both from the decline in volume of business and from narrowed margins. Then, in belatedly reversing its policy in order to counteract the slump the Bank made money cheap and plentiful, so widening bill-market margins again and helping to offset the fall in the amount of commercial bills. Meanwhile, the concentration of power on the supply side of the call-money market was working to the discount houses' advantage. Collusion over rate fixing tended to make the rate for seven-day money 'sticky' and because of the slump conditions it left a good margin below Bank rate.[15]

As noted above the authorities, in preparation for an early return to gold, stepped up the pace of their conditioning of the market in mid-1923, when Bank rate was raised to 4 per cent. As rates rose in New York the Bank operated to push market rates nearer to Bank rate, in order to support the exchange, but because no action was taken to cause the banks to increase their rate for fixtures[16] the discount houses enjoyed widening margins as discount rates rose. Throughout, the Bank of England was aided in its task of preparation by the closer relationships that were developing within the constituent parts of the money market. The concentration of power among the clearing banks and the emergence of common policy among the discount houses produced identifiable groupings upon which the Bank could the more easily bring influence to bear.[17]

The restored gold standard endured from 1925 to 1931. To meet the strain on the balance of payments during these years, caused by the imposition of an over-ambitious overseas lending programme, on capital account, on an insufficiently strong balance-of-trade position, the Bank continued the policy of raising Bank rate only when absolutely necessary but of keeping market rates well braced up.[18] This policy had previously worked to the benefit of the discount houses but now the Bank indicated to the clearing banks that they should support the general strategy by reducing the margin between Bank rate and their rate on fixtures. The establishment of a narrower rate gap in conjunction with the reduced returns available on prime bank acceptances (the result of the foreign competition referred to above) worked to bring discount houses years of low profitability between 1924 and 1927.

The policy of keeping money dear without if possible, raising Bank rate was continued in the last years of the decade, although Bank rate was raised in late September 1929 in order to offset a rise in the Federal Reserve rate which was attracting gold away from London.[19] In 1927 and 1928 open market operations were for the first time reinforced by direct guidance, from the Bank to the representatives of the discount houses, as to the level of rates to be maintained in the market. Business was more profitable for the discount houses during the last two years of relative prosperity, 1928 and 1929, as discount rates rose and the volume of commercial bills increased. Nevertheless, compared with 1913 the market suffered from the secular decline in the amount of good-quality bills coming forward for discount.[20]

ECONOMIC DEPRESSION AND THE
CARTELISATION OF THE DISCOUNT MARKET

If discount market hopes of a return to pre-war 'normality' had persisted, however attenuated, into the last years of the 1920s, they were to be utterly dashed by the events of the decade that followed. A number of factors – the world slump in trade, production and employment; the 'cheap money' policy introduced in Britain as a restorative measure; and the special conditions that appeared in the money and bill markets in London in the early 1930s – combined to put the discount houses into an impossible position. The mode of the houses' salvation, in the arrangements made on both the money and bill sides of their business, was to provide a framework for the houses' operations that would remain long after the circumstances which gave rise to it had disappeared.

In late 1929 the American economy crashed into the start of a slump of unprecedented severity that had far-reaching consequences for the rest of the world. International trade ceased to expand and fell into a period of contraction. Within two years, in September 1931, Britain was to abandon the gold standard that she had struggled for so long to restore.

The abandonment was caused by the crisis of 1931, which itself was brought on by the confluence of three effects of the slump. First, both the balance of payments and the balance between current earnings and overseas lending deteriorated sharply. Secondly, confidence in the pound was shaken by the emergence of a budget deficit that was the product of falling tax yields at a time of increased spending to relieve unemployment. Third, the failure of the Austrian Credit Anstalt in May 1931 initiated a widespread loss of confidence that weakened the liquidity positions of banks in Europe. The attempt to restore these positions withdrew short-term funds from London, while a large part of Britain's short-term credits to European countries became frozen.[21] Gold payments by the Bank of England were suspended from 21 September.

The Bank had previously pursued a policy of successive reductions in Bank rate to a level of $2\frac{1}{2}$ per cent in May 1931 but under the impact of the crisis had raised the rate in two steps to $4\frac{1}{2}$ per cent in July. Now, as Britain left the gold standard, Bank rate was raised to 6 per cent, as a gesture of reassurance for those who feared that inflation would ensue.[22] Nevertheless, the outcome of the crisis indicated that the economic situation at home had priority; the deflationary effects of the gold outflow during the summer being neutralised by increases in the fiduciary note issue and by open market purchases of government securities.

Although discomforting, the 1931 crisis did not seriously threaten the discount market and no houses failed. The houses carried heavy contingent liability on German and Austrian bills but there was no real danger because mostly good quality bank paper was involved, the banks and accepting houses were sound and the Bank stood ready to rediscount bills frozen by the Standstill Agreement. The comparative healthiness on the bill side helped to avert the danger on the houses' securities book, on which they suffered heavy 'paper' losses. They were thus enabled to hold on without having to realise the losses until gilt prices surged upward in early 1932. On balance, interest rate movements over the period were helpful to the discount houses:

between October 1929 and May 1931 the trend was downward and the rises in Bank rate during the crisis itself were comparatively modest; in 1932 the last gleam of relief before the onset of 'cheap money' was provided by the fall in Bank rate from 6 to 2 per cent within a period of six months.

Once the crisis was over and the worst fears about the departure from gold had not been realised, the government embarked in earnest upon a policy of cheap money and reduced Bank rate to the 2 per cent level at which it was to stay until late 1951, with only one brief exception in 1939 when it was raised to 4 per cent at the time of the outbreak of war. The strategy of low Bank rate and associated rates was intended to provide whatever inducement low borrowing costs could provide to industry to expand out of depression and to stimulate expenditure in general. With the very high level of unemployment home affairs definitely had priority over the foreign exchanges, and in any case a depreciating currency could bring welcome benefits by way of a stimulus to exports. In February 1932 the Exchange Equalisation Account was created which was intended to manage the foreign exchange value of sterling in accordance with official policy. In place of the principles of 1844, by which the money supply was subject to regulation by fluctuations on external account, the supply of domestic credit would now be a function of government policy and the note issue would be determined by the preference of the public for currency.

The authorities' debt management policy during the 1930s was to be of major significance for the discount houses. The great weight of debt piled up during the war posed serious problems and it was part of the argument for low interest rates that they would strengthen the gilt-edged market and facilitate the conversion of war debt. It was to gilt-edged securities that the houses were to turn when the volume of bill business was no longer sufficient to sustain them. The bill business was itself affected in that the authorities had since the war sought to reduce the supply of Treasury bills and when the public's demand for longer-term debt increased during the slump the authorities took the opportunity to press their policy.[23] This was the more serious, of course, because Treasury bills had provided the houses with an alternative to the shrinking volume of commercial bills – where the effects of the decline in the *use* of the bill of exchange as a means of finance were exacerbated by the slump in world trade.

The diminution on the supply side of the bill market hit the discount houses the harder because of a contemporaneous rise on the demand side. The slow-down in economic activity brought a reduction in demand for bank loans and advances and caused the clearing banks to expand their holdings of bills and bonds. Their appetite for bills was also increased because of the excessive liquidity they enjoyed as a result of the cheap money policy. There was an added demand for Treasury bills as an investment for the short-term foreign funds attracted to London.

The discount houses were rapidly put into an impossible position. The reduction in supply and the increase in demand squeezed down discount rates on bills. From early in 1932, as Bank rate was falling from its peak, competition at the Treasury bill tender in anticipation of the falls forced issue rates for the bills below rates charged by bankers for loans at call and short notice. After June 30 when Bank rate had attained its 'cheap money' – 2 per cent – level this applied also to the rates on fine bank bills.

The cheap money policy caused the clearing banks – the houses' main source of funds – to modify the relationship between the rate they charged on call loans and Bank rate. Prior to 1932 they had maintained a rigid structure of borrowing and lending rates with the deposit rate fixed at 2 per cent below Bank rate. When Bank rate was reduced to 2 per cent the old structure was abandoned and the deposit rate was set at an absolute level of ½ per cent with a minimum rate for call loans of 1 per cent. When competition pushed down the rate on Treasury bills to a level below the minimum call loan rate the discount houses were involved in losses on all their Treasury bill holdings.[24] By the end of 1932 newly issued or almost newly issued Treasury bills were being quoted at 1¼ per cent, a level which left a slender though positive margin over cost of funds. Beginning early in 1933, however, competition from the clearing banks was so fierce that the rate was forced down to ¼ per cent, around which level it fluctuated until October. As far as possible the discount houses substituted cheaper funds by borrowing from non-clearing bank sources, for example overseas banks and merchant banks which were generally lending at ¼ per cent. The clearing banks, however, were their largest suppliers and were in the anomalous position of refusing to lend at less than 1 per cent on the security of bills similar to ones which they themselves were discounting at ¼ per cent or less.

Loss-making on such a scale could not continue without change of some sort taking place, and it was reasonable for commentators at the time to forecast failures, mergers and the abandonment of traditional lines of business. One house had withdrawn from bill business in late 1931. In 1933 two firms retired and two others, White and Shaxson and King and Foà, merged to form the present house of King and Shaxson. It could of course be argued that the discount market was too big and that a period of stringency would strengthen the apparatus by weeding out inefficient firms. A contemporary observer interpreted the attitude of the banks, in enforcing difficult conditions for a period of over two years, as possibly being due to the fact that

> they felt it desirable to reduce the number of houses competing in the bill market. Once acceptances have become scarce and most of the dealings are Treasury bills, many of the justifications for the existence of an intermediary in the bill market lose part of their force whilst banks are inclined to buy their bills direct through the weekly tenders.[25]

On the other hand, a more recent writer has claimed that the same result could have been achieved by allowing full free competition in the money and bill markets and that the action taken by the banks to restrict competition was but a further stage in a longer-term development of the cartelisation of British banking.[26] This argument is based on the proposition that contrary to opinion both contemporary and more recent (e.g. *The Economist*, June 1955) a free market would not have resulted in chaos in the rate structure and widespread failure of firms. Rates were low because of the authorities' cheap money policy and the structure they attained was due to the action of the clearing banks in colluding to keep their call loan rate at a level considerably higher than the free market rate. Competition between the banks on the other hand would have produced a rate structure on which no efficient discount house need have failed.

This argument carries conviction. The arrangements made to resolve the crisis do seem to indicate that the clearing banks had decided that it was in their own interest to preserve the discount market, in its traditional money-market role, in a manner that would maintain the cartelised minimum rate structure. In addition, there was pressure from the Bank of England in support of the preservation of the houses. The Governor (Montagu Norman), especially, considered the market to be a vital and distinctive feature of the City. The arrangements themselves took the form of agreements, involving the clearing banks and the discount houses, that had the effect of modifying the degree of competition in the money market and the Treasury bill market. These agreements brought into being a market structure that was to endure until 1971. Consideration of them raises the broader question of the parts played by various agencies in the longer-term restriction of competition in the London markets for money and bills.

Regulation of competition in the discount market was essentially a product of the 1920s and 1930s but for the clearing banks the process had begun many years before. In the mid-nineteenth century the British banking industry can be said to have been competitive, in that there was freedom from domination by a few large banks and there was no permanent collusion between banks. There were tentative approaches to collusion after the crisis of 1857, and in the 1870s, following the accommodation bill frauds of 1875 and the depression of 1876, the banks agreed not to pay interest on current account deposits.[27] The banks' agreement to pay interest on deposit accounts at a fixed margin below Bank rate dates from May 1886. These cartel arrangements were, however, loose compared with the rigidity of the system operating after 1920.

It was the impact of the First World War that was to prove of crucial importance for the shape of banking in Britain. At first, the banks were criticised for failing to expand loan finance sufficiently in spite of a guarantee of indemnity to banks and discount houses against bill losses. Later on, the banks became increasingly involved in the financing of government war expenditure. In 1917–18 a series of mergers reduced the number of clearing banks to five and increased their share of total deposits from about 50 per cent to 80 per cent. This reduction in numbers made possible the development of a rigid cartel, which the banks desired on the grounds that it would facilitate the financing of post-war reconstruction, enable them to meet the competition of German banks and maintain London's international financial status.

On this evidence it would appear that the development of cartel arrangements cannot be explained solely by reference to the joint profit maximisation motive. Rather it was a response to public criticism, arising from the insecurity of the banking structure in the nineteenth century and from the banks' failure to respond sufficiently to national needs at the beginning of the First World War. There was also the desire of the authorities to ensure effective war finance. The banks played their part in the provision of necessary funds and developed the cartel in response to the need for public regulation of banking without the imposition of formal controls.[28]

Until after the First World War the Bank of England never stood in the way of concentration and cartel arrangements in banking. Rather, the Bank generally adopted a policy of encouragement towards the development of restrictive practices, taking advantage of a market situation made more easy to control in terms of short-term interest rate policy and the extent of bank advances. It was seen in the previous chapter that between 1844 and the 1870s the policy was that Bank rate should always follow market rate. Policy then changed so that Bank rate was set to lead the market rate, with Bank rate changes being determined by movements in the foreign exchanges.

Bank rate had then to be made effective by keeping the discount rate on bills close up to the public rate.

The Bank's task in this matter was facilitated by its encouragement of three specific agreements: the clearing banks' agreement on a maximum deposit rate (after 1886); the clearing banks' agreement on the minimum call-loan rate (from the mid-1920s); the agreements between the discount houses and the clearing banks (1933–5, see below). Through the working of these agreements the Bank could ensure that a movement of Bank rate would be followed closely by the Treasury bill rate, which would move only between limits set by Bank rate and the minimum call rate. However, in enforcing interest rate control through these means the Bank was forced to supply cash to meet changes in demand so as to avoid undue strain on the agreements through competition between the participants.

The increased cohesion among clearing banks and discount houses resulting from collusive action strengthened the Bank's position, in that rate movements could be influenced via direct 'requests'. The first examples of the use of 'moral suasion' occurred, as was noted earlier, in 1927 and 1928 when the Governor indicated to the discount houses the level of rates he desired to see in the market.[29] In 1935 the custom was begun of weekly meetings between the Governor of the Bank and the senior officers of the discount houses at which the Governor gave his views on the market situation and the conditions the authorities were seeking to create.[30]

The collusive arrangements among the discount houses and between the discount houses and the clearing banks were made within a period of roughly ten years between the mid-1920s and mid-1930s and must be viewed as a reaction to the restrictive policies of the Bank of England and the clearing banks. Primarily they were a reaction to the enforcement of a minimum rate for call loans from the banks, when lending to the discount houses came to be dominated by the 'Big Five'. It was Bank of England policy actively to encourage cartel arrangements for minimum call-loan rates at that time, partly because it was believed that sales of Treasury bills would be maximised by stability of the Treasury bill rate and partly because the Bank wished to push up market rates close to Bank rate as part of the strategy for the return to gold (see above, pp. 41, 42).

It was these circumstances plus direct competition by the banks for Treasury bills that gave rise to the informal collusion among discount houses in 1924. Now, to meet the crisis of 1933 a series of three agreements was drawn up in order to try to push the Treasury-bill tender rate above the call-money rate. That this particular approach was adopted seems to indicate that the clearing banks wished to retain the call-money system because call money was preferred to Treasury bills as a short-term asset;[31] also that they wished to preserve a minimum rate so as both to maintain their profitability and to observe the wishes of the Bank of England, to which the agreements were shown.

In September 1933 the clearers agreed informally among themselves that : (1) while they would maintain the minimum rate on call money at 1 per cent they would attempt to raise the bill rate by bidding at the tender at an agreed price which would provide the discount houses with a margin of profit; (2) also, they would buy and sell in the resale market at the same rate. The operation of this agreement brought a temporary improvement, for the bill rate rose from slightly less than $\frac{1}{4}$ per cent in September 1933 to slightly less than $1\frac{1}{4}$ per cent in December 1933. Unfortunately, the rise in the bill rate had the effect of increasing the attractiveness of Treasury bills as compared to banks' deposit accounts. The increased 'outside' demand that ensued at the tender pushed down the bill rate during 1934. The parties to the clearing banks' agreements were forced to bid at rates lower than the minimum call rate to discount houses in order to obtain any bills at all. By October 1934 the bill rate was down to $\frac{1}{4}$ per cent and the discount houses were returned to a loss-making situation with the banks holding the minimum call rate at 1 per cent.

The second attempt to effect a 'rescue' was made in November 1934 with an agreement entered into for a trial period of three months. The clearing banks agreed to reduce the minimum rate on call money from 1 per cent to $\frac{1}{2}$ per cent for money secured on Treasury bills and other bills eligible for rediscount at the Bank of England but for money secured on bonds and ineligible bills the rate was maintained at 1 per cent.[32] This agreement had the effect of reducing the cost of call money, but competition at the tender was such that by January 1935 the bill rate had fallen to just under $\frac{1}{5}$ per cent. In February 1935, at the end of the trial period, the situation was reviewed by a special committee of the Clearing Banks Committee which submitted a proposal to the Bank.

A new agreement was then drawn up which enjoyed the support of all the banks and the approval of the Bank of England. It contained the following provisions : the clearing banks would lend call money at $\frac{1}{2}$ per cent to the discount houses for bills for their own portfolios; they would not buy bills in the resale market at less than $\frac{1}{2}$ per cent; they would no longer tender directly for Treasury bills for their own account, so as to avoid undue pressure on the rate; they would not buy new bills within eight days of issue. The discount houses, although they had negotiated with the clearing banks on a collective basis, had until this stage not systematically colluded in bill dealing.

Now, however, they entered into a more formal arrangement for bidding at the weekly tender that was intended to regulate inter-house competition.

This change in policy on the part of discount houses was occasioned by the comparative success of the third agreement, which raised the bill rate to a fraction over $\frac{1}{2}$ per cent even when bills were scarce. This bare margin of profit provided an incentive to those dealing in bills to increase turnover. Competition for bills at the tender intensified so that participants might expand their resale business. This 'stagging' threatened to vitiate the effects of the new agreement so the discount houses, at first the bigger ones but then all of them, began in May 1935 to submit collective bids of agreed amount – the bills being divided among the participants on the basis of each firm's capital resources, though with the amounts weighted in favour of the smaller houses. Provision was also made for individual houses to give notice that they intended to avoid taking up bills, by submitting a lower price than the rest of the group. This was the beginning of the syndicated tender system, so familiar to students of the market down to 1971. It was extended in 1940 to include the provision that the discount houses would be prepared if necessary to take up all the bills on offer – the counterpart of which was the assurance of last-resort facilities at the Bank. The full Treasury bill tender mechanism will be the subject of a more complete examination in later chapters.

Although the arrangements were later modified to provide more flexibility of action for individual houses, in the life and death situation of the later thirties the houses were forced to accept the loss of freedom that the 'rescue' operation imposed upon them. The role and some of the motives of the Bank of England in the matter have already been mentioned. The Governor, Montagu Norman, seems to have taken a personal interest in the market's survival, believing that the houses' role as buffer between Bank and banks was valuable enough to warrant his intervention with the representatives of the clearing banks in February 1935.[33] With the crisis itself resolved Norman, with the support of the Bank, sought to strengthen the discount market on the same principle of 'rationalisation' as was currently being applied in industry in general. The process of amalgamation was hurried on by advice and encouragement from the Governor and the threat of withdrawal of rediscount facilities at the privileged rate from firms not considered sufficiently strong. Between January 1933 and March 1936 the number of firms in the market fell from twenty-two to eighteen.

C

THE MOVE INTO BUSINESS IN BONDS

The agreement of 1935 and succeeding arrangements were successful in that they had the effect of stabilising Treasury bill rates at the tender and on bills nearer to maturity, at levels which would provide houses with some measure of profit, however slender. Temporary relief was also provided by the rise in supply of Treasury bills that followed a large influx of gold into the Exchange Equalisation Account – although the authorities continued to press their policy of reducing issues. In terms both of margins and volume Treasury bill business was no longer sufficient and houses turned their attention to the possible alternatives, commercial bills and bonds.

It was noted above that technological and economic factors in the 1930s had resulted in a serious decline in the availability of the best quality commercial paper favoured by the discount houses as their proper business. The immediate reaction of the houses to the shortage was to attempt to increase the supply of bank bills through approaches to possible users and to the acceptors themselves; also to foster the growth of trade acceptances which, though they commanded a more limited market than bank bills, could provide secure and relatively lucrative business. In this endeavour the houses found that they enjoyed the approval of the Governor of the Bank, who believed that a stable and prosperous money and discount market had to be based on business in the finest commercial paper. However, conditions at that time were not propitious for the significant expansion of bill business through individual enterprise, though such an approach was to be more successful some years later. There was a decline in demand for finance from any source and bill finance had in any case to compete with direct lending by the banks. The net result was that in the field of private-sector paper houses were forced to take bills of a quality hitherto considered inferior.

It was not increased business in commercial paper that was to provide any substantial support of the houses' lean portfolios during the 1930s. It was, rather, a reluctant but necessary advance into dealing in short-term government securities. Prior to 1914 houses had held their own capital in bonds and during the First World War bond dealing had begun on a small scale. As can be seen from Table 1 bond business remained very limited in amount during the early 1920s but it increased rapidly after 1925. The big expansion came in the 1930s with peak holdings in 1936, from which there was a decline prior to the large-scale growth of wartime. A bond book is inherently a potentially more profitable and a more risky proposition than a corresponding bill book but the bill famine that accompanied the Depression coincided with the low interest rates – and therefore the firmer bond prices – of the cheap money period. In these circumstances bonds became eminently more attractive to the discount houses than hitherto.

Apart from the risks involved in bond dealing the houses had also to overcome entrenched attitudes towards bonds, held by the clearing banks and by the Bank of England. Prior to 1934 the clearing banks had treated discount-house bond business with some misgiving and had allowed the houses to borrow 'bond' money on the strength of security which included only about 10 per cent of bonds – and thus effectively limited the extent to which borrowed funds could be employed in bond business. Formal recognition of changed circumstances came in the second agreement of 1934 (see above, p. 50), by which clearing banks agreed to lend money against bonds at a margin over money secured against bills. For the Bank of England, Montagu Norman's expressed preference for bank bills as the mainstay of discount market business gave a measure of the official attitude towards the perils of a bond book. Nevertheless, in the difficult times of the 1930s, the Bank at first accepted bond business as a necessary expedient for discount house survival but recognised increasingly the potentially useful role of the houses as jobbers at the short end of the gilt-edged market.

A *sine qua non* of a dealer of any consequence in bonds is the ability to withstand capital losses on his holdings. It is in this regard that the 'rationalisation' and capital strengthening campaign of the 1930s assumed specific operational as well as general economic validity. In general, while individual houses regulated the extent of their bond holdings by reference to the size of capital resources and hidden reserves and tended to restrict purchases to securities with only a few years (preferably less than five) to run to maturity, there was no formalisation of rules for bond dealing such as emerged during the 1950s. Following the low money rates and rising bond prices of the first half of the 1930s there was a downturn after 1935 and thereafter gilt prices continued to move downwards into the war period. Consequently, the estimates of holdings for the three public companies (Table 1) for 1938 and 1939 are only about half the figure for 1937.

4   War Finance and Reconstruction, 1939-51

For the discount houses the approach of the Second World War appeared to offer no comfort at all. The only distinctive contribution that the houses could offer to justify their existence in the later 1930s was their provision of the call-loan market, based upon bill dealing. Because bill business yielded no profit the houses subsidised it through their bond dealing, which itself was hardly tolerated by the authorities. The 'rescue' operation of 1934–5 had been mounted in the hope that because the existence of a separate call-money market suited both the Bank of England and the clearing banks, it might again, one day, become a profitable activity for the houses as the business in commercial bills revived or as the return on Treasury bills was increased by the ending of the cheap money policy. Now the houses faced the possibility that a major war would not only dash all hopes of a revival of commercial paper but would demand finance on such a scale that the authorities would be forced to modify the financial process – to the possible exclusion of the discount market.

In fact, although the predicted shrinkage of commercial bill business did take place and despite the fact that the authorities did introduce a system of direct borrowing from the banks, the effect of the war was to provide the discount houses with a new justification and role, based upon profitable dealing in bonds, and to guarantee their continued existence for at least a decade. Indeed it will be argued that the implementation of the internal borrowing programme, both in terms of bond issues and residual borrowing techniques, operated to safeguard the traditional discount market mechanism at the centre of the financial system.

First, the demands of the government's financial programme, both during the war and the post-war years of reconstruction, provided the discount houses with the opportunity to fulfil a function for which they were uniquely fitted – that of helping to make a market in massive amounts of short-term bonds. Apart from the official approval for their bond business which automatically followed, the houses acquired an expertise in dealing and a familiarity with the operation of the bond market that laid the foundations for business in bonds as a major item in portfolio, during the future years of peace. Secondly, the enormous expansion in demand for temporary borrowing that the war produced, led not to the irrevocable dislocation of the traditional money and bill markets but instead to the introduction of an emergency borrowing technique that took the brunt of the burden and thus left the discount market to handle Treasury bill business, albeit in greatly increased quantities, in their accustomed manner. Consequently, the resumption of normal conditions found the discount houses still in their traditional place at the centre of the mechanism of monetary control. Thirdly, the new opportunities offered to the houses also imposed requirements in terms of further 'rationalisation' of the discount market, by means of withdrawals and amalgamations and a general strengthening of the capital base, both during wartime and the immediate post-war period. This produced a market of greatly enhanced strength and resilience and enabled the houses to take the fullest advantage of new avenues for expansion when they opened up in the 1950s.[1]

THE STRATEGY OF WAR FINANCE

The central economic objective of the government in a situation of 'total war', such as obtained between 1940 and 1945, is to achieve maximum mobilisation of resources for the war effort. Because the usual system of incentives and disincentives of the market economy, whereby resources are transferred from one employment to another, do not operate forcefully enough for wartime conditions they have to be supplemented and reinforced by more direct methods of control. Unless direct compulsion is to take over completely the business of resource allocation, then financial measures can have an important part to play. This 'mixed' approach to economic policy was the one employed in Britain.

Given that normal, albeit modified, methods of resource allocation are to continue, the government must inevitably face the problem of inflation which, if it gets out of hand, can bring in its train the dangers of economic and social (and hence military) disruption. Increased taxation, because of its disincentive and other effects which could react adversely on the war effort, cannot provide a complete answer, so that to the extent that the absorption of purchasing power by taxation falls short of the absorption of real resources in the war effort, the Government spending-machine must in other ways be provided with purchasing power . . . There must, that is to say, be adequate saving and what cannot be done without inflation will ineluctably be enforced by inflation.[2]

In other words, if inflation is repressed, involuntary saving will operate by way of queues and shop shortages, while unrestrained inflation will produce forced saving out of incomes which fail to keep pace. The necessary and preferable alternative to these solutions is 'voluntary saving which directly reduces demand without injustice'. Consequently a goal of financial policy must be the encouragement of voluntary saving.

From the viewpoint of the central authorities, the excess of public expenditure over revenue from taxes, judiciously chosen, must be financed through borrowing. In formulating an effective borrowing policy the authorities must have regard to the following considerations : (1) that consumption will thereby be restricted for the maximum period of time by enticing voluntary savings into the less liquid (longer-dated) kinds of debt, that is those less likely to be realised at a later date and spent; (2) account must be taken of the probable implications of current borrowing both for the post-war financial situation and for the maintenance of confidence, internally and externally – that is the burden of post-war maturities and refinancing must be considered and also the impact of policy upon the propensity for foreigners to hold sterling balances; (3) although the authorities will aim where possible to borrow on the longest possible terms they must also have regard to the needs and preferences of a wide variety of lenders and issue a suitable range of securities to meet them.[3]

It was within this broadly Keynesian theoretical framework that the authorities set about devising their wartime borrowing policy. In so doing they were very strongly influenced : by the experience of the 1914–18 war, in at least the early stages of which they had been found badly wanting in expertise; but also by their experience of continuous management of the money market during the inter-war years, in which they had achieved considerable success. Both sets of experience, in fact, provided support for the decision on the key question of the general level of interest rates at which the Second World War was to be financed.

From the beginning financial policy operated on the premise that this was to be a cheap money war. Specifically, it was to be a 'Three Per Cent War' : that is throughout a possibly long period of hostilities the range of interest rates to be offered on government debt would not be allowed to rise beyond the low level that had become familiar and accepted since 1932. The key interest-rate band of 3 per cent and thereabouts was to apply to long-term borrowing and small savings, while for shorter-term borrowing rates were to be kept to the levels current prior to the outbreak of war, namely 1 per cent and upwards. A brief examination of the factors which led the authorities to this position by 1939 will provide considerable insight into the conduct of financial policy after that date.

In the first place, borrowing in the coming war would take place within a strong framework of controls : controls on the foreign exchange position in order to insulate the domestic situation from foreign disturbances, and controls on the home economy in order to regulate consumption, prices and capital issues. During the First World War, by contrast, London had remained an open financial centre and interest rates had been allowed to rise in response to conditions abroad, possibly because it was expected that at home they would both promote an increase in savings and help to draw the proceeds into government hands. As well as becoming increasingly difficult for the authorities to handle as the war dragged on, the dear money policy had created problems, both monetary and budgetary, for the post-war period. There was in any case a fear that if the authorities were to repeat the policy after so short an interval, lack of City confidence in its success might well ensure its failure the more quickly.

The second factor involved the authorities' new confidence in their ability to manipulate the money market, based to an extent on the cheap money experiment of the 1930s but also by virtue of earlier operations in support of debt financing and foreign-exchange policies. Interestingly, although the authorities adhered to the principle of cheap money after 1932 their activities were in general confined to the short end of the rate structure. The long end of the market was, with some exceptions, left to itself. Where intervention did take place it was in order to operate on the same side as market forces so that, for example, when the trend in long-term rates turned upwards, no attempt was made to reverse it.[4] Worthy of special mention, however, was the Bank's intervention in support of the series of conversion operations, in which the resources of the Issue Department were employed to underwrite the issue of the new stock. Such operations, though novel at the time, later became standard tactics in the Bank's pursuit of an orderly bond market (see Chapter 10). Because it was generally believed that the authorities were incapable of altering market trends, the control of long-term rates at a low level during the coming war would, by implication, have to be accomplished by means of restrictions placed upon 'non-essential' employments for capital.

The third factor concerned the reasons which brought about the choice of 3 per cent, rather than any other rate, as the basis for official borrowing. In deciding on 3 per cent the government took into consideration both their estimate of what the public would expect (i.e. they thought it would be very difficult politically to justify a higher rate and in any case the market had become used to that sort of return on capital during the cheap money period of the thirties) and also their estimate of the very lowest rate that the gilt-edged market would accept.

Having established the key rate for their borrowing scheme the government intended to act as a discriminating monopolist, by negotiating terms separately with each of a number of subdivisions of the market for loanable funds. It was hoped by this means to keep down the average level of borrowing rates paid.[5] In addition, there were indications from outside Whitehall that the government had made the right decision. Although no public announcement of the basic rate for government borrowing was made until March 1940,[6] *The Economist* had in January 1940 published an article entitled 'A Three Per Cent War'. This had argued that because the vastly increased amount of savings that would be needed could only be raised by direct means, the rate of interest could well be reduced to a level more in line with the government's wider strategy. Furthermore the current state of the gilt-edged market suggested that even at that time a medium-term issue at 3 per cent could be contemplated without much preparation.

The arguments in favour of 3 per cent must have seemed very compelling, for the decision to conduct financial policy on this basis was 'taken without formal discussion among ministers; the informal discussions left little trace in the papers and evidently did not occasion any systematic discussions on the official level.'[7] It was apparently taken by a small group of key men who were unanimous in their enthusiasm for the policy – namely the Prime Minister (Neville Chamberlain), the Chancellor (Sir John Simon) and the Governor of the Bank (Montagu Norman), who initiated consideration of the scheme. There was no consultation with J. M. Keynes or other outside economists on the immediate issue although a pre-war report had indicated that academic opinion was in favour.[8]

BOND ISSUES AND THE DISCOUNT HOUSES

As noted above the government's strategy for minimising the cost of war borrowing involved the division of the market into a number of compartments, each of which was to be dealt with separately on appropriate terms. For one compartment, divided off in 1939 and consisting of the small savers, the Treasury employed National

Savings Certificates and Defence Bonds. Further market compartments were formed following the failure of a general-purpose issue in March 1940 (of 3 per cent War Loan, 1955–9), which had been intended to appeal to a wide range of potential lenders. To provide for immediate needs a Bank of England plan for direct borrowing from the commercial banks, via Treasury Deposit Receipts, was put into effect in June 1940. For the rest, the authorities henceforth thought in terms of separate provision for two different groups of lenders : Savings Bonds (which were longer term) for large private investors and institutional savers; and National War Bonds for the business firms and other temporary savers who were accumulating funds earmarked for spending immediately after the war.

There was also a change of tactics after the unsuccessful War Loan issue of March 1940, in that bonds were subsequently supplied through the tap. Of the successful 2½ per cent National War Bonds, six successive series were offered with terms of between six and ten years, from June 1940. Within three years more than £2000 million had been raised on these bonds. In addition, there were large issues of the longer-dated Savings Bonds from May 1942. Such was the scale of operations in both short and longer-dated stocks that it threatened to paralyse the normal operation of the gilt-edged market. Supported only on their own resources the gilt-edged jobbers found it increasingly difficult to 'make a market', when faced not only with normal day-to-day movements caused by the readjustment of (much-enlarged) portfolios but also with the need of the financial institutions frequently to engage in large-scale switches.[9]

It was in the face of this threat to the continuance of the cheap money policy that the authorities began to prepare the discount houses for their new shock-absorbing role in the gilt-edged market. Once put on a sound capital footing the houses, with their access to surpluses of cash all over the money market and to loans from the Bank of England, and armed with the expertise they had gained before the war, would be uniquely placed to become bond dealers of the size necessary for successful jobbing in the new conditions.

For the houses themselves war conditions had already quickened the process of rationalisation that had begun during the 1930s. Between 1939 and 1943 the number of firms in the market fell by seven, to eleven :[10] one firm, Brocklebank and Co. Ltd, retired from the market in 1940 and another, Fairfax and Co Ltd, withdrew from bill business. The merger of Cater and Co. Ltd and Brightwen and Co., planned before the war, took place in October 1939 and subsequently the new company absorbed Roger Cunliffe, Sons and Co. in 1941 and Daniell Cazenove and Co. in 1943. There were also mergers between Ryder,

Parker and Co. and Jones and Brown in 1940, and between Gillett Bros. Discount Co. Ltd and Hohler and Co. in 1942.[11]

The Bank now made it clear that the process of consolidation should continue so that each house might eventually enjoy a minimum capitalisation of £1 million. Further, dealing was in general to be confined to the shorter-dated bonds, with total holdings being held to within eight times total resources. In return for the observance of these conditions and on the understanding that the houses would perform a jobbing function (see below, p. 61), the Bank indicated that in future bonds of less than five years to maturity would provide eligible collateral against last-resort loans.

Official encouragement apart, bond dealing had become an increasingly attractive proposition for the discount houses. The extensive sales of National War Bonds over the period 1940–3 had increased the amount outstanding, of bonds suitable for houses' portfolios, by over £900 million. Also, the authorities' policy with regard to tap issues, that is of worsening slightly the terms on which successive issues were made – ensured conditions of steadily rising bond prices that generated capital profits on holdings and removed the possibility of capital loss. In addition to automatic capital gains the houses also enjoyed healthy running profits, with the cost of day-to-day money at $1\frac{1}{8}$ per cent from outside banks and no more than $1\frac{1}{4}$ from the clearers, as against running yields of up to $2\frac{1}{2}$ per cent on the bonds.[12]

The tide for the discount houses had turned, though the fact was not then fully apparent to them. Attempts to raise new capital, both as a way of complying with the Bank's guide-lines and in order to exploit the new opportunities to the full, produced a response that 'led to a significant influx of outside capital – probably the first concentrated movement since the company flotations boom of the early eighteen-sixties'.[13] During 1942–3 seven houses issued new capital which in the majority of cases brought in outside finance, generally from insurance companies and merchant banks by way of subscriptions to preference shares – though in the biggest single case it was by way of an equity issue.[14] So successful was the programme of capital strengthening, both by way of amalgamation and the attraction of new finance, that by spring 1944 all the houses apart from one had raised their capital to at least the £500,000 specified as an acceptable interim target.[15] As a result of individual increases in capital the published resources of the market rose to £14,440,000, but after allowance for various omissions the true amount of resources has been estimated at about £22 million.[16]

Although as a result of the Bank's preparation the discount houses had by this time emerged as fully operational bond dealers on a sound financial basis, it must not be thought that the Bank had engaged in a special form of 'industrial retraining', with the intention of guaranteeing the houses a lifetime of profitable employment. The measures taken were, rather, a development of the pre-war policy of general market strengthening, now adapted to the needs of the moment and carrying no implications for the future. Nevertheless, the discount houses developed their bond market role to such a degree during the last two years of the war that the authorities began to appreciate its possibilities as a more permanent feature of the financial mechanism.

Houses both big and small came to perform the jobbing function with increasing frequency, that is moderating the severity of fluctuations by standing ready to buy in stock on a falling market and letting out stock, more gradually, when the generality of dealers was buying. Because of the strength of their resources and the high degree of expertise they attained in dealing, the larger houses acquired a reputation for being able to handle larger blocks of business than was normal for the Stock Exchange and also, on occasion, to quote keener prices. On the basis of their wide range of professional contacts these houses increasingly took business direct from financial institutions and from other commercial and industrial enterprises. Also, apart from business that by-passed the Stock Exchange altogether the houses benefited from business that came to them direct from stockbrokers, though after 1944 the rule was that quotations had always to be invited from Stock Exchange jobbers before business was confirmed with a discount house.

The general tendency, however, was for business to come to the houses direct or from the brokers only when, because of the set of the market, the gilt-edged jobbers were either short of stock or unable to absorb any more. It was in such circumstances, when only the discount houses were standing in front of the government broker, that the houses could have an important influence on market prices. In normal market conditions, the influence the houses exerted on prices stemmed from the preferential treatment they received, as professional bond dealers, for tax purposes. Their operations had the effect of keeping short-term bond prices, on a yield basis, well below what non-professional buyers would tend to expect.

RESIDUAL BORROWING AND THE DISCOUNT HOUSES

The government's greatly-expanded need to borrow on short- and medium-term bonds during the war had the effect of transforming discount houses' business in a wholly unexpected and beneficial way. The houses were also centrally involved in the residual-borrowing programme and here, it seemed, there were developments that might fulfil their worst fears of extinction. By introducing a method of borrowing from the banking system that by-passed the discount houses completely the authorities appeared to be depriving the houses of their most characteristic and functionally legitimate activity – that of providing a market in short-term borrowed funds both as between bankers and also intermediate between the banks and the authorities.

The reality of the situation was, however, somewhat different. By means of the new Treasury Deposit Receipts the authorities were enabled to raise large sums of money very simply and very quickly, thus taking the weight of large-scale temporary borrowing off the traditional system and ensuring that it would continue in its familiar form. While the houses were undeniably deprived of business which would otherwise have arisen from even greater issues of Treasury bills, it must be argued that in their arrangements for residual borrowing – as in those for the bond programme – the authorities provided a vital phase of regeneration for the ailing discount market that was to set it firmly on its way through the opportunities of the post-war world and beyond.

The approach adopted to residual borrowing was again a legacy of experience obtained during the Great War, when borrowing on Ways and Means advances had grown alarmingly.[17] Policy throughout the inter-war period was directed towards the reduction of this borrowing to the irreducible minimum necessary to meet unforeseen shortfalls overnight on the Exchequer Accounts. This policy continued during the Second World War and it was only exceptionally and with great reluctance that the authorities were driven to borrow heavily on Ways and Means advances during the crisis conditions of 1940.

Instead, residual needs[18] were met where possible from the weekly issues of Treasury bills. At the time of the outbreak of war over £1100m of the bills were in issue, of which £411m were market bills, issued through the tender, and £707m were tap bills, issued direct to government departments.[19] The large proportion of tap bills was swollen by the holdings of the Exchange Equalisation Account, which had acquired hundreds of millions of sterling to invest as a consequence of the rush to withdraw foreign-owned balances from London. As the Account bought Treasury bills the sterling proceeds flowed to the Exchequer Accounts where, for the first six months of the war, they greatly eased the strain of war finance. When exchange control was introduced the sterling flow came to an end and the authorities were forced to seek alternative sources of funds in a situation made worse by the failure of the War Loan issue in March 1940 and the subsequent depression of the gilt-edged market by almost continuously bad war news.

At first it was estimated that 'spare capacity' in the banking system could provide the extra finance by the absorption of larger amounts of Treasury bills, but by May 1940 it was decided that further increases in the size of the weekly offer could only result in serious distortion of the money market mechanism. A Bank of England plan for direct borrowing from the banks was submitted to the Chancellor and after some amendment and consultation with the bankers, Treasury Deposit Receipts were put into issue at the beginning of July.

This, however, is not a full explanation. Had it merely been a case of relieving the discount houses of possibly unbearable strains, this could have been accomplished by instructing the banks to hold firmly larger amounts of Treasury bills or by making sales of tender bills direct to the banks – as had been the arrangement before 1934. But the war situation was now so grave that in considering the Bank's plan the Treasury had to allow for the possibility that financial business might have to be carried on away from London. In order to achieve the necessary simplification of the system and also to provide the degree of flexibility that the exigencies of war might require, it was clear that there would have to be direct dealings with the banks.

In the circumstances it was decided that direct borrowing could best be effected by using an entirely new instrument – the T.D.R. This would allow the discount market mechanism to continue operating along conventional lines, turning over a relatively stable volume of bills. It would also prevent undue inflation of the banks' liquid asset ratios via acquisition of Treasury bills.

In the T.D.R. the Bank had attempted to devise an instrument that bankers would find sufficiently liquid to be acceptable, but at the same time somewhat less liquid than the Treasury bill. Consequently, the life of the new instrument was set at six months rather than three, and it was made non-negotiable. On the other hand repayment before maturity was possible under specified conditions, for example in emergencies, when the Bank would charge discount at the penal rate, or in payment for the purchase by a bank of a newly issued government bond or Tax Reserve Certificate. The rate on T.D.R.s was set at the lowest possible margin over Treasury bill rate, i.e. $1\frac{1}{8}$ per cent as against 1 per cent. They were to be sold only to the London clearing banks and Scottish banks together with certain central banks which operated directly in the London market. The amount of borrowing for the following week was fixed by the Treasury and announced to participants by the Bank of England, which also arranged individual allocations.

In introducing the new scheme the authorities had intended both to protect the 'cheap money' rate of interest and to prevent excessive liquidity from being generated in the banking system. In practice the acceptability of the new instrument to the banks depended upon the authorities instantly making good any cash deficiency which might threaten the conventional cash ratio.[20] Because the cheap money policy demanded that there be no upward pressure on short-term rates the cash had to be supplied at the ruling Treasury bill rate (1 per cent). It was at this point that the new scheme became dependent upon the traditional money-market mechanism provided by the discount houses. Faced with pressure on their cash base the banks would reduce purchases of Treasury bills from the discount houses, so creating a cash shortage and forcing the houses to borrow from the Bank. So as not to disturb the current rate structure the cash would be supplied through the special buyer ('the back door') who would take up Treasury bills at the ruling rate.

The advent of the T.D.R.s did not mean that discount houses ceased to do business on a large scale in Treasury bills. Total allotments of Treasury bills for 1940, when T.D.R. issues began, were £3182 million, of which the syndicate took £1282 million. Thereafter, issues rose steadily to £3745m (£1155m) for 1941, £3900m (£1406m) for 1942, £4495m (£1507m) for 1943, £5470m (£1826·5m) for 1944 and £6560m (£2465m) for 1945. Despite the greatly increased availability of Treasury bills the business brought the houses virtually no profits. From October 1939 Bank rate was once again fixed at 2 per cent and bill rates fell to a level that gave only the tiniest of margins over the cost of bill money from the banks at 1 per cent. Deprived of any significant level of profits on their Treasury bills and having very little business in commercial bills the discount houses' dependence on their newly acquired position in short-term bonds – in terms both of present livelihood and future development – was virtually complete.

POST-WAR MONETARY POLICY

Although the Second World War came to an end half way through 1945 the cheap money policy together with its attendant disciplines was continued up to November 1951. The discount houses found conditions much the same as during wartime and they continued to perform similar functions in the markets for short bonds and Treasury bills. In some ways indeed they played a more critical part, and accordingly were given preferential treatment that allowed them to embark upon a programme of unprecedented capital growth. Although Treasury bill business became more profitable and there was some perceptible restoration of commercial paper, it was to business in short-term bonds that the houses again looked for the bulk of their profits.

Monetary policy during the six years after 1945 can be divided into two phases. The first phase, from 1945 to 1947, encompassed the drive towards very cheap money that was led by the first post-war Labour Chancellor, Hugh Dalton. Thereafter monetary policy, presided over by Dr Dalton's successor, Sir Stafford Cripps, was 'neutral', in that the Chancellor intended that it should not militate against the wider aim of disinflation – as it was by that time supposed that cheap money had.

Although the drive towards cheaper money was championed by Chancellor Dalton, there was almost universal support at least for the principle of keeping interest rates as low as possible. The efficacy of interest rate variation as a tool of economic management had long been doubted, but the view was that if interest rates were to have any effect at all then it should be as a stimulant rather than a depressant : after a relatively brief transitional phase the expert forecast was of deflationary rather than inflationary conditions. Consequently, it appeared advantageous to maintain the cheap money arrangements during the reconstruction period, supported by a continuation of the wartime direct controls together with budgetary measures. To these arguments[21] Dr Dalton added the force of his own political convictions, quoting from J. M. Keynes's *A Tract on Monetary Reform* (published in 1923) in support of his view that the Chancellor 'must be on the side of borrowers of money as against the money lenders, on the side of the active producer as again the passive *rentier*'.[22]

Dalton had also been impressed by Keynes's assertion of the key importance of expectations in the determination of the market rate of interest.[23] He therefore set out to put credit on a $2\frac{1}{2}$ per cent basis by way of conditioning the gilt-edged market to the acceptance of a long-term rate of interest of $2\frac{1}{2}$ per cent. The strategy adopted was that of using downward pressure on short-term rates and rates on medium-short bonds to force down the long-term rate. It was upon the discount houses in their bond market role that the burden of the leverage thus exerted would fall.[24]

As the war had drawn towards its close the extent and complexity of the houses' bond dealing had grown rather than diminished and the authorities had become increasingly aware of its operational importance for their programme of planned redemptions and refinance of wartime issues. In particular, the preferential tax treatment the houses received enabled them to smooth the market by performing the function of 'bond gatherer' of imminent maturities.[25] Now, in the face of the Chancellor's intention to achieve a significant reduction in the long-term rate of interest, this function became of crucial importance in maintaining market stability during a period in which large sales of short-dated bonds were expected, upon reconversion of the Debt. Before further expansion of bond-dealing facilities was possible, however, the houses needed to strengthen their capital base. Even where companies had raised new capital in 1943 they were now operating at full stretch. In the case of the Big Three companies (Alexanders, National, Union) the total portfolio of bills and bonds at the end of 1945 bore a ratio to published resources of twenty-nine to one; while for the smaller companies the ratio probably exceeded forty to one.[26]

In other circumstances the Chancellor might have found it difficult politically to justify giving priority to discount houses at a time of severe capital rationing, and the possibility of new issues seemed remote when the houses raised the question in the late summer of 1945. Nevertheless, a crisis in the gilt-edged market in mid-September was to convince the Chancellor of the importance of giving the houses a bigger trading base. During the course of the autumn savings drive Dr Dalton gave the first intimation of a move towards lower rates by giving notice of the reconversion of 3 per cent Savings Bonds into a lower (2½ per cent) coupon. This greatly increased the demand for the remainder of the 3 per cent and brought a corresponding flood of financing sales of shorter bonds. The discount houses, which had been gathering in the very shorts throughout, found themselves unable to absorb any more. As selling continued prices fell and yields on the shortest bonds rose to the 2½ per cent level that the Chancellor had in view for the 'medium longs'. Permission for the houses to raise new capital was quickly given.

Consequently, during 1946–7 all eleven of the houses raised new capital : in just over a year the discount market's true resources expanded by about 50 per cent, from £22 million to about £34 million.[27] Six of the houses registered as public companies and obtained quotations on the Stock Exchange. There was also a new formation, the Clive Discount Co. Ltd, founded in December 1946 on capital obtained to a large extent from merchant banks. Overall, as compared to the pre-war position, the number of houses had fallen by one-third while aggregate resources had increased by 70 per cent. In terms of market operations the growth had been even greater because of the smaller multipliers (ratios of assets to published capital resources) in use after the war. 'Normal' bond carrying capacity was now about £270 million – with the possibility of an appreciably larger position in time of strain. Similarly, the houses' 'deposit' liabilities grew during wartime faster than those of the banks, so that compared with 1938 they were one-third larger as a proportion of bank deposits.

In line with his general strategy the Chancellor began to operate on short-term rates as a prelude to exerting pressure on the longs. In

October 1945 the rate on T.D.R.s was reduced by ½ per cent to ⅝ per cent and the ruling 1 per cent rate at which the Bank would turn Treasury bills into cash was cut to ½ per cent. From the shorts the Chancellor advanced through the mediums and into the longs, progressively conditioning the market to the acceptance of lower rates by means of statements of intent and a programme of conversions and new issues at lower coupons.[28] The crucial test came with the tap issue of the new 2½ per cent Treasury Stock 1975 or after ('Daltons') in October 1946 and the conversion into it of the 3 per cent Local Loans Stock.[29] The experiment was not to succeed.

The view of the market was that much of the issue was taken up by the Departments and that the failure of the public to take up the 'Daltons' forced the government to borrow heavily from the banks. Bank deposits did indeed rise rapidly during 1946 but the rise was more a reflection of the scale of government borrowing than of debt management. After 1946, however, the scale of borrowing declined and the rise in bank deposits was more moderate. Dr Dalton had not intended that a decline in interest rates should have been accompanied by a corresponding rise in the money supply, the psychological conditioning approach seeming to preclude the inflationary evils of a rise in bank credit. Nevertheless, on the Liquidity Preference principle the achievement of a lower long-term rate should have involved the authorities in bidding up the price of bonds by means of purchases in the open market. Financing needs of the government would then have demanded expansion of the short-term debt with a concomitant increase in bank deposits.

On this reasoning the slower rate of growth of bank deposits after 1946 may have contributed powerfully to the failure of Dalton's policy. Furthermore, widespread fears in the market that cheap money could not be sustained were strengthened by the increasing opposition to the policy that found its most telling expression in the annual statements of the clearing bank chairmen published at the beginning of 1947. At first the government broker intervened to keep prices up but support was soon withdrawn. Under the impact of the power crisis early in 1947 and the dollar crisis in August, gilt-edged prices fell to an extent that pushed the yield on 2½ per cent consols above 3 per cent by the end of the year.

In November 1947 Dr Dalton was succeeded as Chancellor by Sir Stafford Cripps, who announced continued support for cheap money but who shortly afterwards (early 1948) recognised its failure by putting long-term borrowing and lending on a 3 per cent basis. Cripps adopted what has been called a 'neutral' monetary policy, in that monetary trends were to conform to the wider aims of general economic policy. While short-term rates were to be maintained at a low level, yields on gilts were to be much less supported – except for specific purposes.[30] The upward trend of the long-term rate (the yield on 2½ per cent consols stood at 3½ per cent in 1950) was given impetus by funding operations designed to contain the growth in supply of liquid assets to the banks.

For the discount houses the government's post-war interest rate policy was to a large extent a continuation of the dealing environment they had known during wartime. Where there were changes of emphasis in market conditions the houses found them on the whole to be to their advantage. The quantity of Treasury bills available for discount house portfolios was increased, successively, by the demands of Dalton's cheap money drive, by the reduction in demand from 'outside' buyers (overseas official holdings, as sterling balances declined) and by the substitution to a substantial extent of Treasury bills for T.D.R.s in 1949 and 1950.[31] There was during this period some evidence of a revival in commercial bill business, partly as a response to initiatives by acceptance houses and discount houses, but the amounts involved were modest and added little to the houses' profitability.[32] It was in short-term bonds that they continued to find the greatest rewards – firmly poised as the houses were on a much-strengthened capital base and with the continuing concern of the authorities that they should be able to make a market at the short end of the maturity spectrum. The authorities' less obtrusive handling of the gilt-edged market after 1947 provided for greater flexibility of bond prices but continued to give assurance that any collapse of bond prices would not be tolerated. Bond dealers could therefore expect higher running profits from the somewhat improved yields, and more substantial dealing profits from the freer movement of prices, but not that they might have to suffer heavy capital loss.[33]

The discount houses' prosperous voyage among the short bonds took place upon a relatively calm sea of borrowed funds. For the remaining six years of the 'cheap money era', which was to end in November 1951, Bank rate was fixed at 2 per cent. The rate for money secured against Treasury bills stood throughout at ½ per cent. Bond money was at first priced at ⅝ per cent and money against fine bank bills at ½ per cent, but with the upward trend of bond yields and rates on bank bills after 1948 these money rates also began to rise. By 1951 rates on both bond money and bank bill money could be as high as ¾ per cent. The banks took advantage of the situation by prescribing the proportions in which they would accept bills and bonds as security, so ensuring that they got as much as possible of the higher-priced money.

In the context of a policy of officially managed interest-rates the houses had little difficulty in obtaining the money required each day to balance their books. Given that key short-term rates were not to be allowed to rise the houses knew that the volume of funds necessary to maintain them at the $\frac{1}{2}$ per cent level would always be forthcoming. To ensure that the market received just enough money each day to effect a balance, the authorities would estimate for the succeeding week the amount of funds that would flow out to the private sector through official transactions. By issuing an amount of Treasury bills for the week somewhat in excess of this figure the market would be left with a net deficit. The shortage could then just be supplied each day through the normal smoothing operations of the special buyer. The funds would be released in the mornings by buying Treasury bills from the clearing banks, which would then have less to call from the discount houses. Where the houses nevertheless found themselves with a deficit near to the close the Bank would make it good via direct or indirect help or, if the amount were small, the clearing banks themselves would provide overnight loans by means of a temporary depletion of their cash reserves.[34]

Thus in marked contrast to the conditions that the houses were to experience later, money dealing during the first six post-war years was a routine and comfortable business : the 'evils' of official squeeze, penal borrowing and high rates for scarce money being totally absent.

Part Two

THE MODERN DISCOUNT
HOUSES IN OPERATION:
I, 1951-70

5 British Monetary Policy: a Context for Operations

INTRODUCTION

Because of the very nature of their operations and of the peculiar position they have occupied at the centre of the British monetary system, the way in which the discount houses have at any time been able to conduct their business has been profoundly and immediately influenced by the goals of official monetary policy and the techniques employed to achieve them. This would be sufficient reason for an examination of the theoretical framework of official action in the monetary field between 1951 and 1970 but, in addition, interesting questions arise in connection with the part played by the houses in the process of monetary control itself. In the present chapter there is a general assessment of the aims and theoretical bases of British monetary policy during the period with indications of the discount houses' strategic role. In Chapters 7–11 this role is analysed in the context of the houses' operations in individual markets. Chapter 12 presents a close analysis of the discount houses' role in the mechanisms whereby the Bank might have sought to regulate the level of bank deposits, via leverage on reserve ratios.

THE APPROACH TO MONETARY CONTROL IN THE 1950s

The conduct of monetary policy after 1951 was constrained by the implications of the conditions on which the war had been financed, the conditions imposed by post-war budgetary policy and by certain assumptions made by the authorities about the behaviour of operators in the gilt-edged market.

The policy of financing the war at low rates of interest involved borrowing at shorter term, which had the effect of increasing the liquidity of the financial institutions' asset structures and occasioning earlier and more frequent debt conversion operations. In addition, the government ran budget deficits through the 1950s.[1] Consequently, in the capital market the authorities had to manage continuous and large-scale conversion operations together with a substantial annual net borrowing requirement. The goal of inducing the private sector to buy and then to hold government debt assumed a position of paramount importance.[2] The authorities believed that demand in the gilt-edged market was marked by instability. In the terminology of the current debate over the reappraisal of Keynesian economics, investors were believed to have elastic rather than inelastic price expectations, at least in the short term. This would imply that a fall in bond prices would occasion substantial sales rather than purchases of gilts. In policy terms, investors' confidence had at all costs to be sustained. This was to be ensured by maintaining a buoyant market of stable bond prices in which holders of gilts could be assured of being able to liquidate their holdings without, at the same time, having the wish to do so. Stability was to be maintained through purchases and sales of debt so as to moderate market-produced movements in prices. The important part played by discount-house bond dealers in the management of the gilt-edged market, through the purchase of the less popular very short dated debt, is examined in Chapter 10.

Given the nature of fixed interest securities price stability implied stability of yields. There could thus be no active interest-rate policy except among the shortest rates. Conversely, constrained as to its price, the monopolist producer of money in the economy (the Bank) could not attempt any effective short-term regulation of the supply.

An interpretation of the authorities' behaviour in the 1950s, in terms of the theory implicit in that behaviour, is as follows.[3] The constraints imposed by the policy adopted in the gilt-edged market were not found to be onerous : (*a*) because the interest elasticities of private expenditures were generally regarded as having a small absolute value, interest rates were not regarded as being key variables in the transmission mechanism : they merely affected the non-bank demand for gilts; (*b*) similarly, the resulting loss of short-term control over the money supply (bank deposits) was not regarded as necessarily a disadvantage, first of all because of the prevailing views on the role of interest rates and also because there is no evidence to suggest that the authorities held a 'monetarist' theory, whereby changes in the real value of money holdings would result in *direct* substitution for a wide range of goods and services. If this analysis is correct it can be argued that the authorities must have held an availability of credit theory. Moreover, because they regarded the market for loanable funds as being composed of a number of imperfect and segmented sub-markets it was thereby held that a restriction of *bank* finance was roughly equivalent to a restriction of finance in general. The authorities' attention was therefore directed not at the level of bank deposits but at the level of bank advances, that is they sought to influence the level of aggregate demand through operations on the level of bank advances.

There is evidence apparently opposed to this view, for example in November 1951 the authorities funded £1000 million of Treasury bills in exchange for a new short-dated stock. The banks were obliged to take half of the total, thus switching this amount from 'liquid assets' to 'investments' and reducing their liquid assets ratio from 39 per cent to 31 per cent – at a time when the conventional liquidity ratio was 30 per cent. This device, usually associated with leverage on the volume of bank deposits, was imposed on the clearing banks at that time by informal agreement with the Bank. J. C. R. Dow,[4] following the Radcliffe Report, interpreted these moves as indicating an attempt by the authorities to restore control over the volume of money. Elsewhere they have been interpreted as two arms of a common Exchequer financing policy, both 'lengthening' the maturity of outstanding debt and at the same time guaranteeing a market for short-term government debt through the imposition of the liquidity requirement.[5] In other words the ratio[6] formed part of the mutually beneficial cartel and other arrangements – the 'quid pro quo trade-offs between the Bank, the clearing banks and the discount houses'. In addition the Bank had officially stated that neither the cash ratio nor the liquidity ratio had been used as a fulcrum of deposit control.[7] While this was no doubt the case it could still be consistent with an interpretation that viewed the imposition of a 30 per cent ratio as an aid to the regulation of the growth of bank *advances.*[8]

The characteristic approach to monetary policy during the 1950s can be summed up in what was later called the 'package deal' of measures :

> When restrictive action has been thought necessary, their inclination has been to make a general call for restraint, and to announce several restrictive measures together, or almost together, usually a rise in Bank rate, stern words on bank advances, hire purchase controls, and a pruning of capital programmes in the public sector – all at once.[9]

The merits claimed for this approach comprised : the enhanced effect on would-be spenders; the impression made on external opinion by the comprehensive nature of the measures; the appeal to fairness made by a wider spread of measures; the possibly more than proportionate effect of applying all together measures which individually might command little confidence in their efficacy.

The most noticeable change in the measures employed after November 1951 lay in the use of Bank rate variation. With the exception of August to September 1939 Bank rate had lain unchanged from June 1932 to November 1951. Thereafter, up to the time the Radcliffe Committee reported in August 1959, it was changed twelve times. Because the rule was that Bank rate variation should always be included in a package of monetary measures, it provides a useful indicator of policy.[10] Generally, monetary measures were employed in response to the promptings of the balance of payments situation, which itself tended to be judged on the basis of movements in the reserves. Bank rate variation was always emphasised in this context, although the precise effect it was intended to achieve was never made clear.[11]

Of the other measures included in the package deal the rationale for the use of one of them – direct influence on bank advances – has already been discussed. The first requests for restraint had been made soon after the outbreak of war in 1939 and the device was employed by all three post-war Labour Chancellors : Dalton, Cripps and Gaitskell. As an integral part of monetary policy in the 1950s controls became, in 1955, *quantitative* and not merely *qualitative* and, in 1957, *requirements* rather than *requests*. Another hang-over from the war was capital issues control which, though of minimal significance, was retained on the same availability rationale as control over bank advances. The new kind of direct control on aggregate demand, first imposed in February 1952, was that of statutory regulation of the minimum terms for contracts of hire purchase finance. The availability effect was exercised indirectly in that some attempt was made to restrict the supply of funds to finance companies from the banks and new issue market.

THE FINDINGS OF THE RADCLIFFE COMMITTEE

From the mid-1950s there was increasing unease in official quarters about the efficacy of monetary measures. In May 1957 the Chancellor set up the Committee on the Working of the Monetary System, the Radcliffe Committee, 'to inquire into the working of the monetary and credit system and to make recommendations'. For the Chancellor at that time,

> the problem that was pressing itself most urgently on his attention was that of controlling inflation. In the preceding two years a number of measures had been introduced to check the very rapid expansion which had been so marked a feature of the economy since 1954 . . . There was a feeling that the restrictive measures adopted

were not achieving the results which would have justified the great difficulties which they imposed upon the working of the monetary machine.[12]

The measures alluded to were those discussed above, namely increases in Bank rate, pressure on bankers to contain the growth of advances, plus hire purchase restrictions. To these, however, had been added a new element through the conviction of the Chancellor, Mr Thorneycroft, that the defeat of inflation must fundamentally involve restriction of the money supply.

The Committee reported in August 1959.[18] Their view was so opposed to that of Mr Thorneycroft and academic economists sympathetic to his 'monetarist' ideas that it brought forth publication of a volume of alternative analysis and conclusions.[14] In this context the Committee's most contentious conclusion was that the authorities must '. . . regard the structure of interest rates rather than the supply of money as the centre-piece of the monetary mechanism.'[15] While this did not mean that the supply of money was considered unimportant it did mean that its control was regarded as incidental to interest-rate policy. Because of the far-reaching importance of this conclusion the way in which the Committee arrived at it is worth examining in some detail. The argument proceeded as follows.

The way in which monetary measures would work to push the economy in the direction decided by the government would be through their influence on the total pressure of demand for goods and services. In theory the authorities could exert influence on the level of demand in two ways: (1) via the 'interest incentive effect', that is through changes in interest rates to induce a change in the *incentive* to purchase capital goods and so to cause a change in actual spending on labour and other means of production of those goods[16] (it was believed that only very limited reliance could be placed on this route); (2) via the 'general liquidity effect', whereby the authorities would bring about a change in the liquidity condition of financial institutions and of firms and households so that those wanting money to spend would find it more or less difficult to obtain than before. This route, therefore, concerns the *availability* of funds to would-be spenders. It was in this regard that the Committee considered that the magnitude relevant to spending decisions was not the money supply as such but the 'whole liquidity position'. In this sense spending would not be limited by the amount of money in existence (immediate access to money) but by the amount of money people thought they could get hold of, whether by receipts of income (e.g. from sales), by disposal of capital assets, or by borrowing.

The next step is to understand that all other kinds of liquid assets (for example savings bank deposits or building society shares) were considered inferior compared to the ultimate liquidity of money (currency and bank deposits) and for this reason offered the compensation of the payment of interest. Because in a highly developed financial system many close substitutes for money would be available, restriction of the money supply alone would have a minimal effect in terms of rises in interest rates. It would be up to the authorities to accentuate the interest rate movement either by forcing penal-rate borrowing of money, against the next most liquid asset, or directly through operations in the gilt-edged market. Interest rate movements across the maturity spectrum would affect the behaviour of an indefinitely wide range of financial institutions, whose lending influenced total demand, through changes in the capital value of their asset portfolios : 'A rise in rates makes some less willing to lend because capital values have fallen and others because their own interest rate structure is sticky. A fall in rates, on the other hand, strengthens balance sheets and encourages lenders to seek new business.'[17]

Because the effects of operations on interest rates were considered to be so pervasive it was thought to be possible to avoid the use of a complex system of direct controls over the lending behaviour of numerous institutions.[18] However, in 'times of emergency' the authorities might see fit to employ direct controls against the base of the liquidity structure. That is, because of the position of the clearing banks as 'key lenders' in the system, the authorities might choose to impose advances control. If they should find themselves inhibited in their interest rate policy then advances control could be supplemented with other measures of the package deal, for example capital issues control and the control of hire purchase finance.

On the face of it, the Radcliffe view represents a complete departure from the theory apparently held by the authorities, that whereas the view prior to Radcliffe had been that interest rate effects at the medium and longer end of the market were valuable only in helping to maximise private sector holdings of government debt, the very same rates were now to be regarded as the centrepiece of monetary action. A reconciliation of the apparently opposed views is simple. The Committee, as is clear from the above summary of their views, agreed with the prevailing orthodoxy regarding the interest elasticity of investment expenditure but reinstated the importance of interest rate changes through the 'general liquidity effect' on the lending behaviour of financial intermediaries. The transmission mechanism implicit in the Committee's position was therefore similar to that of the authorities in that : (1) the market for loanable funds was considered to be dis-aggregated into a number of imperfectly related sub-markets; (2) of key importance for potential spending decisions was the *availability* of funds through a pyramid-shaped structure of institutional channels of which the banks formed the apex. The Committee's position dif-fered from that of the authorities in that (in normal times) the avail-ability of funds would be influenced via interest rate effects on lending institutions, and the 'liquidity' magnitude which now had to be con-trolled was wider and more imprecise than the variable at which the authorities were aiming.[19]

For the 1960s, the Committee found that they were unable to offer any 'positive and simple' recommendations with regard to the employ-ment of monetary measures. In concluding that 'monetary measures cannot alone be relied upon to keep in nice balance an economy sub-ject to major strains from both without and within', they could only foresee that the government would have to employ 'in combination, and probably with changing degrees of emphasis, three groups of measures [direct, budgetary and monetary] all of which have substan-tial disadvantages'.[20] They believed that in ordinary times the authori-ties should make more deliberate use of interest rates, especially at the longer end, so as to influence the general liquidity situation. Because the banks were seen as being in a uniquely strong position to frustrate interest rate policy their lending would have to be restrained by the use of a strictly observed liquidity ratio, given added leverage when necessary through the use of Special Deposits or Treasury Deposit Receipts.[21] In conditions of more extreme economic imbalance mon-etary measures were to be employed as follows : in a slump it was recommended only that monetary conditions should be made 'propi-tious' while conditions of 'headlong inflation' were to be tackled via measures which would strike directly and rapidly at the liquidity of spenders – namely control of bank advances, capital issues and con-sumer credit.

THE USE OF MONETARY MEASURES IN THE 1960s

In the decade after the Radcliffe Committee reported the approach to monetary policy adopted by the authorities involved no apparent radical departure from that followed previously. By their own declaration, that approach was broadly Radcliffian in that there was no exclusive concentration on the control of a single variable such as the money supply and attention was consistently directed towards influencing the cost or availability of credit flows to the various sectors of the economy.[22] However, the economic environment in which the authorities had to operate differed in several respects from that with which the Radcliffe Committee were immediately familiar.

Although the economic problems themselves had not basically changed, they had become more intractable. Within the continuing overall need to maintain a state of full employment the principal goals of British economic policy were on the one hand to increase the sustainable rate of growth of the economy and on the other to solve the balance of payments problem. Increasingly, there developed a state of short-term conflict between the position on external account and expansion of the domestic economy. Sterling became increasingly over-valued as the years went by and rectification of the balance of payments attracted a growing proportion of the weight of economic policy measures. The Radcliffe Committee had foreseen that monetary policy would be for the most part permissive and would have to be employed in severe doses only relatively infrequently, in 'emergency' conditions. Instead the authorities made prolonged use of stringent measures of all kinds. Moreover, the packages contained a growing proportion of monetary measures as the limitations of budgetary and incomes policies and exchange controls became apparent. It has been argued that because action taken to influence the balance of payments position would carry adverse effects for the 'growth' goal the authorities appear to have delayed taking action for as long as possible, using movements in the reserves as indicators, and thus had to look to drastic remedies for quick results.[23]

Official interest-rate policy fell far short of what the Committee expected of the 'centre-piece of the monetary mechanism'. Although the 1960s saw marked fluctuations in interest rates there was no active use of debt management policy to influence the general liquidity position. Even in 1969, when a policy calculated to give more flexibility at both the short and long ends of the gilts market was adopted, it is possible that the authorities were merely taking advantage of the easier conditions offered by a budgetary surplus.[24] It was rather the case that, as previously, the authorities believed that the market's re-actions to interest rate changes could be perverse or unpredictable, so that their desire to maintain 'effective' markets for government debt really meant that they had to maintain 'orderly' markets.

This overriding constraint had important implications for the possibility of employment of other forms of monetary control. In the first place, the authorities were not able to pursue an interest rate policy which would have allowed them to control bank lending via leverage on the cash base – even if such a technique had been considered feasible on other criteria. Similar problems attached to control via the liquidity ratio, although the authorities were able to exert some pressure by this means – especially when the pressure was increased by calls for Special Deposits.[25] It was often the case, however, that such pressure was felt to be necessary at times when market weakness would have made large-scale sales of government debt to the non-bank public difficult at prices which would have fulfilled the criteria for orderly markets. In such circumstances the effect of necessary sales to the banks was often to expand their liquid asset holdings. However, in the later years of the decade the authorities were aided by a considerable decline in the proportion of government debt in the banks' total assets in that the banks were not able so easily to escape a pressure by switching their lending from the public to the private sector. Nevertheless, the incompatibility of the desire to exercise control through sales of longer-dated debt with the possibility of doing so at non-disruptive prices, persisted. The authorities defended their adherence to the 'orderly markets' constraint on the grounds that there was 'little evidence that a more active approach would have been more effective'.[26]

The methods actually employed for implementing credit policy during the decade after 1959 were seen by the authorities as being essentially a continuation of developments in progress before the Radcliffe Committee was set up. The chief advance was that the controls had become more specific in their application and more direct in their mode of operation. Hire purchase controls were in operation for much longer periods than was envisaged by the Committee and were subject to quite frequent changes of terms. There was also specific control through the effects of interest rate operations by the authorities on the behaviour of financial intermediaries involved in private housebuilding. As suggested above, the authorities found it necessary, over much of the period, to bring about the sort of drastic effects that could only be achieved by means of direct controls. Here restraint took the form of ceilings imposed on bank lending. Of course, the deposit banks had been prevailed upon to curb their lending on several occasions during the 1950s and in July 1961 a request for restraint was issued in conjunction with a call for Special Deposits. On this occasion, both on grounds of efficiency and equity, a call greatly to reduce the rate of increase of advances was issued to all groups of banks and a wide range of financial institutions. In 1965 all banks and hire purchase finance houses were asked to keep their lending, during the ensuing twelve months, to within 105 per cent of the March 1965 level; in addition there was qualitative guidance as to officially favoured priority borrowers.[27]

Overall, on the basis of their experience of the 1960s, the authorities became convinced that even though certain effects of monetary policy could be discerned (for example marked changes in expenditure on goods following significant changes in the rigour of terms control; private housebuilding and the availability of mortgage finance; investment expenditure and the cost or availability of funds; consumers' expenditure and sharp restriction of bank lending – both directly and indirectly via its effect on stock market values), it could never be relied upon primarily for short-term stabilisation purposes, and that for maximum effect monetary and fiscal policy would always have to be employed in conjunction. In this respect then, the authorities' experience was in accord with the predictions of the Committee.

THE ROLE OF THE DISCOUNT HOUSES

Whatever particular bundle of monetary measures the Treasury and the Bank of England decide to put into effect at any time the ordinary day-to-day tasks of financing the central government, maintaining the liquidity of the banking system and managing the foreign exchange position have to be carried on as usual. Often, shorter-term policies can conflict with longer-term aims. It is for this reason that the Bank of England, which carries the main burden of responsibility for continuous management and support of the financial system, is, and has been, anxious to make the ongoing tasks as automatic and as secure as possible. One manifestation of this concern has, in the past, been the tacit acceptance of and positive encouragement by the Bank of agreements in restraint of competition between key members of the markets through which finance was arranged and control exercised (see Chapter 3).

The argument so far in this book has shown that the discount houses became increasingly important as the centre of the apparatus through which the Bank both guaranteed the continuance of day-to-day responsibililties and concentrated the channels for the implementation of 'conventional' monetary control. The call-money market provided by the discount houses enabled banks to adjust their liquidity positions continuously and meant that any net loss of cash from the banks to the Exchequer accounts would immediately become apparent in one place, that is the discount market. The Bank could then decide, in relieving the shortage, what effect it wished to create in the money market. Call money formed an important part of the liquid assets which the banks held as a minimum ratio to total deposits and in so far as the discount houses used call money to purchase bills and bonds these assets could be viewed as being held indirectly by the banks. The discount houses also played an important part in the supply of the bills (Treasury bills and commercial bills) that, with cash, made up the balance of the liquid assets ratio.

Another aspect of day-to-day business in which the houses provided the requisite support operations was that of government finance. As professional dealers in short-term government securities the discount houses tended to concentrate on their books a fair proportion of gilts nearing maturity. In so doing they simplified the government broker's task of planning the refinancing of the public debt and so helped to keep the market 'orderly'. They also performed a limited jobbing function which contributed to market stability. In respect of the floating debt the houses provided the guarantee that the whole of the offer of 'tender' Treasury bills would be taken up and that there would be relative stability of the Treasury bill rate.[28]

Between 1951 and 1970 the authorities were able to impose hire purchase controls, ceilings on banks' advances and capital issues restrictions without in the first instance utilising the discount houses' services. Similarly, in the scheme put forward by the Radcliffe Committee the discount houses and the rest of the short-term market were accorded no specific role and the part to be played by short-term interest rates was not made explicit. Nevertheless, there was a general presumption that short-term rates would be in sympathy with a wider interest-rate policy. Therefore, although the Committee only explicitly recognised a real significance in Bank rate movements in relation to the external situation, inasmuch as Bank rate was the keystone of the structure of short-term rates, the discount houses had a positive part to play in making Bank rate 'effective'.

Broadly, Bank rate had effects in three main ways : (1) by the 'demonstration' effect of a change, i.e. as an intimation of official attitudes; (2) by the 'conventional' effect of a change, i.e. by the fact that other short-term rates moved with and kept a fixed margin in relation to Bank rate; (3) by being made 'effective', i.e. by being the rate at which the discount houses were forced to borrow when they were 'in the Bank'. By varying the volume and frequency of borrowing at the Bank the authorities could, *ceteris paribus*, enforce any chosen regime in the short-term market. For whatever purpose, but generally in response to movements in the position on external account and in the level of employment at home, over the years from November 1951 to September 1971 Bank rate was changed forty times.

During this period the authorities did attempt to exercise control over the banks' lending by means of pressure on the liquid assets ratio, and for this reason the houses' function in providing the necessary assets – commercial bills as well as Treasury bills and call money – will be examined in the following chapters. No attempt was made by

D

the authorities to use the cash base as a fulcrum for leverage. Nevertheless, because of the importance for British monetary economics of the debate over the control of bank deposits via the cash ratio and also because of the crucial questions raised about discount houses' behaviour in the relevant markets, the whole question will be considered in detail in Chapter 12.

6 Principles of Daily Operation

INTRODUCTION

Individual chapters below are devoted to the sources of discount houses' borrowed funds and to their major assets, both traditional and new. The business of the present chapter is to outline concisely the principles which governed discount house operations and to provide a framework into which the detailed analysis of the later chapters can be fitted. The framework utilised is the houses' daily routine of buying and selling bills, bonds and certificates of deposit and of borrowing and repaying the funds necessary to finance them, culminating in the all-important 'daily balance', or squaring of books at 3 p.m.

THE MONEY BOOK

During the period 1951–70 each of the discount houses was a profit-making limited liability company[1] operating within a set of historically determined institutional constraints. They borrowed money on a day-to-day basis from banks and other institutions that had surpluses to lend and invested it in a variety of assets with terms that ranged from three months to five years. Profits were made from the difference between borrowing and lending rates plus jobbing profits and commissions. The vast bulk of funds borrowed by discount houses was secured by the deposit of collateral with the lender.[2] Collateral consisted of the assets in which the houses had invested the funds borrowed. Because the market prices of the securities lodged were liable to fluctuate the banks insisted that their value should exceed the value of funds borrowed by a specified margin. All funds borrowed were invested so that the extra value of securities for margin had to be purchased with a house's own capital resources. The extent of a house's operations was thus limited by the size of its capital. The ratios maintained of asset holdings to capital were known as 'multipliers'. In exchange for certain obligations the Bank of England acted as lender of last resort – on its own terms – and so enabled the discount houses always to meet their liabilities.

Each day, therefore, discount house officials would be engaged in borrowing money, repaying loans, purchasing bills and bonds, and selling or redeeming matured securities. Money would flow into a discount house: (a) as funds were borrowed and (b) as bills and bonds were sold or they came to maturity. Money would flow out: (a) as banks called funds previously borrowed or overnight loans were repaid and (b) as a house took up bills on days previously arranged or purchased bills or bonds. The working tool that was at the centre of operations and illustrates better than anything else the way in which the houses functioned was the money book, in which were recorded all daily transactions involving money and which showed the money position at any time. This was very important because it was upon such information that the officials had to decide what steps to take to ensure that the flows of money in and out balanced by the time the banks closed.[3]

Money coming into the house was shown on one side of the money book (this would also reflect movements of assets out of the house), and money going out was shown on the other (this would also reflect the movement of assets into the house). Practice among the houses varied as to which side of the book was used for 'Money Out' and 'Money In'. In the following example only the main headings of each type of transaction are shown although there may have been up to fifty or more entries on each side of the book.[4] For the 'rough' money book, kept in the main dealing room as an indicator of the overall position at any stage of the day, the entries were recorded only in round amounts.

Money Out

Purchases of Treasury bills including any commitment to take up bills purchased at the previous week's tender.

Commercial bills (bank bills and trade bills) discounted.

Purchases of government stocks.

Take-up of local authority bills and bonds.

Purchases of negotiable certificates of deposit (denominated in sterling).

Repayment of overnight money or fixtures due, and other money called by banks.

Money In

Bills, bonds and sterling negotiable certificates of deposit maturing.

Sales of Treasury and other bills both to private customers and to the Bank of England.

Sales of government stocks.

Sales of sterling negotiable certificates of deposit.
Any money borrowed on the morning rounds.
Fresh money borrowed after lunch to meet the deficit on the
day : from the banks
: privilege money
: from the Bank

Each payment or receipt of money required a movement of security
so that the volume of security handled each day was very large.
Further, while a house's turnover could be up to £70 million in a day,
the daily balance was effected to the nearest £10,000, which was the
smallest dealing unit in money.

At the start of each day discount house officials knew that they
would have to find a certain amount of money to pay for Treasury
bills due to be taken up by that house as a result of the previous
Friday's tender.[5] In addition, some of the money (including any
privilege money – see below, Chapter 7) borrowed the previous day
would be due for repayment, as would perhaps any seven-day or
overnight money borrowed from the Bank. In addition to scheduled
repayments much of the money running on from day to day would
be called in the course of the morning. To set against the outgoings
there could be receipts in settlement for bonds sold on the previous
day. By the 'close' each house had to find the net sum of the known
amounts plus the amount called less any receipts.[6]

THE ORGANISATION OF BUSINESS

For the transaction of their business each house was organised along
the same lines with dealers in money and bills, bonds and other securities grouped around dealing tables, each of which would be equipped
with a multi-line telephone system. Differences between the houses
arose from the amount of space that could be devoted to each activity
(a function of the size of the house) with the larger companies having,
for example, a separate room for the bond dealers and for the official
whose responsibility it was to effect the disposition of suitable security
on borrowed funds. As the houses moved into business in the newer,
'parallel market' securities, they initially kept it separate from the
traditional business. Until very late in the period certificates of deposit
(C.D.s) and currencies were traded through subsidiaries. As the period
progressed the technical complexity of telephone systems increased so
that dealers could talk instantly on private lines to each of the other
houses and to each of the banks with which business might be negotiated. A remarkable advance was the installation of closed-circuit

television which allowed details of business currently being transacted to be conveyed to all in the house who would need to take action. It was this same television system that allowed discount house officials to be notified in comfort of changes in Bank rate and so ended the necessity for representatives to go personally to the Bank.

THE DAILY ROUTINE

The business day ran from 9 a.m. to 5 p.m. and was divided by well-established routine into a clearly defined timetable with 'deadlines' at 2.30 and 3 o'clock. While much business was transacted through personal contact the use of the telephone came to assume greater and greater importance:

> . . . the telephones are always ringing. Stockbrokers constantly report movements in the gilt-edged market. Commercial bill business is discussed by potential and established suppliers. Borrowers in the local authority market are seeking funds, lenders are seeking outlets. New business may be proposed and analysed, old contacts may be renewed. Visits to industrial companies in the United Kingdom or to banks on the Continent are planned or their results discussed.[7]

The first job of the day was to deal with business received through the post and if, for example, it included bills for discounting an entry recording their purchase would be made in the money book and payment prepared. The next task was to establish the conditions that a house's dealers would have to contend with in the various markets. When houses began to deal in dollar and sterling C.D.s, in the late 1960s, the first enquiries to establish opening rates would be made by dealers in those instruments. At half-past nine it was the turn of the gilt-edged dealers, as the stockbrokers telephoned to give the opening prices of short-dated government stocks. Until gilt-edged jobbers began to deal on the floor of the Stock Exchange, half an hour later, dealing was carried on by telephone.

Between 10.15 and 11.45 a.m. contact was made with all the London banks either on the telephone or through personal calls made by the house's representatives. According to the number of suitable staff available, the total of banks to be visited was divided into 'rounds' of so many banks each. It was on the morning rounds that discount house representatives wore their traditional black silk hats.[8] In the age of the telephone and closed-circuit television, top-hatted personal visits seem a somewhat anachronistic luxury. In the first place, however, personal contact played a crucial part in the building up of a discount house's business – when houses dealt largely in commercial bills – and the funds to finance them were sought in the same way. With the growth of the inter-bank market in sterling funds in competition with the call-money market the discount houses considered that the benefits that flowed from personal relationships amply repaid the extra effort involved.[9]

Whilst at each bank the representatives would ask whether the bank wished to lend money, or needed to call money, or wished to adjust rates on money already with the houses. Enquiries would also be made as to whether the bank wished to buy or sell Treasury bills, commercial bills or C.D.s. From the banks' viewpoint discount market representatives

> are each seen for a matter of a few minutes – the visit is formal, proceedings pleasantly informal. The bank's representative indicates the bank's requirements – calls money and specifies the rate from which it is called, or offers to buy bills or lend money, as the case may be. The question of the rate for bills or money lent sometimes leads to a little resistance on the part of the market, but it is usually possible, without difficulty, to negotiate a rate satisfactory to both sides. A few words on market conditions or some topical subject may follow, after which the first visitor leaves and is followed without delay by the next in the queue.[10]

It was a jealously guarded tradition that the deals made were by word of mouth with no written confirmation. With a large number of banks to visit, however, and the consequent possibility of confusion, it was acknowledged that, once outside, the prudent representative would make a discreet note of the name of the bank and details of the deals in his notebook.

On completion of his round each representative would enter the details of the deals he had negotiated in the money book. The televised information would instantly reach those whose action was required; for example if a bank were calling money, the necessary payment would be prepared by the cashier, the security manager would make arrangements for the withdrawal of suitable security from the bank and the interest department would cease to credit interest on the loan.

BALANCING THE MONEY BOOK

By midday the rounds would have been completed and the money position established, by adding up both sides of the book. The result at this juncture would usually be a large net deficit because banks knew their commitments in the morning and consequently called money to cover them; on the other hand even if a bank knew that it would be receiving money later in the day it would usually be unwilling to lend until the actual payment was received. Between 12 noon and 1 p.m. the Bank of England's agent in the discount market, the 'special buyer' (Seccombe, Marshall and Campion Ltd, the smallest of the discount houses), would telephone to establish the money position in the market as a whole. This would then enable the Bank to decide what action to take so as to effect a desired adjustment (see Chapter 7).

Between midday and about 2.20 p.m. houses would attempt to replace funds lost during the morning by fresh loans from the banks. About ten minutes before the Discount Office closed to the discount houses at 2.30 p.m. the final money position would be established and a decision taken on whether or not to borrow from the Bank of England in order to balance the book. The decision would be based on an assessment of the market situation, in that senior officials would attempt to estimate whether sufficient funds would 'come out' before the banks closed at 3 p.m. Indications given by the special buyer of the attitude of the Bank and knowledge of privilege money available would influence the decision.[11]

The periods before the two deadlines at 2.30 and 3 p.m. involved a certain amount of tension and excitement as attempts were made to borrow the requisite funds. The money book would be closed at 3 p.m. and payments received paid into the house's clearing bank. If a house had not balanced its book in that it had a surplus, interest would have to be paid on it – unnecessarily. On the other hand a deficit would have to be covered by fresh borrowing if the house's clearing bank account was not to be overdrawn – which was 'not acceptable vis-à-vis one bank and another'.[12] The final task would be to balance the ledgers for the day and to prepare the opening money position for the following day. At 3.30 stockbrokers would telephone with government security prices at the close of business on the floor of the Stock Exchange. Telephoned transactions could continue until 5 p.m.

7 Borrowed Funds

INTRODUCTION

During the course of each day, discount houses borrowed money under a variety of heads, the various categories of loans being distinguished as to : the source from which the funds came; the term for which the funds were taken; the rate that was paid on the funds relative to other rates in the structure. Within this rough framework of analysis the present chapter examines the factors which shaped the houses' daily money position and the operations by means of which the daily balance was achieved. Indication is given of the main changes that took place in the relative importance of various lenders to the discount houses, the varieties of loans taken by the houses and the interest rate structures they encountered.

The houses borrowed funds from three main categories of lender :

   (i) the clearing banks;
  (ii) other banks and institutions, including non-bank and foreign sources;
 (iii) the Bank of England.

The Bank of England is dealt with separately because of its role as lender of last resort and the implications for monetary control that flowed from the exercise of that function, and because of the general regulatory influence it exerted over the market. Category (ii) is a rather heterogeneous collection and is merely meant to represent non-public-sector sources other than the clearing banks. Throughout the period from 1951 to 1970 the most important single group of lenders to the discount houses was the London clearing banks, consistently lending a higher percentage of the houses' total funds than any other group. In the later years its importance in percentage terms increased, with the peak (75·6 per cent) in 1969.[1] A description of the lending operations of the clearing banks can, consequently, be treated as the standard case against which other lenders can be compared.

BORROWING FROM CLEARING BANKS

All funds lent by the clearing banks to the discount houses were lent returnable 'at call or short notice'. On the other hand, the total amount of funds lent on this basis was divided up into 'regular money', 'overnight money' or 'night money', and 'privilege money'. Before examining the differences between the various types of money it will be helpful to look at the process from the lender's point of view so as to show how the total volume of funds to be lent was determined and how it was divided up between the rival borrowing houses.

The banker's dilemma is that of trying to find the proper balance in the assets he holds between those that yield greater profit but carry greater risk, and those that are more liquid and therefore more readily available to meet demands for cash but which yield only little or no profit. The resolution of this problem has traditionally been found in the maintenance by banks of commonly accepted ratios between certain liquid assets and the bank's total liabilities. While originally adopted for reasons of 'bankers' prudence' the ratios became obligatory through the requirements of monetary control as envisaged by the central bank.

In more practical terms, liquid asset reserves are vitally necessary to a bank to enable it to meet the calls made upon its cash position not only by movements of funds between institutions within the private-sector banking system but also by flows into and out of the system brought about by international trade, government budgetary and debt operations and by speculation in sterling. Some idea of the magnitudes involved can be gained from the following figures. In the mid-1960s the aggregate turnover of all the accounts maintained with the commercial banks was estimated at around £750,000 million per annum (perhaps between £2000 million and £2500 million per day); towards the end of the 1960s the annual figure could have risen to £1,000,000 million with the daily turnover between £3000 million and £3500 million.[2]

The major movements of funds followed recurrent patterns both annually and on a weekly basis. The annual movements of funds were reflected in very similar fluctuations in clearing banks' deposits. There was almost invariably a high peak in gross deposits at 31 December; a heavy fall followed in the first quarter of the year, after which came a partial recovery to a lesser peak at 30 June. There was then a shallower fall followed by a progressive increase which became very marked immediately before the December high peak.

The weekly pattern was similarly well marked. Monday was a day of uncertain conditions, while on Tuesday there was a distinct shortage of money brought about by transfers from the commercial banking system to the Bank of England on account of the Inland Revenue. Wednesday tended to be steady, while on Thursday outflows on government account gave easier monetary conditions. Friday and (until 1970) Saturday were also typically easier. Despite the multitude of factors at work, the stability of the overall pattern was guaranteed by the relatively large scale of government operations.

As a consequence, the commercial banks required a disposition of their liquid assets that would enable them to accommodate the effects on their cash positions of both the shorter- and longer-term movements. As was explained in Part One of this book, the operations of the discount houses had come to assume a central role in the working of the portfolio adjustment mechanism that was developed. The following analysis of the banks' requirements and the ways in which the discount houses helped to supply them goes some way towards an explanation of the continued acceptance of the peculiar arrangements for money dealing between clearing banks and discount houses – especially as regards the rate structure on borrowed funds – that obtained up to September 1971.

The banks' first requirement was for cash to meet, for example, public demand from the branches and for settlement at the daily clearing. In this regard cash equivalent to 8 per cent of total deposits was held in the form of notes and coin in tills and balances at the Bank of England.[3] The second requirement was for liquid assets that could be used to adjust the cash position. It was this requirement that gave rise to the call-money system. Money was lent out at call and short notice, that is overnight to seven days. Of the total figure published by the banks for call money the discount market took, in the second half of the 1960s, a proportion that declined from about 75 per cent to 70 per cent; the balance comprising loans, for example to money brokers, Stock Exchange jobbers and brokers and other bankers.[4] The third requirement was for reserves to accommodate the seasonal movements. These were provided largely via investment in Treasury bills, the maturity dates of which could easily be arranged – on the basis of past experience – to meet regular commitments. Similarly, the banks invested in suitable commercial paper, although its usefulness in this regard was more limited because of its lack of flexibility for the arrangement of maturity dates in comparison with that of Treasury bills.

In connection with the last requirement, the banks had prior to the early 1930s purchased graded parcels of commercial paper from the discount houses but had largely satisfied their demand for Treasury bills by competing directly at the tenders. However, under the terms of the 1935 agreement between clearing banks and discount houses (see Chapter 3) the clearing banks ceased to tender for bills for their own portfolios but took them instead from the discount houses after an interval of at least seven days. The houses subsequently sold Treasury bills to the clearing banks in parcels made up on the basis of the maturity dates of the bills – so ensuring a flow of maturities tailored to meet the banks' liquidity requirements.

In addition to the 8 per cent cash base, therefore, the banks held bills and call money in their liquid assets portfolio to give a ratio of liquid assets to total deposits of 30 per cent, a minimum that was reduced to 28 per cent in October 1963.[5] The liquidity of Treasury bill holdings was guaranteed by the official policy of maintaining stability of short-term interest rates (because it implied that the bills could be turned into cash on demand), while that of call money was assured by the Bank in its role of lender of last resort. The liquidity of commercial bill holdings derived from the expertise of the discount houses in choosing good-quality paper bearing names of high standing and backed by the houses' own guarantee on paper they had sold.

Bankers naturally demanded that where possible their liquid assets should be not only liquid but also profitable. Cash holdings, of course, did not earn interest, though on occasions when the authorities forced the banks to make Special Deposits these earned the current Treasury bill rate, because Special Deposits were designed to enforce a reduction in earning liquid assets, that is, not cash. Earnings on call money depended upon the level of Bank Rate, conventions applying to the various types of money lent (see below, pp. 95–7) and the state of supply and demand in the market at any time. Earnings on bills depended upon the types of bills held and their life to maturity, for example rising from the shortest-dated Treasury bill to the longest-dated trade bill. Taking bills and call money together it has been estimated that in 1969 a movement of rates of only one quarter of one per cent could affect gross earnings from these assets to the extent of approximately £5 million per annum and that total earnings on these assets could well account for about one-fifth of a bank's total gross earnings for the year.[6] Given the level of Bank rate the banks could influence their earnings on call money, making up say one-third of total liquid assets, through the cartel agreements on interest rates. For the rest, earnings on bills would be influenced by the market Treasury bill rate, the basis of which would be the result of the weekly tender in which the discount houses played a key (though by no means independent) role.

Treasury bill business is analysed in Chapters 8 and 12, and attention at this stage can be confined to asking how the banks calculated each day the amount of money that would be lent to or called from the market. Early in the day each bank made an estimate of its likely inflows and outflows of funds for that day using a system very like the discount houses' money book. On both sides of the book would be shown transactions in cash, and cheque and credit clearings, each having a net value 'in' or 'out'.[7] Also shown on the 'in' side would be : bills and bonds maturing, interest and dividend payments, the repayment of privilege money and government disbursements. Also shown on the 'out' side would be payments on account of government departments, the largest being those to the Inland Revenue. These items together with others would be totalled in amount and a net figure, 'in' or 'out', found. To this figure the banks would add the closing balance of cash and the balance at the Bank and then deduct cash for reserves. If the final result were found to be negative the banks would call funds from the market. If, however, a surplus were found it would either be lent to the market or invested in bills, the decision taking into account the amount of money already being lent overnight, the value of bills maturing over the next seven days and the extent of known future commitments.

Of equal interest is the question of how the banks discriminated between one house and another for business purposes. In general they related their requests for bills, offers of money or calls for money to the size of the house, as measured by capital resources. This meant that except where individual houses had abnormally large amounts outstanding overnight no house would be hit disproportionately hard by calls. Also, requests to houses for bills would be calculated on the same basis as they took up bills at the weekly tender.

THE CATEGORIES OF BORROWED FUNDS

The literature of the call-money system employed a confusingly large number of terms to describe the commodity that was being traded. Money nominally lent 'at call and short notice' was variously described as 'regular money', 'basic money', 'good money' and 'night money'. Apart from 'good money' which was a blanket expression referring to money not likely to be called, the various terms did provide a useful means of categorising borrowed funds. The primary distinction was between regular money and night money, where regular money referred to more permanent lending and night money to lending which was more temporary, being more subject to fluctuation in amount and implying that the banks would probably need to call it back the following day. The distinction was reflected in the way in which the rate on each was determined prior to the abolition of the bankers' cartel. Regular money was lent by the banks at rates fixed in relation to Bank rate and was subject to 'fixtures' between individual houses and banks, that is *ad hoc* agreements concerning the size and term of loans. Rates paid on night money, on the other hand, were much more the product of the market conditions obtaining from day to day.

While this is a useful generalisation it must be noted that not all regular money was lent at the same rate and that alternatively – on the basis of rates charged – money could be classified as follows : (*a*) basic money, that is the more or less permanent part of regular money that was lent at the minimum call rate which was fixed in relation to the clearing banks' deposit rate, which was itself fixed in relation to Bank rate; (*b*) the regular money that was lent at rates above the basic rate : this together with (*a*) gave an average rate for regular money; (*c*) true 'night' (overnight) money, the rates for which fluctuated both daily and during the course of the day according to the state of supply and demand in the market.

The apparent paradox in the use of terminology will bear closer examination, for although it was commonly accepted that regular money was more permanent money and that night money was lent 'overnight', both categories were technically money 'at call' from the clearing banks, which had the right to withdraw it at any time. This problem obviously perplexed the members of the Radcliffe Committee, as their questioning of L.D.M.A. representatives shows.[8] The L.D.M.A. were asked (Q. 3485) whether the references in their *Memorandum of Evidence* to basic or good money meant the same as regular money. The L.D.M.A. agreed that the basis of good money was that the houses always had it with them. They further agreed, however (Q. 3486), that good money was also on a day-to-day basis and that in fact (Q. 3487) all money borrowed was on a day-to-day basis. Pressed for the reason for the distinction between regular money and night money when all money was nominally at call, Sir A. Macnaghten replied for the L.D.M.A. : 'Because that is the way the market has always been, going back a long way. We have got money on our books which we may have borrowed for over a hundred years.'

Because the rate on regular money tended to be less subject to fluctuation than the (market) rate on night money its continuation was seen as being advantageous to both discount houses and clearing banks. It was explained that when the rate on regular money was below market rate the discount houses benefited but when it was above market rate the bankers gained (Q. 3489). In order to ensure that he had a good proportion of his money out at call at a *reasonable* rate *all* the time the banker was willing to forgo higher rates some of the time.

This being the case, how was the total amount of money lent divided up between regular money and night money? In reply to Q. 3488 an

L.D.M.A. representative said that in the case of his own house they had about four times as much regular money as night money. In other words a clearing bank that had, say, £10 million of regular money would have perhaps £2–£2½ million of overnight money. The position was summed up for the Committee by Lord Harcourt as follows :

> What it really boils down to is, as far as the clearing banks are concerned, for eighty per cent of the market's requirement there is steady money, and for the remaining twenty per cent you bid if you want money. You bid up if you are very short of money; on the other hand you refuse to take it if you do not want it and therefore it is unworkable or workable only at a better rate. It is the marginal money which is open to bids from hour to hour.

The L.D.M.A. agreed that this was a fair summary.[9]

In addition to the categories already described the discount houses had for many years possessed the right to borrow from the clearing banks small sums of money which would enable them in difficult times to balance their books. This 'privilege' money was provided at a fixed rate over the minimum call-money rate after the late 1950s and before that at the basic rate itself.

More specifically, if towards the close of business the discount houses found that they could not obtain sufficient funds from other sources to balance their books they had individual agreements with various clearing banks which gave them the right to claim a small additional loan. Loans ranged from £25,000 to £100,000 and in total amounted to about £5,000,000. They were provided on the understanding that they would be taken only if all other sources of funds had failed and that they would be repaid automatically on the next business day. A house would, however, be able to count on taking privilege money before resorting to the Bank. The privilege money principle appears to date well back into the nineteenth century with the agreements, at first informal and later formal, stemming from regular contact between individual houses and banks and their mutual recognition of the needs inherent in a money market that was not so closely regulated by the authorities as it later became. The spur for bankers to promote the regularisation of privilege arrangements and therefore their outlets for money came with the persistence of very easy money conditions in the 1890s. In the mid-1920s the loans assumed a crucial importance in that they allowed houses to purchase American cotton bills which because of the time difference between London and New York, were presented for discounting just prior to the close. In general, after the Second World War the frequency of resort to privilege money depended upon conditions obtaining in the money market.

NON-CLEARING BANK SOURCES

Although the London clearing banks remained the biggest single suppliers of funds to the discount houses during the twenty years after 1951 they were by no means the only important ones. The houses also took money regularly from the Scottish banks, members of the Accepting Houses Committee (the accepting houses), overseas banks with offices in London, other banks in London and foreign banks with London branches. In addition money was taken from banks on the Continent and from lenders outside the banking system, for example insurance companies, mining companies and other commercial and industrial concerns that wished to put out funds for even a single night at the clearing banks' deposit rate or at $\frac{1}{4}$ per cent over that rate for money placed at seven days' notice.

In common with the clearing banks the other lenders used the call-money system for the regulation of their own cash positions, because the surplus or reserve funds not only retained the required degree of liquidity but were also profitably employed. However, as will be shown later (see Chapter 11), from the late 1950s the importance of the call-money market for this purpose declined with the growth of rival outlets for short-term money.

An indication of the magnitude of lending to the discount houses and also of the changing relative importance of the various groups of lenders can be obtained from a brief examination of Table 3. For each group of institutions the volume of lending outstanding at the year's end is shown together with figures expressing each amount as a percentage of total borrowed funds. Despite the changes of series that occur in the table the overall picture of the pattern of borrowing that it presents is clear.[10] The London clearing banks not only remained the most important single source of funds but also increased the extent of their dominance of the discount houses' call-money market during the course of the 1960s. On the other hand, excluding the Bank of England whose lending was determined upon other criteria, the relative importance of the other groups declined. It is significant that, as the figures show, the major movements took place during the 1960s. Shifts in the relative importance of various groups of lenders to the discount houses themselves reflect changes in the share of the market for very short-term funds enjoyed by the discount houses. Until quite recent years the houses themselves took the overwhelming proportion of these funds but the development, in the late fifties and early sixties, of new outlets enlarged the size of the market and reduced the discount houses' share of the available supply of funds. The result was that lending to the discount houses became increasingly dominated by the clearing banks while funds which had previously been deposited with the houses were diverted to the new market in local authority loans, in which the non-clearing banks and other financial institutions were the lenders, and the new 'inter-bank' market in sterling funds, in which non-clearing banks were both borrowers and lenders.

In addition to financial, commercial and industrial sources, so-called 'hot' money from abroad could provide a substantial amount of funds. Foreign funds were attracted to London, assuming a sufficient degree of confidence in sterling, to take advantage of an interest rate differential, for example following a rise in Bank rate. For the most part, when a discount house borrowed money from a bank in London it could not know whether or not it was borrowing foreign money. Some foreign money, however, was deposited directly with the houses on a daily basis by continental banks which did not possess a London office,[11] and, as a subsequent concomitant development, money came in via the sale of bank and Treasury bills to these same bankers. Technically, the operations were not fundamentally different from business with banks that did possess London offices except that they were conducted through a London correspondent bank. In the 1960s, much of the foreign money was denied to the discount houses by the more attractive rates, with which the houses could not compete, offered by local authorities and by banks operating in the inter-bank market.

One final possible source of funds from within the private-sector banking system must be mentioned. In addition to the normal inflow of funds from the banks in response to telephoned requests and the fixed quotas of privilege money that could be taken up before resort to the Bank, there occasionally existed the opportunity for one discount house to borrow funds from another. The possibility would arise in a situation in which for some reason funds were unevenly spread. All the houses were business competitors but such transactions could obviously be to the advantage of both surplus and deficit houses. The rate charged was normally reckoned as equal to the highest rate reached during the day in other transactions.

THE STRUCTURE OF INTEREST RATES

Brief reference has already been made to the subject of the cost of the discount houses' borrowed funds and to the rate differentials that obtained as between the various categories of money. The time has come for a closer look at the rate structure.

The whole structure of short-term money rates was built ultimately upon the keystone of Bank rate. Bank rate was, until its replacement by minimum lending rate in October 1972, the rate at which the Bank of England was prepared to discount paper of a specified quality or to lend money on the security of such paper in the execution of its role as lender of last resort to the discount houses. Traditionally the raising of Bank rate signalled the pursuance by the authorities of a restrictionary policy and its concomitant of tight money conditions; the lowering of Bank rate signalled the reverse. When Bank rate moved up or down a large number of other short-term interest rates moved in sympathy. Though they would all follow Bank rate for economic reasons the amount by which they would move might be governed by convention – as with the London clearers' deposit rate. During the twenty years after 1951 the announcement of a Bank rate change was normally made at the traditional time of 11.45 a.m. on Thursdays at the Bank of England. The clearing bankers then fixed their common deposit rate and the minimum rate for call money to the discount houses. On occasion, however, because of extraordinary circumstances this practice was departed from. During the financial crisis in the autumn of 1964 the announcement of a Bank rate change was made by the Chancellor of the Exchequer in the House of Commons at 10 a.m. on 23 November, a Monday.

In terms of the routine and techniques of borrowing money for the daily balance there were no significant changes during the quarter century after 1945. Over the years, however, the structure of interest rates that directly affected the operations of the discount houses underwent a number of changes. Certain events provide useful, analytical boundaries between sub-periods of widely different conditions each of which produced a distinctive climate for money dealing.

November 1951 marked the end of the authorities' policies of cheap and neutral money with their carefully regulated monetary conditions and the beginning of the new monetary policy, which involved flexible interest rates, the opportunity for enterprise and the dangers inherent in the new uncertainty. Another convenient landmark was provided by the publication of the Radcliffe Report in 1959. Apart from the wealth of new information it provided, the report influenced the way in which the authorities attempted to manage the monetary sector during the ensuing decade. It can also be seen as providing a very rough division between eras of 'traditional' discount market operations and the growth of new types of business with the creation of new markets. A third line of demarcation was provided by the implementation of the Competition and Credit Control proposals in September 1971 (see Chapter 13). Cartel and convention in interest rate determination were swept away and a new regime of greater competition, in which the allocation of credit was to be determined primarily by its cost, was inaugurated. The periods of cheap and neutral money and the consequences of Competition and Credit Control are dealt with elsewhere (see Chapters 3, 4, 13, 14) and for the moment attention is focused on the twenty years of flexible Bank rate after 1951.

The era of low and rigid rates was ended in November 1951 when the incoming Chancellor introduced his 'new monetary policy' and raised Bank rate from 2 per cent to 2½ per cent. An attempt was made to ease the market gently into the changed circumstances by the introduction of a concessionary rate of 2 per cent at which the Bank would make last-resort loans to the houses. These special arrangements were continued until September 1953 when Bank rate, which had been raised to 4 per cent, was reduced to 3½ per cent.

There were also changes at this time in the rates charged by the clearing banks for day-to-day money. They introduced different rates for loans against the three main classes of security, namely 1¾ per cent for Treasury bill money, 2 per cent for loans against commercial bills and 2⅛ per cent for bond money. The banks were thus still lending a part of the money at their own deposit rate which at this time stood at 1¾ per cent and it was not until February 1955 when Bank rate was increased from 3½ per cent to 4½ per cent that the clearing banks fixed their minimum lending rate at a differential (¼ per cent) over their deposit rate. The banks also took this opportunity to introduce two other changes. They fixed their deposit rate at its familiar 2 per cent below Bank rate; and the discrimination in money rates between different types of security was ended. The net result was, with Bank rate at 4½ per cent, a single basic rate of 2¾ per cent at ¼ per cent over their deposit rate of 2½ per cent.

Further modifications to the structure were made in November 1958 on the occasion of a reduction in Bank rate from 4½ per cent to 4 per cent. The clearing banks reduced their deposit rates by ½ per cent but only reduced their money rates to the discount market by ⅜ per cent, thus effectively increasing the differential between deposit rate and basic rate by ⅛ per cent. With these changes there came into being the clearing banks' rate structure that remained in force until September 1971. For the sake of example, when Bank rate was raised to the post war record level of 8 per cent the positions of the other relevant rates would be as follows :[12] the clearing banks' deposit rate would stand at 6 per cent for money at seven days' notice, that is at Bank rate minus 2 per cent.[13] The discount houses by agreement with the clearing banks gave as a maximum the same rate for deposits from lenders outside the banking system but took them on a day-to-day basis rather than at seven days; deposits taken at seven days' notice would earn a maximum of 6¼ per cent.

The clearing banks would look for a margin of profit between the rates at which they borrowed and lent money. For the discount houses the minimum rate for call money came to be fixed at ⅜ per cent over the clearing bankers' deposit rate (i.e. 6⅝ per cent). This rate would constitute the 'basic rate' charged on a proportion of the regular money which together with a rather higher rate charged on the rest of the regular money would give an average rate of approximately 7⅛–7 5/16 per cent. Night money was, as previously indicated, lent at a rate determined each day by market conditions. Given a Bank rate of 8 per cent and a shortage of funds in the market the rate for night money could be as high as 7⅝ per cent. Privilege money was charged for at a fixed concessionary rate : this used to be at the basic rate but in the later 1950s with higher money rates obtaining the rate was raised to ½ per cent over basic. In the example given the rate for privilege money would stand at 6⅞ per cent.

The rate structure described is that which applied to loans from the discount houses' biggest suppliers of funds, the clearing banks. Also it was the model upon which other banks tended to base their own lending rates. The Scottish banks in London adopted the clearing banks' base rate as their own minimum for loans, and while with other banks the cost of money was fixed by free negotiation between individual banks and discount houses the usual practice was for the non-clearers to adopt the pattern described. However, although they conformed to the general pattern, the rates on loans from non-clearing banks were subject to considerable fluctuation depending upon whether conditions in the money market were tight or easy. Though the average rate the houses might have to pay on these funds might be a little higher than that for clearing bank money, the non-clearers had to reckon on getting rates much lower than the minimum rates of the clearing banks when the money market was easy.

Rates on the 'parallel' markets (e.g. the inter-bank and local authority markets) tended to be higher on the same range of maturities than those obtaining in the traditional market. The existence of the differential was, as will be shown later, the result of the different trading conditions obtaining; for example, transactions in the inter-bank market were unsecured and there was no lender of last resort to guarantee the liquidity of borrowers.[14]

A record of changes in the structure of interest rates gives only the bare bones of the changing monetary environment. The ending of the policy of low, carefully managed interest rates and the introduction of flexibility in Bank rate presented the discount houses with a completely different set of constraints within which they had to obtain their funds. Certainty and dull routine disappeared, to be replaced by greater freedom and scope for the exercise of initiative and skill in dealing. New opportunities for profit making were accompanied by the possibility of suffering significant losses.

The most apparent facet of the new situation was, of course, that interest rates were subject to fluctuation during the course of the day. Freed from minute control by the Bank, rates could now rise sharply as money tightened towards the close, and always in the background loomed the possibility of having to make good a net deficit with money borrowed at penal rates from the Bank. A change in Bank rate, decided (quite arbitrarily from the market's point of view) by the authorities, could shift up or down the whole rate structure and with it the prices and yields of the securities and other assets in discount house portfolios.

Another significant change in the daily round was that banks were likely to call more heavily than previously. On the average perhaps 10 per cent of funds lent would be called, but if the proportion rose as high as 20 per cent the expectation would be that tight conditions could prevail.[15] For money dealers anxious to temper enterprise with safety it became necessary to attempt to gain greater control over conditions of supply. 'Fixtures' between individual houses and banks became much more common and attempts were made to widen the range of potential sources of funds.[16] The tendency was to increase the number of banks to be visited each day.

COLLATERAL SECURITY

Against nearly all the money that they borrowed the discount houses had to lodge collateral security. Security and margin requirements have already been mentioned and will be dealt with in the context of individual assets. For the present, attention is directed to reviewing some general principles involved in securing loans and to a brief examination of the effects of collateral and margin requirements on discount houses' investment policy. The subject is worth looking into for the following reasons : (1) because of margin requirements the extent of a house's resources exercised a very real constraint on the size of its portfolio; (2) qualitative restrictions that lenders placed on the type of security they would accept could strongly inhibit a house's lending policy.

The security that a discount house gave consisted of the bills and bonds in which it had invested its borrowings. There was, therefore, a two-way process. Funds flowed from a bank to a discount house, which invested the whole amount in assets. These assets, upon which a discount house was making either a profit or a loss against the cost

of the borrowed money, were then lodged as security against the
funds with which the assets were purchased. In addition, however,
lenders required that borrowers should provide some margin of security, that is some value of assets over and above the value of funds
borrowed. The amount of margin varied with the asset : for bonds the
figure was 5 per cent at current prices over the amount of the loan;[17]
in the case of bills the margin had to be sufficient to cover the discount
at current rates.

The question then arises of how, if all money borrowed had been
invested – because houses did not carry idle balances – a house was
to provide extra security as margin? It was in this connection that the
extent of a house's own resources was of such great importance, for
it was out of those resources that a discount house purchased the
required extra assets. The result is shown in Table 3; the total value
of assets held exceeded the value of borrowed funds, excluding capital
and reserves, by the amount of margin on bills, bonds and so on. The
amount of margin for each year is given as a percentage of total
assets, which were equal to the total of funds invested.

The term 'resources' requires some further explanation. A more
useful term to describe the items involved would be 'shareholders'
funds', which comprised capital and reserves. Because houses were (and
still are) allowed to maintain hidden reserves it is not possible to know
the exact figures. In general, the aggregate published figure for shareholders' funds of the L.D.M.A. amounted in mid-1969 to over £55
million; if hidden reserves are taken into account the true figure could
well be around £70 million.

Because a discount house's borrowing power was limited by the
necessity to deposit collateral security for an amount exceeding the
value of the loan, shareholders' funds were important in that they
constituted the trading base for the whole operation of the house. A
house's total borrowing did not normally exceed thirty times its shareholders' funds. As an everyday rule of thumb for dealing, simple
'multipliers' – the ratios of published resources to investments – were
used. There was no rigid rule about the proper size of multipliers and
fair judgement of the suitability of any given multiplier could only
be made with knowledge of the inner reserves of the company in
question and of the composition of its portfolios. However, multipliers
of from eight to ten for bonds and about twenty for bills were generally accepted.

The second major point made above was that the borrower of funds
was constrained not only quantitatively but also qualitatively. Because
the security that was lodged consisted of those assets in which the borrowed funds had been invested, the discount houses' choice of assets for

their portfolio would be influenced by the conditions of acceptability laid down by the lender. In short, security requirements exerted an influence on the composition of a house's portfolio.

With regard to Treasury bills and bonds the requirements were quite straightforward : the quality was guaranteed and it was only the tenor of the bill and the life to maturity of the bond that were in question. In the case of commercial bills, however, the attitude of the banks towards various classes of acceptances would exercise a powerful influence on the quality of commercial bills that a house might discount. As a consequence of the relative decline in importance of the Treasury bill in the portfolios of both discount houses and clearing banks, the banks had to take more commercial bills both for their own portfolios and as security on loans. Coupled with this development there was the movement of the clearing banks into a position of greater dominance as suppliers of borrowed funds. The most important lenders of funds were thus given scope for the exercise of greater influence over the composition of discount house portfolios.

Although most of a house's borrowed funds were secured in the way described, a small proportion was borrowed unsecured against a deposit receipt. Unsecured or 'clean' money was borrowed in the non-clearing-bank money markets and particularly in the inter-bank market. The danger inherent in using unsecured money to finance asset purchases was that if the funds were to be withdrawn they might have to be replaced immediately with secured money, that is funds might have to be borrowed from sources that required the placing of collateral. For this reason it was considered prudent to ensure that there was in the portfolio sufficient uncommitted security to cover the clean money. In some houses there would be specific allocation of available assets to clean deposits.[18]

THE BANK AS MARKET REGULATOR AND LENDER OF LAST RESORT

There were many channels through which the Bank of England exercised control over the British banking system, broadly defined. For the discount market virtually all its activities were subject, in some shape or form, to supervision or control by the Bank. Each of the asset chapters deals with the discount houses' relations with the Bank in the context of the houses' business in that asset and market. Relations with the Bank are also central to the discussion in the chapters dealing with the question of the control of bank deposits. Here attention is focused on the question of discount house borrowing from the Bank and the management of the money market.

The amounts of money that the discount houses borrowed from

the Bank represented only a very small proportion of the houses' total funds, as Table 3 clearly shows. Nevertheless, borrowing from the Bank and the possibility of having to do so weighed very heavily in discount house calculations, because it was through the discount houses that the Bank lent 'at last resort' to the whole banking system. The Bank's duty in this regard meant that, as in earlier periods, it stood ready to lend sufficient amounts of cash to maintain desired levels of liquidity when financial crisis threatened. The operation of this system guaranteed that commercial banks would work to fixed reserve ratios rather than vary them between times of boom and stringency.

The Bank's last-resort role must be seen as a specific aspect of two wider but closely integrated functions. As central bank the Bank of England had among its responsibilities the management of the central government's financial transactions and the management of the money market. The first involved administration of the Exchequer accounts and the second the regulation of the cost and availability of funds to the discount houses, clearing banks and the rest of the banking system.[19] It is appropriate to consider the two tasks together because transactions and operations in either 'sector' had ramifications for the other, so that for the Bank the tasks appeared as a composite problem involving competing goals to be reconciled. The obvious relevance for the discount houses was that because of their role of transmission agency between the authorities and the banks they had to bear the consequences of any net change in financial circumstances between the two.

In its management of the two 'sectors' the Bank made use of a working sheet similar to those employed by the discount houses and clearing banks. The sheet was divided into two parts corresponding to transactions in government finance ('Exchequer') and in the money market ('Bankers'). Exchequer transactions covered a group of accounts in the Banking Department of the Bank, namely the Exchequer proper, the revenue departments, the Paymaster General (including the Exchange Equalisation Account) and the National Debt Commissioners; the Issue Department of the Bank was also included in the group because of the nature of its transactions in government debt.[20]

All government departments kept their working balances to a minimum each day and transferred or lent overnight their surpluses to the account of the Exchequer proper. Similarly, this account plus that of the Paymaster General were together operated so that only a relatively very small balance (£2 million) was left overnight between them. Despite the unevenness of the flows of receipts and payments over the week and over the year the Bank, with the Treasury, had so to manage these central accounts as to ensure that all payments could be met each day but that no large surpluses built up.

'Bankers' referred to the balances of banks and discount houses that had accounts at the Head Office of the Bank of England. It therefore covered transactions affecting 'the money market', broadly defined. Beginning with an 'Actual Balance', which referred to the size of bankers' balances at the previous close of business, the Bank aimed at a 'Bankers' Target', which represented the figure for balances that it was estimated bankers would wish to hold at the close of the current day. The target figure was arrived at by projection of available data and by keeping in touch with market conditions through direct enquiry and through consultation with the special buyer.

The Exchequer and Bankers 'sectors' were closely linked by the fact that transactions in the Exchequer accounts would usually result in a debit or credit to the account of a bank or discount house and hence to the total for Bankers. Consequently, the management of the Exchequer accounts was linked to the management of the London money market because : 'The net flow day by day of government payments to and receipts from the Bankers is the main cause of ease or stringency in that market.' A common example of this was the effect on the banks of their payment on behalf of customers of tax revenues to the Exchequer on a Tuesday. The demands made on their liquidity would cause them to call from the discount houses which would consequently be left short of funds. If the Bank in those circumstances chose not to put into the market the required amount of money at market rates to enable them to balance their books the houses would be forced to borrow on last-resort terms from the Bank.

One of the principles of money market management employed by the Bank was illustrated in the above example. The Bank's tactics were always to attempt to ensure that it retained the initiative : that in any situation in which it wished to exert an influence it was left with a number of options and the market was left with none. In practical terms this meant creating a shortage of funds which the Bank could then relieve on the terms it deemed most appropriate. Consequently, and as a matter of course, the authorities left the market initially in shortage each week through the normal operation of the Treasury bill issue. In Chapter 8 the procedure will be examined whereby the authorities put on offer slightly more bills than were necessary to meet the government's borrowing requirements and the discount houses ensured, through their agreement to 'cover the tender', that the desired shortage would be produced.

The Bank did not have this option if the market were initially in surplus. In these circumstances the Bank could sell Treasury bills in the market both to 'mop up' the surplus and to provide planned maturities of bills for days on which funds were expected to be short. Because the market could not be expected willingly to part with funds which it might need to meet a prospective shortage the Bank would be left only with the choice of rate at which to sell the bills.

The daily round of the money-getting process was described above. The principal lending banks by convention made any necessary calls for money from the discount houses by midday : because the size of the calls would be based on the banks' estimated needs at the close of business any general shortage in the market would be most apparent at that time. Between noon and 3 p.m. the houses' deficit would be reduced by the inflow from the banks and there would be a progressive narrowing of the gap between the deficit reported directly from the market and the Bank's forecast of the position at the close. Before the Discount Office closed the houses would have to decide whether or not to go to the Bank, the decision being based upon the size of the deficit and a house's judgement of the amount of money likely to 'come out' before the banks closed. Making allowance for this figure the houses would borrow the minimum sum necessary to effect a balance.

From the vantage point of the Bank, the position at any time during the day could be calculated by taking the opening balance and adding algebraically the results of transactions affecting bankers' balances to obtain an estimate of the closing balance for the day. This figure would be compared with the 'Bankers' Target' to give a measure of the shortage or surplus in the market. If a shortage was forecast and this was unchanged in the early afternoon and broadly confirmed by reports from the market, then the Bank would decide, in the light of its prevailing policy goals, on the manner in which it wished to relieve the shortage.

In the performance of its last-resort function the Bank possessed two 'doors' : a 'front door' and a 'back door'.[21] It used to be true to say that the main distinction between the two was that lending through the front door raised short-term interest rates whereas lending through the back door left them undisturbed. In more recent years, changes in front-door lending policy have made this distinction less clear cut. Lending at the front door referred to advances granted or bills discounted through the Discount Office at the Bank, at which time the market would be 'in the Bank'. Lending at the back door referred to the 'smoothing out' operations of the special buyer who would regulate the availability of funds in the market by buying or selling bills at market rates either *directly* with the discount houses ('direct help') or *indirectly* through the clearing banks ('indirect help'). The functions of the special buyer are described below.

For the discount houses, borrowing from the Bank of England meant borrowing from the Discount Office, which is the office of the Cashier's Department responsible for the management – in the broadest sense – of the money market. This has involved not only the management of front door and back door operations but also the question of 'eligibility' of paper to be used for collateral when borrowing from the Bank. Connected with this is the more general problem of the maintenance of a good standard of paper in the market, and the Office makes regular sample purchases, for the Bank's own account, of the commercial bills discounted by the discount houses.[22]

Throughout, the Discount Office has been responsible to the Governor of the Bank for the liquidity of the banks and other financial institutions in the City. Monthly and weekly returns are called for and balance sheets are taken in and scrutinised. In addition the Principal of the Discount Office spends much time in becoming acquainted with the City institutions and their senior personnel. The task in respect of the discount houses is relatively straightforward and involves checks on the quality of paper discounted in the market and on the maintenance by the houses of a proper relation between the size of their book and the extent of their capital resources.[23]

Although the Discount Office is open until 3 p.m. borrowing requirements have traditionally had to be notified by 2.30 p.m. The minimum amount that a house would consider going to the Bank for would be about £500,000 and on a day of great general shortage, when the Bank would be lending many millions, those houses that delayed and found themselves at the rear of a queue at the Discount Office might find that their needs would be supplied only on penal terms of extra severity, which would involve them in even greater losses.

Borrowing from the Bank has always been against eligible security. Traditionally Bank rate was the rate at which the Bank would be prepared to discount 'first class' bills of exchange. As circumstances changed and new types of debt came into the market the range of paper that the Bank would accept was widened. Prior to 1971, paper eligible at the Bank included Treasury bills, bonds with not more than five years to run to maturity, bills of exchange accepted by first-class London banks and accepting houses, and local authority bills. The Bank took commercial and local authority bills in appreciable quantities from early in 1969 due to the shortage of Treasury bills in the market.

Houses rarely sought last-resort help via the discounting method because the Bank required that the bills must have a life of not less than twenty-one days, which meant borrowing at Bank rate for that length of time. Instead the money was borrowed against the security of bills or bonds. As Treasury bills became scarcer in the market there was increasingly an advantage to be gained by offering bonds, for Treasury bills were widely acceptable to other lenders with only very small margin whereas the Bank required a 5 per cent margin on both bills and bonds.

Although front-door lending was traditionally at Bank rate for seven days, the Bank experimented over the years with several combinations of rates and terms. The most obvious way of varying the cost of borrowing from the Bank was by raising or lowering Bank rate, and after November 1951 the level was subject to continual readjustment. However, Bank rate variation was not always deemed the most appropriate method, because of the desirability of maintaining simultaneously in the domestic money market and the foreign exchange market dissimilar interest rate regimes to meet dissimilar conditions. In addition, special circumstances called for a lending rate other than Bank rate and a shorter or longer term for the loan than seven days.

Between November 1951 and September 1953 (as described above, p. 101) the authorities helped to ease the market into the unfamiliar rigours of the 'new monetary policy' by giving last-resort help at a concessionary rate of Bank rate minus $\frac{1}{2}$ per cent. During the next decade, from September 1953 to January 1963, front-door lending was at Bank rate for a minimum term of seven days.

In January 1963 a pre-war practice was revived when the Bank announced that it would reserve the right to make loans at up to 1 per cent over Bank rate.[24] The Bank wished to be able to vary not only the scale on which the discount houses borrowed but also the price they would have to pay for the facility at any given level of Bank rate. Borrowing from the Bank was seen as providing an indication of the Bank's attitude towards short-term rates and as affecting the average cost of the market's borrowing. It was explained that a rise or expectation of a rise in costs would lead the market to seek a higher return on its assets. The Treasury bill rate was the most sensitive rate and it would tend to become firmer.

The desire of the Bank for greater flexibility in lending technique stemmed from the fact that circumstances might be encountered in which the external monetary situation might call for a rise in the Treasury bill rate and the rates that moved in sympathy with it, while on the other hand the domestic situation might demand a steady Bank rate. Because daily management of the money market was not sufficiently finely tuned to enable the Bank to determine the exact amount that the houses should borrow from the Bank it was hoped that the new arrangement would give the Bank greater power to influence the Treasury bill rate, both directly and by implication.

In the event the tactic was used only once, on 19 March 1963, when the houses were forced to borrow fairly heavily at ½ per cent over Bank rate. It is interesting to note that at the following tender the Treasury bill rate was sharply raised as the syndicate cut their bid price. The whole question of the ability of the Bank to influence the level of the Treasury bill rate has been the subject of some discussion : it is examined below, in Chapter 12.

On 30 June 1966 the Bank employed a new technique whereby advances were granted overnight at Bank rate. The technique was introduced in support of the Bank's policy at that time of keeping money tight in the market and keeping short-term interest rates firm. By lending overnight a shortage of funds could be carried forward from day to day. By charging the loans at Bank rate it was hoped not only to raise directly the average cost of the discount houses' borrowed funds but also to encourage other lenders to demand higher rates for overnight money. It was envisaged that in normal day-to-day management of the market overnight lending could be used to balance out shortage and surplus on successive days, and where necessary market rates could be left unaffected by lending at a level broadly in line with them.[25] This variant was used from September 1966 and was found to be especially useful when neither discount houses nor clearing banks possessed suitable bills to sell to the special buyer and when the Bank did not wish to exert any particular influence on market rates.

On 1 August 1967 the Bank lent, for the first time, for seven days at the market rate. The intention was that repayments should be made at the time when settlement was due for the large official purchases of steel company securities. On 6 September the Bank lent, again for the first time, for five days at the market rate. In July 1969 the Bank lent at market rates for as long a period as eighteen days.

It was not only the terms on which they had to borrow at the front door of the Bank that was of importance to the discount houses, but also the frequency with which they had to do so. Table 5 shows the frequency with which the Bank intervened in the money market and the amount of help that was given. The columns show : (1) the number of days on which no assistance was given; (2) cash released to the market by way of advances, at or above Bank rate and at market rates, and by purchases of Treasury bills; (3) cash taken out of the market to mop up a surplus, by sales of Treasury bills. For the 1960s, allowance is made for cash released by purchases of bills at other than market rates. Judged on the basis of the number of working days on which no intervention was made, the tendency was for the Bank to intervene more frequently in the money market as the period progressed, particularly to give assistance at rates other than Bank rate and above.

The alternative way for the Bank to relieve a shortage in the market was to provide temporary accommodation through the back door via smoothing operations. The special buyer released cash to the discount houses either directly, by buying bills from them, or indirectly, by buying bills from the clearing banks which then lent the resultant funds ('made money') to the houses. In giving either direct help or indirect help the special buyer would purchase bills at a rate deemed by the authorities to be 'the market level'. The reason why the authorities might give help to the discount houses indirectly by taking bills from the banks was because, very often, it was the banks that held the chosen maturities of bills. This would be due to the arrangement whereby the banks' Treasury bill requirements were supplied by the discount houses, which held the bills for only a week before selling them on.[26]

The special buyer would choose to purchase bills maturing on a day in the near future when it was known that the market would be particularly liquid, for example, because of the maturity of a large amount of government stock. By taking in Treasury bills maturing on that day the authorities would help to minimise disturbance to market conditions. In general terms, by relieving a shortage through the purchase of bills due to mature within a few days the authorities could ensure that the stringency would quickly return, so leaving the initiative again with the Bank.

In the opposite situation to market tightness – that of an excess of liquidity and sagging rates – the special buyer would be prepared to 'mop up' ('working in reverse') by *selling* bills to the market. Mopping up would leave the houses free to fulfil their function of taking surpluses of cash from the banks. The necessity for the special buyer to perform this function was reduced to a minimum by careful choice of maturity dates when purchasing bills at other times, as indicated above.

By means of both sales and purchases of bills as necessary it was possible for the Bank to maintain a chosen pattern of market rates. For a period prior to 1951, indeed, market rates had been maintained at a fixed level by the authorities who stood ready to exchange freely cash for bills and bills for cash at the chosen rate.

8 Treasury Bills

In 1951 the 'bills' in a discount house's portfolio meant, overwhelmingly, British government Treasury bills, which accounted for over 60 per cent of total assets (see Table 4). The item 'other sterling bills', which was mainly made up of commercial bills drawn on banks and firms resident in the United Kingdom and on the London offices of overseas banks – but which also included Treasury bills of the Northern Ireland government and bills issued by local authorities – accounted for only one tenth of that figure, i.e. a mere 6 per cent of total assets. By 1969, however, the proportion of British government Treasury bills had fallen by two-thirds, to 22 per cent, while 'other sterling bills' had increased nearly sixfold, to 34·6 per cent. By the latter date, of course, there had been other important changes in the composition of discount house portfolios, but for the moment attention is concentrated on the nature and significance of discount house operations in the Treasury bill market and, in the next chapter, on the phenomenon of the gradual reinstatement of the commercial bill as an important means of finance and medium for discount house investment.

The Treasury bill is an instrument by which the British government borrows money at short term (three months or less) and is the principal constituent of the Floating Debt. Dealings in Treasury bills have been, especially since the 1930s, centred on the discount houses and not, as in the case of government bonds and stocks, on the Stock Exchange. In law the instrument cannot be defined either as a bill of exchange or as a promissory note. The technical objection is that it is not an unconditional order or promise to pay but rather a charge on a particular fund, namely the Consolidated Fund of the United Kingdom. Rather, the bill is a bearer security entitling the holder to a payment of a fixed amount out of the Consolidated Fund at a fixed date, now normally ninety-one days after issue. Under the Treasury Bills Act of 1877[1] Treasury bills may be issued for any period not exceeding twelve months. Between 1917 and 1950 bills offered at the tender were all for a term of three calendar months. In 1950, at the request of the discount houses, a term of ninety-one days was adopted instead. This has been the rule since 1950 'except for a temporary and seasonal use of sixty-three day bills each winter from 1955 to 1962'.[2] Ninety-one days, rather than a longer term, has been found to be a suitable 'tenor' for both sides of the market. Because of cheapness and flexibility (especially given the market arrangements in force between 1951 and 1971) the government has found it advantageous to turn the borrowing over every three months.

The holder of a Treasury bill is not rewarded by the payment of interest : he purchases the instrument at less than its nominal value, that is the bill is issued at a discount. The bills are available in six denominations ranging from £5000 to £250,000. For the issuing agency, the Bank of England, Treasury bill issues fulfil two primary functions : (1) they provide the final means of adjusting the Exchequer's daily cash position, short of the overnight advances used by the Bank when it is too late to deal in Treasury bills; (2) they provide the final means of adjustment – short of borrowing by the discount houses – of the clearing banks' balances with the Bank and enable the Bank to bring about degrees of tightness and ease in the money market, and thus to influence the rate at which Treasury bills are discounted and other short term rates.[3]

In respect of their Treasury bill business the discount houses moved into the otherwise freer market conditions and more flexible interest rate regime that obtained after 1951, still subject to the rigid arrangements produced by the peculiar problems of the 1930s. Down to 1971 the restrictions on competition and the obligation to 'cover the tender' remained as important constraints on the conduct of the houses' Treasury bill operations and therefore on the management of the whole asset portfolio. The existence of an active resale market in Treasury bills meant that the houses were always able to obtain, at the market rate, supplies of bills that had run for some part of their life. In addition, bills entered portfolio via the 'mopping up' sales by the Bank through the special buyer. Nevertheless, the main source of Treasury bills for the discount houses remained the weekly tender at the Bank of England, not only because of the institutional constraints within which they worked but also because of the jobbing profits to be made on resale to the banks and others. The houses' holdings of the bills at any time can be seen as the outcome of the interplay of factors on the supply side and the demand side of the market.

The amount of bills that the discount houses would take up at the weekly tender would be a function of : (1) the amount of bills that the Bank in consultation with the Treasury decided to put on offer each week; (2) the proportion of that amount (more exactly, of the amount actually allotted) that the L.D.M.A. managed to secure.

THE SUPPLY OF TREASURY BILLS

(a) The size of the weekly offer
The size of the offer of Treasury bills to be made at the tender in any week was determined by the authorities, who had to take a number of factors into account. The basic requirement was for an estimate of the flows of funds likely to occur during the forthcoming period between the central accounts of the government, or the accounts of other customers of the Bank, and the general public. The result would show the authorities what action they themselves would have to take to bring about a desired position. The calculation took place as follows. Towards the end of each week the Treasury first forecast Exchequer receipts and disbursements for some weeks ahead; and secondly combined these figures with the amount, which would be known, of Treasury bills maturing each week in the hands of the market and the Banking Department of the Bank of England, that is all bills other than those held by the Exchequer and the Departments. In this way the authorities obtained a rough total of new bills to be issued each week. The rough total would subsume the effects of the size of the government's borrowing requirement and also of seasonal factors (the stage of the tax year reached). Because the flow of government financing was – and is – strongly seasonal in pattern, with a large proportion of the tax revenue concentrated in the last quarter of the financial year, the Exchequer would need to borrow substantially at short-term on current account even if, over the year as a whole, its finances were going to be in exact balance. Consequently, the total of Treasury bills issued declined from December to March and rose from March to December, the fluctuations corresponding to movements in the receipt of taxes.

The final total of bills to be issued was calculated after making allowance for the effects of the following: Treasury bill business or other transactions by overseas central banks and other private customers of the Bank of England; the likely course of official transactions in government stocks; and official transactions in foreign exchange. In addition it was in general the practice to offer slightly more bills than estimates suggested were strictly necessary to meet the needs of government borrowing, both to make allowance for errors and unforeseen contingencies and to create an initial shortage of funds in the market that the Bank could then relieve at its discretion with or without the penalty of forcing houses to borrow at the 'front door'.

E

(b) Official borrowing policy

An important and pervasive influence on the amount of Treasury bills that would come on to the market would be the authorities' overall policy towards borrowing in this very liquid form. The question of the availability of Treasury bills came into great prominence in the 1950s in the context of the debate over the control of bank deposits. For the authorities, who were probably attempting to restrain the growth of advances, the supply of Treasury bills and not the supply of cash had come to be 'the effective regulatory base of the domestic banking system'. This was shown by the increasing attention paid to the liquidity ratio after 1951 and its explicit formalisation in 1955. The adoption of this approach arose from the imposition of constraints that precluded the use of cash base control, namely (1) the Bank's duty to maintain the liquidity of the banking system; (2) the loss of control over the Treasury bill rate that would follow. Stability of the Treasury bill rate was desired because the authorities feared that irregularities would spread first to the short end and then to the long end of the bond market, undermine confidence and so make funding more difficult. In addition, it was believed that the nature of the Treasury bill market was such that it was not necessarily the case that larger amounts of Treasury bills would be taken up by the public at relatively higher rates. It was for this reason that the authorities wished to retain the restrictive arrangements between the discount houses and the clearing banks at the tender : they were thus enabled to retain control over both the quantity of bills taken up and also their price (Treasury bill rate).

Because of the importance of Treasury bills for the banks' liquid asset portfolios (even with the increased availability of commercial bills in the later years) : 'within the total of borrowing needed to finance government expenditure . . . financial policy since the war has aimed, more often than not, to produce the greatest possible contribution from lenders other than the banking system.' Nevertheless, because of the practical problems involved in meeting the Exchequer's needs from day to day : 'as the system works, the banks and discount houses between them find themselves inevitably holding the residual amount of bills necessary to bring into balance the Exchequer's cash position – and the market's.'[4] The problem was exacerbated throughout the 1950s by the pursuit of policies in the finance of central government, on external account and in the bond market, that conflicted with the goal of reducing the availability of Treasury bills.

At the end of 1951 the volume of market Treasury bills in issue, minus known public-sector holdings, stood at about £2700m.[5] From this figure it rose steadily to £3563m at the end of 1955. For the following three years it averaged around £3400m and reached a new peak of £3530m at the end of 1959. Thereafter the figures followed a downward trend, falling to £2642m in December 1966. The total for March 1967 was only £1723m but that for December was over £3000m as were those for March and December 1968 and for March 1969. By December 1969 the amount outstanding had fallen to £2710m and reached only £2244m in December 1970 (the figure for March 1970 was £1443m and that for March 1971 a mere £950m). Quite obviously, apart from the setback over the period from December 1967 to March 1969 the authorities achieved a measure of success in their Treasury bill policy in the 1960s that was denied them during the 1950s. A number of factors contributed to the attainment of their objective.[6]

(c) *Local authority finance*
An important contribution arose from the market borrowing element of local authority finance. The growth of temporary borrowing on their own account by the local authorities meant that to that extent the finance did not have to be provided by the central government. Between October 1955 and March 1964 local authorities were only allowed to borrow from the Public Works Loan Board if they could show that they were unable to borrow funds on their own credit from the market on reasonable terms. It was argued that local capital which would not otherwise enter the gilt-edged market would be attracted into local authority finance and that the central government's borrowing requirement would be correspondingly reduced. The need for the authorities to create liquid assets for banking-system portfolios would therefore decline. In 1955, before access to the P.W.L.B. was withdrawn, there was only about £170 million (4 per cent of total local authority debt) of temporary debt outstanding; by 1965 the total had risen to £18,000 million (more than 18 per cent of total loan debt).[7] Although this development facilitated the funding of Treasury bills, it did constitute 'unfunding' on the part of local authorities, and the creation of large amounts of very short-term debt in this way led to the introduction of restrictions by the authorities in 1964.

(d) *The Exchange Equalisation Account*
The reduction in the availability of market Treasury bills can also be explained by reference to the operations of the Exchange Equalisation Account.[8] In the case of an *outflow* of gold or foreign currency, the Account would acquire sterling in response to sales which would then be lent to the Exchequer by the purchase of tap bills, with the possibility of a corresponding reduction in the amount issued through the

tap. Between the financial years 1963–4 and 1969–70 the figures for the Exchange Equalisation Account of the state of the official reserves show a net increase (outflow of sterling) for only one year (1965–6); in all other years the figures register a net decrease (inflow of sterling).

(e) Funding policy

The effect on the discount houses' Treasury bill take-up of the heavy gold outflow in 1964, for example, was made the more severe because it coincided with successful funding operations in longer-dated debt but was at the same time mitigated by a fall in 'outside' demand for tender bills, as merchant banks and others experienced heavy withdrawals of sterling deposits.

The effects of war and early post-war finance were to leave the banking system replete with liquid assets. In addition the mere passage of time had the effect of concentrating the weight of the Public Debt at the short end of the maturity spectrum. Consequently the policy of the authorities throughout the fifties and sixties was one of funding and lengthening the Debt (that is reducing the amount of Floating Debt and increasing the average maturity of marketable securities outstanding). The effect of a funding operation was to exchange one kind of government debt for another without any change in the total held. When, for example, the banking system took up more stocks the Exchequer was able to sell, through the Issue Department, more stocks and so had less to finance on bills. When settlement for the stocks was made the market's shortage of funds was that much greater and the Bank gave more help by buying up bills to the same extent. The outcome was therefore that the banking system as a whole had exchanged bills for stocks with the Issue Department.

A substantial reduction in the amount of Treasury bills outstanding was made by the special funding operation which began late in 1951, whereby £1000 million of Treasury bills were exchanged for Serial Funding Stocks and where roughly half the amount came from bank holdings. A subsequent rise in market holdings was corrected by a similar operation twelve months later. During the 1960s the years in which the authorities were successful in effecting large increases in the amount of stocks in the hands of the public were also the years in which they achieved significantly reduced levels of Treasury bills outstanding (1966–7 and 1969–70). Generally, however, because of their overriding concern with the maintenance of 'orderly' markets the authorities never pressed their funding operations *à outrance*.

Of the other ways in which a borrowing requirement could be financed the contribution of domestic currency issues was positive and significant throughout the 1960s as the fiduciary note issue expanded.

In the first half of the decade some success was achieved in increased sales of National Savings securities as a response to the improved terms offered.

(f) Reduced availability to discount houses
The extent of the impact of the reduced availability of Treasury bills on the clearing banks' liquid asset portfolios in the 1960s was of special interest to the authorities. As a proportion of the banks' total liquid assets Treasury bills fell from about 63 per cent at the end of 1959 to around 11 per cent at the end of 1970. Correspondingly, commercial bills became increasingly important, as did call money put out with the discount houses and others. There was a contemporaneous fall in the holdings of Treasury bills by the accepting houses and overseas banks. For the discount houses Treasury bill holdings suffered a similar though not quite so drastic reduction during the course of the 1960s. From the figure of £624m (60·5 per cent of total portfolio) in 1951 the holdings fluctuated in amount during the 1950s, reaching £702m (65·8 per cent of total portfolio) in 1952 and falling to £523m (54·8 per cent) in 1956. At the end of 1959 the houses held £635m (56·2 per cent) after which the trend was downward for a decade to a post-1945 low (for December) of £399m (22 per cent) in 1969. In 1970 the position was drastically changed as holdings rose to over £870m, though as a percentage of total assets the figure was only 37·2.[9]

Plainly, the reason that the discount houses had over 60 per cent of their total assets in the form of Treasury bills in 1951 was largely a question of historical necessity. The effects of wars and of international stagnation had deprived them of commercial discounts and, given the lack of suitable alternatives, the demands of Exchequer finance had provided substitutes in the form of marketable securities and Treasury bills. Because of the risk involved in committing a portfolio largely to fixed-interest longer-term paper (see Chapter 10), and because of their obligation to cover the tender, the preponderance of government debt in the houses' portfolios was in the form of Treasury bills. Only in the early 1960s did Treasury bills and bonds come to make an equal contribution, and in 1965 and 1966 bond holdings actually exceeded Treasury bill holdings; from 1967 onwards bonds experienced a relative decline.

The characteristics of the bill made it eminently suitable for use as a discount house asset. It had been designed specifically to resemble as closely as possible the commercial bills to which the houses were accustomed. In addition, the instrument possessed from the start qualities of security and liquidity based on the guarantee of the Treasury : both that at maturity the holder of the bill would be put in funds to the amount of the nominal value of the bill, and that during the currency of the bill it would be redeemable for cash at the Bank at the going rate of discount. These qualities were of particular importance for the type of business that 'lent short but borrowed even shorter'. Finally, the Treasury bill market was characterised by great ease and convenience of dealing, in a commodity that was homogeneous except in respect of length of life to redemption and therefore the rate of discount payable as between one bill and another.

THE WEEKLY TENDER AT THE BANK OF ENGLAND

The weekly Treasury bill tender at which the discount houses and other members of the public, including foreign official and unofficial holders, obtained their supplies of newly-issued bills[10] was begun by an announcement made each Friday of the amount of bills to be offered at the tender on the next Friday, the bills to be taken up and paid for on any business day in the following week.[11] The actual date of issue was left to the free choice of the tenderer and the bills normally matured ninety-one days later. The Bank reserved to itself the discretionary power to allot an amount of bills smaller, though not larger, than the advertised offer. The implication was that if the Exchequer's needs were found to be smaller than was anticipated the exact size of the allotment could be determined after the bids had been received. Tenders had to be submitted through authorised channels, that is a London banker, discount house or broker, on the official forms provided. On the form the tenderer stated : the quantity tendered for (not less than £50,000); the denominations required; the price offered, submitted in £sd for £100 of bills;[12] the date on which the bills were to be taken up and paid for.[13] Separate forms were used for tenders of different dates and for bids at different prices. Bids made in this way were accepted at the Bank up to 1 p.m. on each Friday.

The sealed bid auction was begun by the opening of the forms in the presence of the Secretary to the Treasury and the Governor of the Bank or their representatives. The bids were sorted and the total of bills applied for at each price established.[14] Tenders at the highest prices received allotment in full – so far as the total amount of bills to be issued permitted. When the point was reached at which the amount of tenders at the next highest bid price exceeded the amount of bills remaining available, allotment to such applications was made proportionally. The Bank made a rough calculation of the allotment at about 1.45 p.m. and announced the exact results by 3 p.m. The Bank stated : the total amount of tenders received; the amount allotted;

the average rate of discount for all bills allotted; and the amount of bills to be offered for tender on the following Friday. This last was authorised by the Treasury, which at the same time fixed the rate of discount to be allowed to government departments on tap bills issued during the following week.[15]

The main categories of institutions that tendered for Treasury bills were : overseas official holders of sterling (who tendered through the Bank); other overseas holders of sterling; miscellaneous domestic lenders, including industrial companies with cash surpluses as well as non-banking financial institutions of many kinds; the discount houses; other members of the discount market; the clearing banks – but only on behalf of their customers, not as principals; other banks; the Bank of England, which put in its own bid on behalf of customers (e.g. overseas central banks and its own Banking Department).

The arrangement whereby the clearing banks obtained their bills from the discount houses after seven days of their life had run derived from the agreement of 1935 (described in Chapter 3), drawn up to meet a particular situation. Subsequently, however, the banks found this to be a convenient arrangement for a practical reason – the problem involved in being unable to forecast accurately their cash position on a given day one week ahead was overcome by their being able to purchase the bills in suitable parcels from the discount houses.

Until the implementation of Competition and Credit Control in September 1971 the various categories of tenderers could usefully be divided into two groups : the discount houses' syndicate, bidding at a common price for the total of bills on offer, constituting one group and all other tenderers making up the second group as the 'outside tender'.[16] The importance of making this division stems from the question, which will be considered at some length later, of whether the discount houses' syndicate possessed the power to vary their holdings of Treasury bills and therefore their take-up at the tender, or whether they were merely residual holders whose allocation was determined by the strength at any time of the 'outside tender'. The significance of this question for the operation of the mechanism of monetary control will become apparent in Chapter 12. For the moment, however, attention is confined to a brief examination of the syndicate and the outside tenderers.

FIXING THE SYNDICATE BID PRICE

The price at which the syndicate were to put in their bid was decided at a meeting of the London Discount Market Association held on Friday mornings.[17] The decision was made often after 'bitter argument' by a majority vote in which all houses, irrespective of size, had equal voting rights. It was argued by the members of the L.D.M.A. that the bid price was decided by themselves alone, though the position could be corrected subsequently by the Bank.[18]

Information on which the Association might base its bid price was derived from two main sources : from newspapers and journals (and no doubt from the great amount of information put out by stockbrokers and others for their clients and friends) and from the weekly meeting with the Governor of the Bank, at which an informal discussion of the week's events in the money, bill and bond markets took place and at which the L.D.M.A. sought information on the foreign exchange position. Both the Bank and the L.D.M.A. claimed that there was no collusion or undue influence over the question of the discount houses' bid price.[19] The explanation of the purpose of the weekly meeting as given to the Radcliffe Committee by the then Governor, Lord Cobbold, is worth quotation in full :

> The purpose of the weekly meeting between myself, or the Deputy Governor, and the Chairman and Deputy Chairman of the D.M.A. is that we should personally keep in touch with the representatives of the Market, so that we may know what is in their minds; and that they should have the opportunity of discussing the general situation with us. I often give them confidentially my views on the position and outlook both from the domestic and foreign scene : and they are naturally free to take these views into account in choosing the rate at which they tender. Beyond such expression of views and opinions I do not seek to influence their judgment. The market's independent assessment of the rate at which they should tender, made in the light of all the circumstances (including our own operations and such general views as we may have expressed) as they see them, is of value to us.[20]

Whether culled from newspapers, journals or the personal word of the Governor, the L.D.M.A. used, as special indicators for their decision on the rate at which to bid, the state of the gold and dollar reserves and – where possible – the foreign exchange position in an attempt to evaluate the strength of the pound. These practical aspects of fixing the price (rate) had underlying them a very simple principle : the houses were proposing to lend money to the government for a period of ninety-one days.[21] The profitability of the investment would be a function of the margin between the average cost of borrowed money and the bill rate. Once the bills had been purchased the rate of return would be fixed for the houses until the bills were sold or they matured.

Consequently, the houses' preoccupation was with the price at which they would have to borrow money during the following three months. The rate of central importance in this regard was of course Bank rate, because the clearing banks adjusted their lending rates as Bank rate moved and other sources of funds tended to adopt the pattern of rates imposed by the clearers. At bottom, then, the L.D.M.A. had to attempt to predict what the authorities were going to do with Bank rate during the ensuing thirteen weeks. There was always the possibility that due to their obligation to cover the tender the discount houses would find themselves having to take up a large amount of bills in full expectation of a sharp rise in Bank rate. Such an occasion was the tender of Friday 21 July 1961.[22] The general expectation was that strong measures were to be adopted by the Chancellor to deal with the economic crisis and it was known that some of them were to be announced in Parliament on the following Tuesday. Due to the abstention of many regular tenderers the L.D.M.A. were forced to take up 66 per cent of the bills. Bank rate was raised by 2 per cent on the following Tuesday, taking with it the banks' lending rates. The discount houses thus had to take up their allocation at a loss of 2 per cent per annum.

Under the arrangements for the syndicate, individual discount houses limited the size of their applications for bills in proportion to the extent of their capital resources. The quota for each house was based upon the size of its capital and reserves and was weighted by a variable multiplier, which meant that the houses with the smaller capital resources could go for a rather bigger percentage of their capital and reserves than the larger houses. This was due to the fact that at the time of the agreement the smaller houses were doing a larger bill business in proportion to their capital. This syndicate rule was rigidly enforced during the war and during the early post-war years, but with the more flexible interest rate conditions of the 1950s pressure grew within the Association to allow greater freedom to individual houses. The outcome was that from 1955 houses could, up to a maximum of 15 per cent of their quota, tender at a price slightly different from the syndicate price. There was also provision for houses to 'put bills on the table', thus abstaining in some part of their quota. This flexibility allowed greater freedom for the adjustment of portfolios.[23] There was no requirement for dissenters to declare their intentions unless they had decided to 'put bills on the table'. In that event the Committee of the Association had to decide whether the amounts 'put down' were sufficiently large to require their being taken up by the rest of the Association. In 1957 the rules were changed so that houses no longer abstained but instead tendered at a lower price – which meant that the tender was always covered.

When newly issued, so that they still had three months to run, Treasury bills often found a ready market with the customers of the banks.[24] Bills not sold for a 'jobbing' profit in this way by the discount houses were held in portfolio to yield a running profit – or loss – until they too were sold, for few bills actually matured in houses' portfolios. Most bills went to the clearing banks but there were also sales to other banks and institutions that had failed to satisfy their requirements at the tender. It remained the case that clearing banks refrained from taking bills until at least a week of their life had run and in the early part of the period they bought only bills that had run for at least one month. The trend, however, was for the bills to be taken when they were longer dated, ten weeks or more after the mid-1950s and even longer in the mid-1960s.[25] While in portfolio, Treasury bills were put out as security on borrowed funds, the size of the margin of collateral in the form of bills over call money being equal to the rate of discount – for example, with a discount rate of 6 per cent, margin on bills of three months would be approximately one quarter of 6 per cent, i.e. 1½ per cent actual. In addition to providing a margin of security, the houses supplied bills to the banks in parcels made up on the basis of maturity dates requested, the dates reflecting times of heavy commitment. Finally, bills could be sold from portfolio to the special buyer at times when he was giving 'direct' help.

THE 'OUTSIDE TENDER'

There remains the question of the 'outside tender'. During the war years much of the outside demand for Treasury bills came not from domestic but from 'overseas official' sources, which employed the bills as a liquid investment for their greatly enlarged sterling balances. As the size of sterling balances declined after the war so did this source of demand for bills. In the 1950s, outside competition for Treasury bills came to be associated with 'other overseas residents' and especially with 'other' holders, a category which consisted of domestic concerns both industrial and commercial. The following statement by the Bank of England puts into perspective the extent of competition from this quarter :

> Although rising substantially in the 1950s, Bill holdings outside the banks, discount houses and overseas central monetary institutions have never accounted for more than a relatively small part of the total. In March 1951 they totalled only about £75 million or 2½ per cent of all Treasury bills in the market. By March 1960 they had risen to £772 million (nearly 24 per cent) but by March 1964 they had fallen again to £360 million (14 per cent).[26]

Financial institutions such as insurance companies, building societies, pension funds and hire-purchase finance companies were all very small holders, accounting for only about £20 million at 31 March 1964. The greater part of the residual category, 'other holders', was largely in the hands of industrial and commercial companies. Such companies held Treasury bills largely to give them an income on their temporary surpluses of cash, for example funds set aside for the payment of taxes.[27]

The pattern traced out by changes in the size of these other holdings of Treasury bills and the fluctuations in demand implicit in them is interesting evidence of the movement of funds in response to interest rate differentials. The movement went as follows. Before 1951 the yield on Treasury bills had not for a long time been attractive enough to persuade companies to invest funds in bills rather than hold them on deposit with the banks. Specifically, for several years prior to November 1951 the banks' deposit rate and the yield on Treasury bills had both been at ½ per cent. With the return to greater flexibility in interest rate policy, the general level of short-term market rates increased and a margin appeared between the Treasury bill rate and the bank deposit rate. Holders of large balances on deposit with the banks began to take advantage of the higher income to be earned on Treasury bills and companies' holdings rose rapidly. Subsequently, however, in the 1960s, the still higher yields to be obtained on loans to local authorities and hire-purchase finance houses brought about a diversion of funds from the traditional market to the new markets. The demand for Treasury bills from 'other' domestic and overseas sources declined; holdings were nine times greater in 1960 than they were in 1951 but by 1965 they had fallen to one-third of the peak figure.

As the amount of outside demand climbed towards its peak the Bank of England explained the reason for this closely observed phenomenon to the Radcliffe Committee :

> Since early in 1955 there has been a substantial holding of Treasury bills by industrial and commercial concerns; this interest has continued to a degree having no parallel at any earlier time. The phenomenon is to be associated . . . both with the absolute height of the Treasury bill rate and with the margin between the Treasury bill rate and bank deposit rates. . . . There is some ground for asserting that in the last four years industrial and commercial concerns as a group have been willing to hold up to £400 million or more of Treasury bills at any one time, and the habit may be expected to spread.[28]

Certainly, the experience of the L.D.M.A. (Qs 3473 and 3474) seemed to suggest that the degree of competition from outside sources increased in fairly direct proportion to the height of the discount rate. This general thesis was, however, questioned (Sayers, Q. 2151) on the grounds that whereas the differential in February 1955 seemed to have produced a big industrial demand for Treasury bills, that of October and November 1957, again unusually wide, had produced nothing like the same increase in demand. The Committee suggested that the difference between the two situations was that whereas in the earlier period there was a large positive rise from what was usual before, in the more recent period, while the level reached by the previous rise had been maintained, something like saturation point had been reached. Support for this view came from the Bank. Further (Qs 2153 and 2154), it was the Bank's opinion that – estimating the level of industrial holdings – they were higher than they were when the differential was narrower, that is that they formed a higher proportion of the total liquid assets of industrial companies and that there did not seem to be any closer relationship between the differential and outside holdings of Treasury bills.

It has already been suggested that a general aim of official policy was to borrow where possible from sources outside the banking system. In view of this the L.D.M.A. (Q. 2148) asked whether the increase in outside holdings could not be encouraged by way of regulating the rate that banks could offer for deposits so that it would consistently be below the Treasury bill rate. In fact (Q. 2149) the Bank had never considered such a manœuvre, on the grounds than an arbitrary reduction in the bankers' deposit rate might lead them to lend money more cheaply to the discount houses to finance their Treasury bill book which in turn might make the houses more anxious to compete for bills. This, indeed, was the likely outcome, for heavy outside demand for Treasury bills could and did result in the discount houses being deprived of bills, at times of favourable interest rate conditions when houses could be expected to want them most. In other words, much Treasury bill business would then by-pass the discount houses, which would have to attempt to make good their portfolio deficiencies by purchasing bills in the resale market and from the special buyer on occasions when he was mopping up a surplus of money.

In the 1960s, between 1963 and 1970, there was another large bulge in the holdings of overseas central monetary institutions, that is the 'inside' customers of the Bank of England. From the point of view of monetary control, however, fluctuations in the demand for Treasury bills from other overseas residents and other holders was of greater interest. During the 1950s 'hot money' from abroad normally went into Treasury bills, so that the Treasury bill rate, adjusted for forward exchange cover, was the interest rate that determined the movement of funds from overseas. The analysis earlier in this chapter would suggest that the impact of a hot money inflow would in these circumstances be neutral, because the increased volume of Treasury bills issued by the Exchange Equalisation Account to finance its purchase of foreign currency would be taken up by those abroad who were placing the hot money. With the changed pattern of interest rates obtaining in the 1960s, money from abroad was attracted into the parallel money markets so that the impact on the credit situation would no longer be neutral. The switch from the Treasury bill market also occurred in the case of industrial and commercial concerns at home, which increasingly sought the higher yields to be found on the parallel markets.

9   Commercial Bills

INTRODUCTION

The item 'other sterling bills' in Table 4 is composed mainly of commercial bills drawn on banks and firms resident in the United Kingdom and on the London offices of overseas banks and having a maximum maturity not ordinarily longer than six months. Also included are the Treasury bills of the Northern Ireland government and bills issued by local authorities, but the preponderance of commercial paper is sufficient to allow use of the figures as an indicator of changes in the discount houses' holdings of their traditional asset.

From a figure of £63m (6·1 per cent of total assets) in 1951, 'other sterling bills' fell to £42m (3·9 per cent) in 1952 and during the following three years did not rise above £49m (4·5 per cent). The situation changed dramatically in 1956 when holdings rose to £85m (9·0 per cent of total assets) and despite some slight falling back in 1957 and 1958 the trend was upward, with figures of £118m (10·4 per cent) in 1959, £183m (15·0 per cent) in 1961 and £302m (23·5 per cent) in 1964. Over the following five years holdings more than doubled to a total of £629m (34·6 per cent of total assets) in 1969. In 1970 the total was higher, at £697m, but the proportion of total assets was lower, at 29·6 per cent. After the implementation of Competition and Credit Control in 1971, holdings of other sterling bills fell sharply, but for the present chapter the main interest lies in the phenomenon of the reinstatement of the commercial bill as a major asset for the discount houses – after expert opinion had pronounced on the 'irreversible shrinkage in the relative supply ...'[1]

BILLS OF EXCHANGE

In straightforward terms a bill of exchange can be defined as 'a written instruction by the person drawing it (the drawer) to another person (the drawee) to pay a particular sum either to the bearer of the bill or to the order of a specified person (the payee)'.[2] A 'London bill' is a bill of exchange addressed to a drawee resident in the United

Kingdom and payable in sterling in London. The bill of exchange has two main functions: (1) the more important is to enable a seller or exporter of goods to obtain cash as soon as possible after the despatch of the goods and at the same time to allow the buyer or importer to defer payment until such time as he receives the goods or later; (2) another function is to provide short-term finance for trade and industry – though in this role it often takes second place to the bank advance.

In order to receive payment for the goods before the bill matures the exporter will sell or 'discount' the bill on the London market.[3] The buyer of the bill has the benefit of a discount from its face value representing the interest for the period during which he has to wait until the bill matures and he receives the face value. Thus the difference between the buying price and the redemption value represents the return on the purchaser's investment.[4]

The various types of bills in which a discount house might do business can be broadly categorised by reference to three citeria:[5]

(1) The length of the period for which the bill is drawn. As the question of discounting only arises in the case of bills drawn so as to be payable after a period of time (e.g. ninety days or three months), it is with these *period* bills that the discussion is concerned rather than with *sight* bills, which are to be paid immediately they are presented to the person on whom they are drawn.

(2) The type of institution by which the bill has been accepted. This criterion produces the following list of bill types: (*a*) *fine bank bills*, which are bills drawn on and accepted by London banks and accepting houses of undoubted standing. They command the finest (i.e. lowest) rates of discount;[6] (*b*) *agency bills*, that is bills drawn on and accepted by the London branches of banks whose head offices are located abroad. The high standing of some of these banks meant that at least until the implementation of Competition and Credit Control in 1971 their acceptances could be discounted at fine rates; (*c*) *trade bills* are drawn by one trader on another trader who accepts the bill, so that it does not bear the name of a recognised bank. Because of the higher risk of default they are discounted at rates higher than for bank bills and agency bills;[7] (*d*) *foreign domicile bills* are bills payable in sterling but drawn on and accepted by overseas names: they are less acceptable to discount houses than other types of bill, for although it is possible to use them as security against a loan from a bank they would not be eligible for last-resort borrowing from the Bank.[8]

(3) The nature of the transaction underlying the bill. The distinction here is between bills that are drawn to finance an actual movement

of goods from the seller to the buyer and which have the relevant commercial documents attached at the time of drawing, i.e. *documentary bills*; and what are known as *finance bills*, i.e. bills drawn to finance the holding or processing of stocks of raw materials, or simply to enable the drawer to give credit to his customer. The preference in the City has been for bills that finance an actual movement of goods, and this puts a limit on the amount of finance bills that can be discounted in the market or at the Bank. Their acceptability will, to a greater extent than for documentary bills, depend upon the quality of the names they bear.

The most convenient classification of commercial bills for present purposes is that which distinguishes between *bank bills* and *trade bills*, that is between bills accepted or endorsed by recognised banks and bills that do not bear the name of a recognised bank. The rate which discount houses would pay for bank bills would depend upon : the financial standing of the bank whose name the bill carried; the extent to which a house was already committed in that bank's paper; the life to maturity (the 'tenor') of the bill; and current conditions in the bill market. Before September 1971 the L.D.M.A. observed a common *minimum* rate – the 'fine rate' – below which they would not bid for bank bills. The fine rate was set each week in relation to the rate at which the houses agreed to tender as a syndicate for Treasury bills at the following tender.[9] Bank bills were an attractive investment for discount houses because they gave a relatively high degree of security together with a yield that was higher than that on Treasury bills. Because they were not as secure as Treasury bills, however, houses observed normal bankers' prudence by limiting the extent of their liability with any one bank. In addition, bank bills were not always drawn in such round figures as Treasury bills and so involved a more lengthy computation of discounts.

With regard to trade bills, because traders were considered to be generally less liquid than banks, the bills they accepted were regarded by discounters as carrying potentially greater risk. Every drawer and others who put their names on a bill (endorsers) would have a contingent liability in the event of the acceptor's default. This was reflected in the yield differential over bank bills. The more normal outlet for drawers who wished to discount their trade bills was with their bankers, who would be closely acquainted with the nature of the transaction and the credit standing of the parties. Nevertheless, trade bills drawn to cover particular transactions involving movement of goods and bearing two good names would be considered by the discount houses. The discount rate on trade bills would also depend upon the volume of trade bills in circulation and especially of trade bills bearing the names of the drawer and acceptor and drawn for the type of goods in which they were dealing. In general, there was a recognised market in London for bills drawn and accepted in certain trades and industries in which the use of such finance was traditional – for example the timber trade.

DISCOUNTING AND REDISCOUNTING

When a bill had been accepted it was ready for discounting. The owner of the bill would 'discount' the bill when he sold it; equally, a discount house would 'discount' the bill on buying it. When a discount house sold a bill from its portfolio it would 'rediscount' the bill. When discounting a trade bill a discount house would deal directly with the drawer; the discounting of a bank acceptance, on the other hand, could involve direct dealing with the drawer but more usually the bills were placed in the market by the relevant accepting house or bank.

Bills discounted by a discount house became the property of the house and were held in portfolio until resale. In the same way as other eligible assets commercial bills were employed as security against loans from the clearing banks and other secured loans. After being held in this way for about a month the bills would be sold off to the clearing banks which readily took up good-quality commercial paper, endorsed by a discount house and with about two months to run, for use in their liquid assets portfolio. To make the bills attractive investments for the banks the discount houses employed their expertise in making the bills up into 'parcels' which would provide both security and liquidity by dint of the careful choice of names of drawers and acceptors and the variety of transactions covered. When buying a parcel of commercial paper a bank would be paying for the discount house's ability to assess the credit-worthiness of the parties to a transaction and also for the readiness of the house to assume liability on the parcel. Because of the preference of the banks for bank bills the relative amount of trade bills included in any parcel would be severely limited.[10] This in turn kept down the amount of trade paper in discount house portfolios.

When a discount house purchased a bill of exchange it obviously did so in the expectation of making a profit. Profit would comprise : the difference between the prices at which the bills were discounted and rediscounted or the face value at maturity, i.e. 'dealing profits'; and the margin between the average cost of borrowed funds and the average running yield on bills, i.e. 'running profits'. They also earned commissions from the purchase and sale of bills on behalf of customers outside the banks.

The principle that emerged above, from consideration of various bill types, was that the higher the quality of the bill in terms of the probability that it would be met at maturity and also its eligibility as security against loans from the banks and from the Bank of England, the more acceptable it would be to the discount houses and the lower would be the rate at which it would be discounted. Higher rates of discount and therefore, *ceteris paribus*, higher profits could be earned on bills of lower quality but the temptation for houses to take into portfolio a high proportion of such paper had to be scrupulously resisted because of the likelihood that the bills would not be accepted as collateral against loans from the clearing banks and would be ineligible for purposes of last-resort borrowing. Furthermore, in order to ensure that a house was able to maintain an active turnover of bills in portfolio an important constraint on the choice of bills for discounting was the question of their ultimate saleability to the banks as liquid assets.

Some indication of the rate differentials that could be expected to exist between bills of various types has already been given. The acceptances of banks and accepting houses of the highest standing commanded the finest rates, at a level somewhat higher than the Treasury bill rate. Those of the London offices of foreign banks stood just slightly higher, to take account of any political risk involved. Rates on trade bills were higher, and the spread was greater, in proportion to the risk inherent in the bill.[11] For example, for Thursday 26 March 1970, with Bank rate at $7\frac{1}{2}$ per cent per annum, money market rates were as follows : average rate on allotment of Treasury bills, 7·1776; discount houses' tender rate for Treasury bills, $7\frac{3}{16}$; three months prime bank bills, $8\frac{1}{2}$; three months trade bills of good average quality, $9\frac{1}{4} - 9\frac{1}{2}$; call money, $5\frac{5}{8} - 7\frac{1}{4}$ (the lower rate is the basic rate). For Friday 30 April 1971, with Bank rate at 6 per cent per annum, the rates were : average rate on allotment of Treasury bills, 5·6844; discount houses' tender rate for Treasury bills, $5\frac{11}{16}$; three months prime bank bills, 7; three months trade bills of good average quality, $7\frac{1}{2} - 8$; call money, $4\frac{3}{8} - 5\frac{7}{8}$.

THE EXTENT OF THE HOUSES' BUSINESS

It was noted earlier that the discount houses' remaining commercial-bill business was almost completely destroyed by the effects of the Second World War. It was estimated that at one stage the total of foreign drawn bills had fallen below £10 million, while the outstanding amount of inland drawn paper had fallen to a mere £30 million or so.[12] Nevertheless, within three years after the end of the war there was a detectable revival of the acceptance credit, not only in purely internal financing but also, though less significantly, in foreign trade.[13] At 31 December 1947 the 'Big Three' houses (Alexanders, National and Union) showed rediscounts totalling £33·5m, compared with £18·5m at the end of 1946, £8·5m at the end of 1945 and £7·5m at the end of 1944. Taking together the acceptances of merchant banks, clearing and other banks, plus agency paper, the total available in the market, £100 million, was comparable with what was usual just prior to the war : though making allowance for the increase in the price level indicated that the physical volume of business being financed by bills was still much below the pre-war level.

Despite the problems posed by direct controls on economic activity, the revival of the use of acceptance credits was due mainly to the enterprise of merchant bankers in introducing or reintroducing bill finance to a wide range of trades and commodities, for example wool, paper, hire-purchase finance, timber, cocoa, tea and rubber. In international trade, advantage had been taken of the force of habit among traders, the expertise available in London and the cheapness of finance, to increase bill use. At home, however, there was no great success in efforts made to encourage the use of bills in the classical manner, that is for the finance of a movement of goods from manufacturer to wholesaler and from wholesaler to retailer. Despite the relative cheapness of bill finance, it is likely that traders were discouraged from its use through a lack of familiarity with the procedures of the discount market, thinking them complicated and lacking in confidentiality.[14] As will be shown below, efforts by discount houses to overcome ignorance and prejudice among traders were to be a factor in the revival of commercial bill business on a large scale in later years.

The unpredicted rise to new prominence of the houses' business in commercial bills began during the late 1950s. From the position in 1951 in which other sterling bills occupied only 6·1 per cent of total portfolio, as against 60·5 per cent for British Government Treasury bills and 30·5 per cent for bonds, fluctuations in the level of holdings followed during the 1950s which left the position largely unchanged by 1958 when the figures were : 6·6 per cent for other sterling bills, 56·4 per cent for Treasury bills and 30·5 per cent for bonds. Thereafter, growth was rapid and by 1968 'other sterling bills' was the biggest item in portfolio at 33·7 per cent, as against 28·3 per cent for Treasury bills and 18·4 per cent for bonds. This position was held also in 1969, after which Treasury bills resumed their usual position as the biggest single item.

The increased availability of commercial bills, which the growth of holdings reflected, was significant for a number of reasons. First, there was strong feeling inside and also outside the discount market (for example at the Bank) that the good health and stability of the discount houses would be promoted by a vigorous and growing business in good-quality bills of exchange : it was in their commercial bill business that the houses had most to offer, in terms of specialisation of function and expertise. Secondly, the houses' staple bill diet of Treasury bills was threatened by the eventual success of the authorities' policy of reducing the volume of Treasury bills in issue. Here, not only would the shortage of bills itself pose a threat but so also would the narrowing of margins which would arise *ceteris paribus*, from the increase in competition for the bills. It was seen in the previous chapter that the discount houses' holdings of Treasury bills fell from £624 million in 1951 (60·5 per cent of asset portfolio) to £399 million in 1969 (22·0 per cent). Taking year-to-year fluctuations into account, the trend after 1959 was steeply downward for a decade. Commercial paper provided a welcome substitute for disappearing Treasury bills.

The third respect in which the increased availability of commercial bills was significant concerned the mechanism of monetary control. Because the clearing banks counted good quality bills of exchange as liquid assets for the purposes of their liquid assets ratio, growth in the quantity of the bills available provided an offset to any shortage of Treasury bills brought about by the authorities' funding of the Floating Debt. This gave the banks power to expand their holdings of liquid assets independently of official financing policy. Their chief source of the bills was the discount market. The implications of the development are examined below, in Chapter 12.

An analysis of the reasons for the growth of discount house holdings of commercial bills can be approached from both the demand side and the supply side. The following analysis deals first with the factors that could have influenced the amount of commercial bills that houses would wish to take up and secondly with factors that could have contributed to the increased availability of commercial bills.

FACTORS AFFECTING DEMAND

(a) Characteristics of the business
Within the discount houses' total bill portfolio the business in commercial bills was conducted in a completely different way from the business in Treasury bills. In contrast with the relatively simple process of fixing a syndicate bid each Friday and specifying take-up days in the following week in respect of the homogeneous, characterless and safe Treasury bills, the cultivation of business in bills of exchange was an art that allowed scope for the individual approach. Not only was there the variety of types of commercial bills available but, in addition, each individual bill was different by virtue of the transaction it covered and of the names it bore. To become a dealer of any significance in bills of

exchange it was necessary to become familiar with the financing of a wide variety of trades and commodities and with the credit-worthiness of a vast number of drawers and acceptors. Given the operation of the minimum 'fine rate' system and related rates, competition for bills depended to a large extent on personal contact and the establishment of goodwill. For this reason, if the bills also met the criteria dealt with below, discount houses would not ever wish to refuse good-quality bills for discount. To do so would be to endanger goodwill, future business and future profit.

(b) Eligibility – for the banks

The higher rates obtainable on commercial bills made them more profitable than Treasury bills but also indicated that they were commensurately more risky and therefore less liquid. Thus the question of acceptability, or eligibility, arose with commercial bills whereas with Treasury bills this was not a consideration. For the clearing banks, as the discount houses' biggest single source of funds, commercial bills in a houses' portfolio had to satisfy two requirements. The bills had to be acceptable for use as security against loans at call or short notice, and they had to be suitable for purchase as portfolio investments, in parcels of round amounts varying from £100,000 to £1 million. The banks would inform the houses as to the proportion of agency, finance or trade paper they would allow in each parcel.

In this context it was quite common during the mid-1950s (i.e. prior to the large upthrust in commercial bill business) for banks to take a small proportion of fine trade bills in parcels of bank acceptances at the same agreed rate as for the fine bank bills. In the same way, circumstances often forced discount houses themselves to discount fine trade bills at the rate for fine bank bills. However, the subsequent growth in the volume of trade paper offered for discount forced rates up to a more acceptable margin over rates for fine bank bills, giving a proper return to discount houses for their endorsement of the trade paper.[15] With regard to agency bills, because such paper was not eligible for discount at the Bank the amount that the banks would take was limited; this in turn limited the amount that the houses could take. Even so, the commercial standing of some of the acceptors concerned (e.g. American banks in London from 1959–60 onwards) enabled them to discount large amounts of their bills at fine rates.

The banks, of course, purchased both Treasury bills and commercial bills from the discount houses for use in their liquid asset portfolios. In parallel with the decline in the volume of Treasury bills available there was a fall in the holdings of the banks. At 31 December 1955, for example, the London clearing banks held £1271 million of British government Treasury bills : by 15 December 1965 holdings had fallen to £770 million. Over the same period holdings of United Kingdom commercial bills rose from £129 million to £356 million, providing a partial offset.[16]

> It is not only that the sums they could put into Treasury bills have fallen absolutely, but as a proportion of deposits the fall has been precipitous. Thus the move into commercial bills was almost inevitable, and as an inducement the Market has been able to offer such bills to the banks at an increasingly attractive premium.[17]

The increased demand from the banks allowed the discount houses to speed up their turnover, so that they were able to discount more of the bills as they came forward.

(c) Eligibility – at the Bank of England
Eligibility considerations applied also to the Bank of England, which was the final arbiter of market standards in commercial paper. The Bank was concerned both to maintain the standards of quality long associated with the London prime bank bill, and hence its reputation as a liquid asset of undoubted security, but also to allow reasonable development of bills of all classes as being useful financial instruments (some gave rise to modest net earnings of foreign exchange). The main weight of Bank influence was exercised through the accepting houses because although these houses accounted for only about a third of all bills *accepted* by banks in London, they accounted for a much higher proportion of the bills *sold* in London. This was because the bulk of accepting houses' acceptances were put on to the market whereas a large proportion of the bills accepted by other banks were retained for their own portfolio.

The Bank exercised its influence in the market through three available channels. The first involved prior consultation with the accepting houses, by means of which undesirable finance-bill business could be discouraged. The second was by means of sampling purchases, whereby the Bank was able to test the quality of prime bank bills and later, with the general growth of commercial bill business, of trade bills as well. Although trade bills of suitable quality had always been eligible as security for advances made by the Bank, the practice of the discount houses had for many years been to lodge only Treasury bills or short bonds. This meant that scrutiny of commercial paper was confined to the representative selection of prime bank bills purchased by the Bank for its own portfolio. However, beginning in September 1963 the Bank took a keener interest in trade paper, asking the discount houses occasionally to include some fine trade bills in the security lodged against last-resort loans. Later, the Bank included such trade bills in its regular sampling purchases, at a small margin over the rate for bank bills. For the discount houses this move was especially important as it allowed them to increase sales of good trade bills as 'eligible' bills to a banking system still somewhat reluctant to take them.

In January 1964, as a reflection of the general increase in commercial bill business, the Bank increased its average weekly rate of purchases of prime bank bills by about a third. It was considered that bill purchases constituted an important means of influence in the market, not only through their direct effects but also indirectly, as other banks followed the Bank's lead.

Over the twenty-year period from 1951, the great majority of both bank and trade bills were drawn for a tenor of ninety days. The Bank's policy was to encourage the practice and in 1953 the discount houses were told that ninety days was '. . . a good and reasonable period for drawing . . .' and that only very exceptionally should the period be extended. Nevertheless, in 1964 the Bank agreed to take bills originally drawn for 180 days in their weekly sampling purchases from each house, provided both that there was justification for the original tenor and that the bills had no more than ninety days to run.[18]

The third channel of influence available to the Bank lay through the rediscount facilities it extended to the discount houses. However, especially during the 1950s, the houses rarely sought last-resort help using commercial bills as security, Treasury bills being found more convenient. Consequently this channel was of very minor importance. The Bank's eligibility rule for commercial bills was that the bills should bear two good British names, one of which would have to be the acceptor while the other would, in practice, be the name of the discount house that had endorsed the bill on resale to the Bank. With regard to finance paper, the Bank's attitude had undergone changes : the trend had been for the bills to become more acceptable in the 1930s and this continued during the Second World War. This policy changed at the beginning of the 1950s as the Bank sought to restrict their use. Henceforth, only self-liquidating bills would be discounted at the finest rates at the Bank. The Bank's change of attitude towards finance paper was influenced by the relaxation of exchange control regulations relating to the granting of credits abroad, and also by the feeling that this was more appropriate to peace-time conditions.[19] In the mid-1960s there was a hardening of the market's attitude towards finance paper.

(d) Discount houses' dealing criteria
Quite apart from rules imposed from outside, discount houses had

their own criteria as a basis for bill dealing. The houses would accept as a good commercial bill one that was 'self-liquidating on a short-term basis', so that the bill would represent commodities that would be sold before the bill matured, thus providing funds for payment. The credit would not be renewable. In the same way as the Bank of England, the houses would look for two good names on a bill, the selection of good names being an aspect of the bill dealer's expertise.

Nevertheless, the tendency had been for the amount of the genuine ('classical') commercial bills to decline as a proportion of the discount houses' intake, the decline being due to a number of factors, including the development of a buyer's market in many areas of trade, an increasing resort to overdraft facilities and the rise of factoring.[20] In place of classical bills, houses purchased finance bills of various kinds, examples of which were as follows. The most illiquid and, therefore, the least generally acceptable were those drawn by finance companies, in which the accepting bank was given a general charge on the goods in the underlying transaction. The next least liquid were bills drawn by manufacturers against stocks of raw material in warehouse. More acceptable would be bills drawn by large exporters of manufactured goods, for borrowing purposes, against a general charge over goods in transit but not against a specific shipment or set of documents. Generally, these financial arrangements would employ revolving acceptance credits whereby bills were drawn for large round amounts and carried the understanding that they would be renewed on maturity. Because finance bills did not represent any underlying movement of goods their quality depended much more on the strength of the names they bore.

Other constraints on the amount of acceptable-quality commercial bills that a house could take up would be imposed by the volume and cost of call money available and by factors affecting the holdings of other assets in portfolio. Because call money was a house's stock in trade, the first concern would be to ensure a supply of money which, once in the house, could then be employed to the best advantage. Consequently, although rates would be a matter for negotiation, a house would not wish to refuse money and so endanger its goodwill. The conventions governing money and bill dealing virtually guaranteed a margin of profit, the only real danger stemming from a serious miscalculation over possible future Bank rate changes when setting the syndicate tender rate for Treasury bills and the fine-bank bill rate for commercial bills.[21] With a higher rate of discount on bank bills than on Treasury bills, the houses would gladly substitute the former (when available) for the latter and would be able to do so to the extent that the bidding policy they would necessarily have to follow at the tender did not run contrary to the view of the Bank on the proper level of the Treasury bill rate (see Chapters 8 and 12). The picture cannot be nearly complete until consideration is given to the influence of a house's bond business. In the next chapter this is analysed within the context of the whole portfolio.

FACTORS AFFECTING SUPPLY

(a) The revival of commercial bill business
The supply side of the analysis seeks to explain the reasons for the increased availability of commercial bills to the discount houses during the late 1950s and the 1960s. The increase in supply was the more remarkable because it was so clearly unexpected by those best able to make an accurate forecast. The well-known conclusions of the Radcliffe Committee, that the business in commercial bills was 'vestigial but still large enough to be a useful source of income for the houses most active in it' (*Report*, para. 165), but that the shrinkage in the relative supply of commercial bills was 'irreversible' (para. 584), were based on the memoranda and evidence submitted to the Committee. Certainly the evidence of L.D.M.A. representatives indicated that no significant resurgence in the volume of commercial paper coming forward for discount was anticipated in the discount market. Asked whether they thought the volume of commercial paper would increase or decrease over the next ten or twenty years, one representative said that he thought it likely to decrease while another said that he thought the question to be too difficult to answer.[22]

Although exact figures of the growth of the total commercial bill supply and of its composition by type of bill are not available, the trends can be indicated clearly enough. One estimate of the amount of borrowing from the banking system on commercial bills, that is bills discounted by banks and discount houses, shows that from negligible proportions at the end of the war, borrowing rose to £200 million in 1953 and to £400 million in 1960. In the following four years it doubled again to over £800 million.[23]

Going a step further, although no detailed analysis of the proportions of bank and trade bills in the total supply is available, estimates put the proportions of trade paper as being low and a figure of about 10 per cent might be the most useful to work with.[24] Bank bills were obviously the more important and figures of bank acceptances should provide a good indicator of increased availability of commercial paper. It is not, however, the figures for total bank acceptances that are relevant but those for banks whose acceptances are likely to have entered the market, because : 'since the clearing banks rarely sell bills discounted for clients or purchased in the open market, it is the merchant, overseas and foreign banks in the City who create the supply of bills and influence the rates'.[25] It can be seen from Table 7 that total acceptances of the accepting houses, overseas banks and other banks in the United Kingdom stood at £209m at the end of 1951. At the end of the following year the total had fallen to £123·2m. It then fluctuated until 1957 when it rose to £205·8m. Acceptances rose strongly again in 1961 to stand at £288m. Thereafter the trend was steeply upward : over the next four years the total more than doubled, to a figure of £658·1m at the end of 1965, and after a further four years it had risen to £858m, at the end of 1969. Overall, the figures for discount houses' holdings of other sterling bills, which were dominated by commercial bills, followed the same trend (see Table 4).

The increase in commercial bill business involved both bank bills and trade bills and covered transactions both at home and overseas. A number of factors may have contributed to the upsurge and the most significant appear to be as follows.

(b) Overseas trade

One factor affecting the supply of commercial bills coming forward was the value of foreign and international trade. Members of the Accepting Houses Committee made clear to the Radcliffe Committee that there was still a preference 'on policy grounds' for an international bill.[26] However, asked to elucidate their statement (Q. 5853) that 'a substantial part of the commercial credit business of the accepting houses is now devoted to home trade', L.D.M.A. representatives indicated that roughly 80 per cent of their outstanding acceptances were for home account and about 20 per cent for foreign account. This represented the proportion between domestic and foreign *customers*, but the proportion of new acceptances that would be in respect of trade taking place between one British businessman and another, that is non-foreign trade, would be (Q. 5855) a very much smaller proportion.[27] See Tables 7 and 8, which divide total acceptances into those on behalf of U.K. residents and those on behalf of overseas residents and show that for members of the Accepting Houses Committee alone the proportion on behalf of overseas residents was smaller.

The Accepting Houses Committee also provided information showing the relationship between the supply of bills and the amount of trade. Two charts were supplied (see Figures 1 and 2) which showed the following. Figure 1 : the total of the acceptances of the seventeen members of the Committee outstanding at the end of each quarter; the total value of all bills and promissory notes drawn during each quarter; the value of U.K. trade during each quarter; the exports of the overseas sterling area to countries other than the United Kingdom; the value of world trade (excluding United States special category exports); the level of Bank rate. Figure 2 : the value of U.K. imports and exports; wholesale prices (basic materials) index; export prices (manufactured goods) index.

In interpreting the charts the following must be taken into account. A major part of the acceptance houses' acceptances covered the movement of raw materials and in many cases this movement was seasonal. Consequently, acceptances tended to be used heavily in the first quarter of each year (see Figure 1 but fell off in the middle of each year. Thus bank bills showed a peak at a time of the year when Treasury bills, for reasons of public finance, showed a trough.

Secondly, although the majority of term drafts were drawn for a usance of three months, they could be drawn for periods ranging from three days to six months, so that figures of acceptances outstanding would not necessarily be a reliable indicator of turnover. Thirdly, whether London acceptance credits would be used for the finance of international trade, in preference to other methods or other centres, would depend upon a number of considerations, and changes of preference could cause fluctuations unrelated to economic factors in the total amount of acceptances. Finally, the figures for the acceptances outstanding of the members of the Accepting Houses Committee are not exactly comparable with the figures for all bills and promissory notes drawn : whereas the accepting houses' figures are exact, those for all bills drawn can only be an approximation based on stamp duty figures.

Despite the qualifications the charts indicate clearly that the total of acceptances of the members of the Accepting Houses Committee bore a fairly constant relation to the total of all bills drawn and that the movement of both these totals coincided very largely with the movement of the total value of U.K. trade (that is U.K. external trade, see Q. 5904).[28] These movements show the same tendency as the exports of the overseas sterling area to countries other than the United Kingdom, the figures of U.K. merchanting transactions and the value of world trade. Also there was a relation between all these movements and the movements of import, export and wholesale prices.

Because the indicators move so closely together and assuming that extrapolation is possible, the growth of U.K. external trade in the years following the period of the above analysis can be used to explain the increased availability of bank bills in the late 1950s and during the 1960s. United Kingdom external trade (the value of imports plus the value of exports and excluding re-exports, in current prices) rose from £7083·3m in 1958 to £7509·4m in 1959 and to £8342·4m in 1961.

Over the following four years it increased by over £2000m to reach £10,487·3m in 1965. By 1969, when commercial bills were at their apogee as a proportion of discount houses' total asset portfolios the value of overseas trade had risen to £15,689·1 million.[29]

Following the post-war recovery of trade and commercial bill business, the discount houses' holdings fell after November 1951 (see Table 4) – partly as a result of the collapse of commodity prices during the second half of 1951, as the boom which had followed the outbreak of the Korean War came to an end. The volume of bills coming forward was again set on an upward course by the rapid growth of international trade from 1954 onwards. 'It is relevant, when looking at that curve of bills and acceptances for 1956 and 1957 to look also at the value of U.K. Trade [Figure 1], and, on the other chart [Figure 2] at the value of imports and exports, all of which were showing the same upward tendency at the same time.'[30] Again a check occurred to the growth of the houses' holdings after the September 1957 rise in Bank rate to 7 per cent. A tightening of the exchange control regulations banned the use of bills to finance trade between overseas residents, as well as on refinance credits. In February 1959 the restrictions on the use of commercial bills for financing trade between overseas residents were removed and the market's holdings began to rise again.[31] Thereafter, in each year from 1960 to 1969, the value of discount houses' holdings increased.

(c) Finance paper
Several factors involved in the growth of commercial bill business related to conditions in the home economy and gave rise to an increased flow of both bank bills and trade bills. With the relative decline of the classical self-liquidating bill, discount houses expanded into purchases of finance paper covering a variety of transactions. This business had developed rapidly as finance houses grew to meet the hire-purchase requirements of the post-war boom in consumer goods. By the start of the 1950s this business had grown sufficiently for it to attract the scrutiny of the authorities. Later it came to be accepted that a 'fair proportion'[32] of finance paper would circulate in the market and that some of it, that drawn by some of the country's largest public companies, would command good rates.

In fact, it was in the bills of the large public companies that the real growth occurred, the Bank taking a tolerant view of an increase of credit that was directly related to manufacturing and trading activities. For these finance bills, generally drawn for amounts of not less than £25,000, were used by the companies increasingly to provide short-term working finance, by supplying credit from the time that a

contract was signed to the time at which the manufacturer or entre-
preneur parted with the goods and collected payment. For very large
amounts finance would be provided by syndicates of accepting houses.
Drawers would pay an acceptance commission over and above the
rate of discount in order to get their bills accepted and it was in order
to avoid the cost involved here that the biggest and best names discounted their bills with the discount houses directly, as trade bills. In
circumstances in which banks were 'fully loaned up', the old inhibitions
among discount houses about harming the clearing banks' advances
(overdraft) business faded away and the houses actively pursued this
good trade-bill business, sometimes encouraged by the banks themselves.

(d) Credit restriction

One influence widely regarded as encouraging the growth of commercial bill finance, both bank and trade bills, was its availability as
compared to substitutes and especially the bank advance, which was
subject to restriction during the 1950s and 1960s. In other words, in
the face of government restrictions affecting orthodox channels for
obtaining credit, potential borrowers entered the bill market. The
rationale behind this view was set out in Chapter 5, above. Control
of sections of the credit market would be ineffective inasmuch as
deficit units were driven to parts of the market where credit was still
available. R. S. Sayers, who was instrumental in formulating the 'Radcliffe view', later put it as follows : '. . . the phenomenon was the direct
outcome of the method of restriction used by the authorities : restriction being applied to lenders, borrowers could protect themselves by
establishing connexions with a wider variety of lenders'.[33]

The view that such a movement did occur is given credence by the
statement of the Bank of England which reported that discount houses'
holdings of commercial bills nearly doubled during the course of
1956 '. . . as borrowers who were prevented from obtaining bank
advances because of credit restraint turned to bill finance'.[34] However,
despite the general agreement, one dissident voice was raised in 1958
in evidence to the Radcliffe Committee. Asked whether there was
some association with the credit squeeze, so that some lines of credit
were available through the discount market, after acceptance, that
were not available through the banks, a representative of the Accepting Houses Committee said (Q. 5850) :

It may happen that, if we commit ourselves to granting a line of
credit to a customer which he can use, say until March, 1959, and
if he is not using that in full and he has reached his limit on his

overdraft facilities, he may tend to use the acceptance line to a greater extent . . . but we are facing virtually nothing of a demand for acceptance facilities to replace what I might call a squeezed overdraft.

To establish causation is always a difficult matter but it may not be without significance that not until May 1965 did the authorities take direct action to limit finance through bills. A rigid quantitative restriction on purchases of all commercial paper was imposed – including bank bills.[35] The restrictions caused some resentment in the discount market, for the houses were being asked not only to restrict the creation of credit on their own behalf, through trade bills, but also to control credit creation by the banks, by having to refuse bank bills and so put goodwill at risk.

(e) The cost of bill credit

Another influence on the bill supply was the reduction in the cost of bill credit.[36] Two factors were influential here. Pressure to cut the size of acceptance commissions was exerted by an increased degree of competition in the acceptance business. This development was forced upon a previously sheltered market as a result of the influx of foreign banks, especially American banks, into London after about 1959. Whereas commissions generally stood at between $1\frac{1}{2}$ and 2 per cent in 1952, by 1965 they had fallen by up to $\frac{3}{4}$ per cent. The effect was to make an acceptance credit more competitive *vis-à-vis* bank overdrafts and, in the case of finance companies, more competitive *vis-à-vis* direct bidding for deposits from the public. An influence of longer standing was the growing size of companies, which made them more ready to demand lower rates for the privilege of having their bills accepted.

The second factor was the abolition in 1961 of the *ad valorem* bill stamp of one shilling (five new pence) per £100 and its replacement by a flat rate duty of twopence (slightly less than one new penny) per bill. Because the cost of shorter bills obtained greatest relief the effect was substantially to increase the volume of shorter bills drawn. For banks and discount houses working on the basis of small margins and large turnover the benefit was marked. The effect of the reduction was acknowledged by the Bank, which reported that between 1961 and 1964 '. . . commercial bill business was rising strongly again, having received added impetus from the reduction in stamp duty . . .'[37]

(f) Discount houses' initiative

Given the system of rules and conventions within which they worked prior to 1971, discount houses had the reputation of being institutions in which expertise based upon long experience went hand in hand with a rather 'traditional' and only slowly changing view of the way in which business should be conducted. With regard to the resurgence of trade bills, it has been said that this business would have grown even faster had it not been for the 'inherent conservatism of the whole banking set-up whose responses to the changed credit needs of the 1960s depend a good deal on differing traditions and personalities'.[38]

However, as was pointed out above, once over their initial shyness, the discount houses eagerly sought this business. In bank bills, accepting houses took the opportunities offered by direct controls on bank lending and by the 'encouragement' given by the authorities to the capital market to keep down new issues, to propagate the use of the acceptance credit. 'The accepting houses never failed to adapt their bills to meet new needs even when changes in banking might have appeared to rob them of their very raison d'être.'[39] For their part, discount houses attempted to inform a business community long unfamiliar with bills of exchange – due to the Depression and the Second World War – of the services the houses could offer. As early as 1952 the well-known *Bill on London*, produced by Gillett Brothers Discount Co Ltd, appeared and enjoyed a good sale both at home and abroad.[40] Other houses also sought to publicise their activities through the production of brief guides to the working of the discount market in general[41] and to the operation of specific kinds of financial services. By these means and through personal contacts – visiting regions and individual companies which might furnish suitable paper – the houses' actions belied the view that they were merely passive receivers of business created by others.

It would be difficult to attempt to quantify the contribution made by the houses' own initiative to the development of their commercial bill business during this period. Their endeavours, however, continued to enjoy the support of the authorities. On the eve of the big expansion in the houses' traditional business, L. K. O'Brien justified their role to the Radcliffe Committee[42] in the following terms. He believed that although the same functions could be performed by others, they would be less efficiently performed. The continuing justification of this aspect of the houses' business rested on their provision of an expert market : 'The market is important not only because the amount is still important, but also because where a market does not exist it is always more difficult for people who have to dispose of bills, or any commodity, to have their needs met efficiently.'

10 Bonds

INTRODUCTION

By 1951 discount houses had been carrying on business in short-dated government stocks for more than thirty years. Table 4 shows that in that year houses' holdings of British Government Stocks (end-year figures) stood at £314m (30·5 per cent of total portfolio). In 1952 they fell to £291m (27·3 per cent) but rose steeply in 1953 to stand at £383m (35·3 per cent). Holdings then fell during the following four years to the low figure of £223m (23·3 per cent) but thereafter grew year by year to stand at £488m (39·0 per cent) in 1962. After dipping slightly over the next two years, holdings rose to £500m (34·4 per cent) in 1965 and then climbed to their highest level since 1951, at £544m (31·1 per cent). Holdings fell sharply in 1968, recovered well in 1969 to £364m (20·0 per cent), and then dropped very sharply to stand at £160m (6·8 per cent), their lowest since 1951. In 1971 holdings recovered strongly to reach £391m (12·8 per cent).

It seems clear that the changes in discount houses' holdings over the period contained no underlying trend. Fluctuations were sufficiently marked, however, to warrant investigation as to their cause. The enquiry will throw light on the nature of the discount houses' operations in gilt-edged securities and on the role they played in the gilt-edged market. The first part of the following analysis examines the characteristics of the gilt-edged market, the debt management operations of the Bank of England, the nature of fixed-interest securities; and assesses the market role of the discount houses. Against this background the second part of the analysis examines the reasons for the changes in the size of houses' holdings of bonds during the period, within the context of changes in the composition of the whole portfolio.

THE GILT-EDGED MARKET

In contrast to the other two major assets in which the discount houses dealt during the 1950s and 1960s the securities with which the present chapter is concerned were all traded on the Stock Exchange.[1] The gilt-edged market covered securities issued by the British government, the dominions and colonies, the local authorities and most of the public boards. Apart from stocks issued by the British government itself, there were certain other gilt-edged securities guaranteed by the British government in regard to payment of interest and repayment of principal, for example issues in respect of certain nationalised industries and a few Commonwealth stocks.

United Kingdom local authority stocks were not guaranteed by the central government, though interest payments and repayment of the capital sum were a charge on local authority revenues. Local authority issues were normally medium-dated stocks but after 1964 there appeared as a new element in the gilt-edged market local authority bonds, termed 'yearlings' (though maturities could range up to five years); they were similar in character to short-term British government bonds.[2] The securities issued by Commonwealth central and local governments were, similarly, not guaranteed by the British government, although there were exceptions. The issues of a great many of the British Colonies and former colonies were managed by the Crown Agents.

British government securities could be divided into four categories, corresponding to four sections in the gilt-edged market, according to the number of years they had to run to maturity. The categories were: short-dated (due to be redeemed within five years); medium-dated (with redemption between five and fifteen years); long-dated (over fifteen years) and undated (where either there was no final date for redemption or the date was unspecified and at the option of the government).[3]

Short-dated stocks were sometimes termed 'money stocks' because they provided an alternative to other forms of short-term lending. The rate of commission on purchase and sale was very low ('left to the discretion of the broker'); for example in the case of large amounts it could be as low as $\frac{1}{64}$ per cent on the nominal value of the stock.[4] The discount houses and banks were the chief investors in the short-dated market because they required investments which could easily be liquidated and which could be bought and sold in large quantities. Correspondingly, the great bulk of the discount houses' bond holdings were in short-dated British government stocks, although the houses carried on a smaller and less active business in dominion, colonial and British corporation issues of similar maturity.[5] In February 1964 the discount houses were instrumental in introducing the new local authority 'yearling' bonds.

The discount houses, in common with other investors, bought and

F

sold gilt-edged securities through the medium of the stockbrokers. Estimation of the number of broking firms that regularly transacted large-scale business in the gilt-edged market is difficult but a reasonable estimate would be between twenty and thirty. In addition, three firms of stockbrokers acted as 'money brokers' to the jobbers. In this role they helped to maintain the essential characteristics of gilt-edged dealing – for example, easy marketability, even up to very large amounts, coupled with prompt delivery and payment. The money brokers lent either stocks or money, depending upon whether the jobber had to make or take delivery. Stocks which were scarce in the market were borrowed from institutional investors, while money was obtained from bank and non-bank lenders. The jobbers were unable to do this themselves since they were allowed to borrow only from their banks or the money brokers. Most importantly, it was to a significant extent due to their liaison with the money brokers that the discount houses were able to play their own part in making a market in short-dated gilts. The money brokers enabled discount houses to acquire large amounts of stock at short notice and also to unload and switch large amounts. From their experience, the brokers were able to build up a picture of where stock was being held in the market.

The stockbrokers dealt with the stock jobbers who numbered, according to the evidence of the government broker to the Radcliffe Committee, about twenty in the gilt-edged market in 1957. By 1967, however, the number had fallen to eleven. In terms of the net position of their total buying and selling orders, the government stock held by these jobbers was in 1957 put at well under £100 million. It has been estimated that in the mid-1960s average daily purchases and sales of gilt-edged stocks amounted to about £70 million.[6]

DEBT MANAGEMENT POLICY OF THE BANK OF ENGLAND

Of very great importance in influencing the discount houses' approach to bond dealing was the policy being pursued in the gilt-edged market by the Bank of England. The Bank's interpretation of the nature of that market and of the goals and tactics which followed from it were examined in Chapter 5. In essence, these remained unchanged between 1951 and 1971. There was, however, a detectable shift in emphasis between the first and second decades. In the ten years or more prior to 1971 the conduct of debt management was dominated by the 'support' function of the Bank. The government's borrowing requirement had grown rapidly in the 1960s and the prevailing belief, that the number of willing holders of the debt would be reduced if it were felt that the market was being manipulated for monetary policy purposes, forced the Bank to follow the cautious policy of 'leaning into the wind'.

This policy produced the following list of priorities for the 1960s and therefore a corresponding dealing environment for the discount houses. Later, at the end of the 1960s, the Bank's responses to the desires of investors became less automatic and a more flexible attitude towards price changes was introduced. In this respect the Bank was reverting to an emphasis that had been more apparent during the 1950s.

The primary aim of the Bank was to sustain the confidence of investors, that they would always be able to deal readily in substantial amounts of stock, and to this end the Bank stood ready to smooth market fluctuations, to encourage breadth of dealing and to promote efficiency of operation. Further, success in this direction took the Bank a long way towards the achievement of the closely related goal of obtaining favourable terms for the government's longer-term borrowing. This, in turn, brought into consideration factors affecting the demand for stocks from various sections of the market and hence of the effects of borrowing policy upon the liquidity of the banks and others. A fourth aim was to avoid serious repercussions in the money market, by so arranging the maturity dates of the market debt that they were spread as evenly as possible. Refinancing of maturing debt at longer term was a continuing preoccupation, as noted earlier, as was restriction of the proportion of short-term debt. Finally, in pursuit of these various aims the Bank had also to attempt to achieve that pattern of interest rates deemed most appropriate given all the circumstances.[7]

In common with the discount houses and other dealers in the gilt-edged market the Bank worked through a firm of stockbrokers (the government broker), and traditionally two senior members of Mullens and Co. have devoted themselves to government business. As noted in previous chapters, market operations could broadly be divided between operations in maturing debt and the issue of new stocks. In the first case, the Bank had developed the practice of gradually buying in maturing stocks as their final maturity dates approached and holding them in official portfolios. Successfully achieved, this policy would ensure that final repayment would involve only book-keeping transactions with no disruption of the money market. In the second case, to avoid distortion in the gilt-edged market and subsequently in the money market as payment was made, the Bank again employed the tactics of gradually easing new issues on to the market at a pace governed by the appetite of investors. By offering the whole issue to the market on one day and at a price very close to comparable investments the Bank would ensure that demand for the stock could be satisfied at ruling market prices. The preponderance of the stock would then be purchased for official holdings and trickled out through 'the tap' as opportunities for sales became apparent.

A third case, intermediate between the other two, involved the government broker in 'switching operations' – that is offering longer-dated stocks in the market in exchange for shorter-dated issues, so as to maintain an even distribution among maturity dates. To enable the government broker to perform these three basic functions the Bank utilised the securities held in the Issue Department as cover for the note issue. It was thus possible to maintain a large and varied portfolio of stocks which could be used, on terms advantageous to the Bank's chosen policy, to supplement the resources of the market jobbers. The Bank thus acted as 'jobber of last resort' and gave the gilt-edged market a breadth and depth which it otherwise would not have had.

Of more immediate importance from the point of view of the discount houses' bond dealing was the question of the Bank's ability to achieve that pattern of interest rates that seemed best suited to the prevailing needs of general economic policy. The view of the Bank was that it was unable to impose a pattern of rates on the market. Although, as shown earlier (Chapters 3 and 4, covering the period 1914 to 1951), the Bank possessed significant powers to influence short-term rates, the situation with regard to long-term rates was not comparable. The very size of the Bank's operations was bound to have some effect on longer-term borrowing rates, but clearly the Bank was unable to dominate a market on which the total amount of gilt-edged securities quoted was (in March 1967) £21,775 million nominal. In sum, the Bank claimed that apart from smoothing operations and giving the market a lead, '. . . fundamentally the level and pattern of long-term interest rates depends not on . . . [the Bank's] operations but on the overall pattern of demand for and supply of long-term funds'.[8]

PRINCIPLES OF BONDS AND BOND DEALING

Gilt-edged stock is customarily quoted in terms of £100 nominal upon which a fixed rate of interest (the 'coupon rate') is paid. When the stock stands at par in the market the yield will be equal to the 'coupon' but fluctuations in the 'market rate of interest' will cause the market price to stand above or below par. Due to the state of knowledge in the market and the existence of alternative forms of investment (e.g. Treasury bills) the yields on short-dated bonds will tend to move together.

The 'running' or 'flat' yield on a stock is obtained by dividing the coupon by the market price, expressing the result as a percentage.

Further, stocks bought in the market and held to redemption will involve an element of capital gain or loss when calculating the overall return from the investment : a 'redemption yield' is obtained which consists of the running yield plus or minus the difference between the market price and the redemption price, amortised over the remaining life of the stock. The longer the life of the stock, the smaller the difference (differences in coupon apart) between the running yield and the redemption yield for any given price.[9]

As the yield on any particular stock moves in direct relation with the 'market rate of interest' the coupon on that stock is brought into line with the market rate through fluctuations in the market price. As a consequence, the market price of a stock will vary inversely with changes in the market rate of interest. Prior to October 1972[10] the market rate would itself move in response to changes in Bank rate. Prices of stocks would, of course, change for reasons other than changes in Bank rate, for example their length of life to maturity, the effects of market operations by the government broker, portfolio adjustments made by individual investors, or because of buying or selling operations by the institutions. The degree of effect that any given purchase or sale of stocks would have on the market price of stocks of that type would depend upon the degree of 'thinness' of the market, that is how much of the stock was being dealt in.

It follows from what has been said about fluctuations in bond[11] prices that discount-house bond dealers stood to make a capital gain or loss (a 'dealing' profit or loss) depending upon how prices moved between date of purchase and date of sale. Also, as with the Treasury bills and commercial bills in portfolio, a profit or loss would be made consequent upon the relationship between the running yield on the bond, which would be fixed at the time of purchase, and the cost of the money with which the holding was financed ('running' profit).

Because bond prices moved inversely with changes in the market rate of interest, it is now possible to appreciate how disastrous an unexpected rise in Bank rate could be for the discount houses. With a rise in Bank rate the cost of money would rise immediately with it, while the yields on bonds and bills already in portfolio would be left at the level fixed at time of purchase. Consequently, running losses would be sustained until holdings either matured or were sold – at a loss – and were replaced with new investments based upon the higher level of Bank rate.[12] In this way, the houses' bond dealers could be put into a painful dilemma in a time of generally rising interest rates. Unless the stocks were at or close to maturity, dealers would have to choose between continuing to take a running loss or to accept a dealing loss. For this reason dealers would have a preference for the shortest bonds, which involved the least risk of dealing losses; unfortunately the shorter the maturity held the less would be the scope for making substantial dealing profits.

Of course, a capital loss incurred because of a rise in interest rates would only be a 'paper loss' unless the bonds had to be sold before maturity. Nevertheless discount houses regarded a paper loss on bond dealing as a serious matter because of the following considerations : (a) the written-down value of bond holdings would show as a loss in a company's published accounts; (b) the ratio, of bonds held to published resources, which houses used as a guide for prudent dealing, would be reduced; (c) when bond prices fell a house had immediately to provide, out of its own resources of capital and reserves, additional margin on its call money to compensate for the fall in the value of the bonds lodged as security.

In an attempt to reconcile the opposing elements of profit and risk inherent in bond business, dealers developed general principles of dealing, of which the following three were central : (1) mention has already been made of the desirability of restricting holdings to the shortest of eligible stocks because of the smaller amount of risk involved : it may therefore be concluded that in anticipation of a rise in Bank rate a house would attempt to shorten the average life of its bond portfolio in order to minimise the inevitable losses; (2) as a further precaution in the same situation a house would endeavour to have as small a holding of bonds as possible; (3) in the expectation of a general rise in rates, a house would prefer to have as much of its holding as possible in higher coupon issues, for the extent of gain or loss after a change in Bank rate would depend to some extent on the coupon of the stock in question.

To expand the last point a little, it can be said that for a given change in Bank rate low-coupon bonds were subject to greater price fluctuations than high-coupon bonds – that is, with a given change in the level of interest rates there would be greater 'volatility' (change in price in relation to change in yield) the *longer* the term of the stock and the *lower* the coupon.[13] The following example will illustrate this principle :

Coupon	Nominal	Market price	Yield
1	100	50	2
10	100	50	20

Interest rates now rise by 1 per cent

1	100	33·3	3
10	100	47·6	21

In the latter half of the period the generally higher coupons on bond issues did much to protect houses' bond books against sharp falls in bond values. Not only did they reduce the danger of capital loss but also the higher running yield on these stocks provided better cover against high rates on borrowed funds.

The size of the coupon on stock issued was, clearly, a factor under the control of the Bank, though houses would, where possible, choose the higher couponed of available stocks. On the other hand, principles (1) and (2) could be implemented by discount-house bond dealers themselves. The principles found expression in the adoption of a policy device which took into account the size and average length of a house's bond book. This device was the 'bond multiplier', referred to earlier, which indicated the ratio of bond holdings to published resources. Although multipliers of eight or ten to one would have been regarded as normal during the 1960s, the multipliers of individual houses would be calculated with regard to the extent of hidden reserves and the maturity distribution of the book. It will be shown below that experience of Bank rate movements during the period 1951–70 caused some revision of thinking on the use of the bond multiplier.

Of the two main influences that bore on the ratio of bonds to published resources, one, hidden ('inner') reserves, is quickly dealt with for there are, by definition, no published data. It is possible, however, to examine more closely the sort of maturity pattern that a house's bond book might have taken. R. S. Sayers's history of Gillett Brothers Discount Company Limited reveals a classification of bond maturities which that house adopted in the late 1940s. The classification was Gilletts' own but it reflected the prevailing attitudes of the Bank of England and of the clearing banks and other banks from which Gilletts had to borrow most of their funds.[14]

The bonds were arranged in five groups in order of decreasing liquidity, depending upon the length of life to maturity of the bonds and the status of the issuing authority. Thus, Group 1 consisted of bonds within six months of maturity, headed by British government bonds but also including issues of dominion and colonial governments and approved British local authority stocks. Gilletts had traditionally regarded bonds in this group as bills, because prior to 1914 many bills had been for a six months' tenor. Because British government bonds in Group 1 could be regarded as 'long Treasury bills' the banks were generally willing to take them as security against loans without the addition of 'margin'. Although the Bank normally made no distinction between these and other short bonds, an exception was made in the mid-1950s as a way of helping discount houses out of difficulties on their bond business.

Group 2 of the classification, consisting of British government bonds with between six months and five years to run, contained the balance of bond holdings which were eligible for the purposes of lender-of-last-resort borrowing from the Bank. The remaining categories of bonds in portfolio, consisting of the issues of other borrowers and of British government 'long' bonds (more than five years to run) and 'very long' bonds (up to about twelve years to maturity), generally offered higher yields, but this advantage could be entirely offset by the higher rates charged by banks for the money to finance these, less liquid, bonds.[15] On the basis of the classification adopted Gilletts could hold bonds to the extent of ten times their own capital resources, excluding bonds in Group 1, with the actual amount being limited by the amount of bond money available from the banks, and the extent to which estimated depreciation of bond values could be matched with additional cover to be provided out of own resources or hidden reserves.

THE MARKET ROLE OF THE DISCOUNT HOUSES

It was noted above that one of the main reasons for the encouragement by the Bank of England of the discount houses in their bond dealing, derived from the need to provide a wider and more effective gilt-edged market to cope with the growth of the government's funded debt. In summary of what was said in Chapter 4, concerning the bond-market role acquired by discount houses during the Second World War and the post-war period of reconstruction, the service the houses provided was that of extending the facilities afforded by Stock Exchange gilt-edged jobbers and in particular of making a market in unpopular short-term bonds. In increasing the liquidity of these bonds the houses helped to reduce the cost of borrowing on them. In acting as they did the houses made official refinancing operations smoother and more efficient and so obviated the necessity for the Bank itself to operate more actively.

An assessment of the part played by discount houses in the short-dated bond market during the 1950s can be made on the basis of evidence given to the Radcliffe Committee by representatives from both the Bank and the discount houses. It is likely that what was said held also for the 1960s, for no contradictory evidence was presented to the Select Committee on Nationalised Industries in 1969.[16] In fact, it becomes clear that the principles originally established during the war held also for the following quarter-century.

In the Radcliffe evidence the Bank confirmed that by dealing actively in short-term bonds the discount houses conferred upon them a higher degree of liquidity and therefore made them more attractive to investors (Qs 531, 535). By demonstrating to would-be investors that a purchase of bonds would not prove to be a 'lock-up' of funds, the houses assisted the Bank in the achievement of its long-term goal of funding the floating debt. The Bank considered (Qs 536–7) that a jobbing function was part of the houses' operations, and while they accepted no formal obligation in this regard, the more important members of the market were always ready to deal. The element of 'passivity' that entered into the jobbers' role, for example of standing ready to buy when the public wanted to sell, was present in the discount houses' operations but made a contribution of only marginal importance to the degree of liquidity that the houses conferred on the bonds (Qs 538–9). The Bank observed that the houses' function of making bonds more liquid by their dealing could be viewed as another facet of their bond-gathering function. Large industrial and commercial companies with resources to invest in liquid form had to some degree been tempted into short bonds as an alternative to Treasury bills : although yields on bonds were relatively attractive there had still to be the assurance of a high degree of liquidity.[17]

The views expressed by representatives of the L.D.M.A. with regard to the houses' role in the short-bond market gave support to the view of the Bank. The L.D.M.A. believed (Q. 3450) that they could successfully combine bond dealing for profit with the 'passivity' supposedly inherent in the jobbing function. While the jobber had to make prices, he could make very wide prices and in very limited amounts. Therefore, it could be said (Q. 3451) that the houses performed the service of a jobber but in such a way that the price reflected pretty quickly and pretty fully the feeling of the market as a whole.

Overall, the houses considered that the market in the short-term bonds they dealt in was infinitely superior to the market in any other government securities : a great volume (perhaps £20m) could be dealt in without moving the price by more than a very small fraction. There were of course (Q. 3452) other factors at work, for example the Departments and the oil companies, but broadly speaking it was at any one moment the discount houses that made the prices in short bonds. Whether the houses acting as a jobber could substantially steady prices would depend upon the volume being sold.

A final point, keeping in mind the experience of wartime (see Chapter 4), concerned 'direct dealing' (Q. 3464). One member of the L.D.M.A. said that although houses' dealings were done almost entirely through a stockbroker, there were occasions when discount houses did business direct with a bank. However, the Chairman of the L.D.M.A. said that the broad basis was that they dealt with brokers and that transactions went through a jobber in the Stock Exchange: they could not deal direct. Obviously, direct dealing was seen as very much an extraordinary activity.

MANAGING THE BOND BOOK IN THE 1950S AND 1960S

Having examined a number of factors, both institutional and technical, that were of importance in influencing discount houses' business in short-term bonds, the next and final step is to trace the course of the houses' bond strategy within the context of the whole portfolio.[18] The fluctuations in the size of the houses' total bond book have already been described and it will be shown that the most important cause of planned expansion and contraction of discount houses' bond holdings and of planned changes in the maturity pattern of the bond portfolio was expectations of changes in Bank rate. Two subsidiary influences were: (*a*) variations in the levels of other asset holdings – especially Treasury bills – and (*b*) availability of borrowed funds.

The relevant monetary policy background to activity in the gilt-edged market and to the conduct of discount houses' portfolios during the two decades after 1951 was given in Chapter 5. In fact the period divides fairly neatly into a number of cycles of monetary policy measures indicating attempts alternately at restriction and expansion. The cycles occurred because of the tendency, described in the Radcliffe Report (para. 434), for the authorities to amplify the shock effect of a set of measures via the 'package deal' approach.[19] Furthermore, because the authorities always included Bank rate changes in a 'package' of measures, Bank rate can be used as an indicator of policy.

Consequently, although it is obvious that Bank rate cycles were integrally coincident with the cycles of the general package of measures, it was with the changes in Bank rate that the discount-house bond dealers were mainly concerned. Taking into account the incidence of crises in 1955 and 1957, with their important concomitant changes in Bank rate, observed Bank rate movements over the relevant period produce the following series of sub-periods: November 1951 to December 1954; January 1955 to August 1957; September 1957 to December 1959; January 1960 to January 1964; February 1964 to September 1967. The evidence of each sub-period provides full support for the hypothesis that the key influence on discount houses' bond dealing was houses' expectations as to the future course of Bank rate, and that the requirements of other assets in portfolio and the availability of bond money were factors which also had a part to play. Space does not allow for detailed examination of every sub-period but the main points can be illustrated by reference to the events of two of them, namely January 1955 to August 1957 and September 1957 to December 1959.

Following the reintroduction of an active Bank rate policy in November 1951 discount-house bond dealers conducted their books in a predictable manner : in response to phases of rising and then falling Bank rate the houses, in accordance with their expectations, respectively shortened and reduced their holdings and then expanded them again with the recovery in bond prices. By the end of 1954 the houses' bond multiplier of holdings to published resources stood at a dangerously high eleven-and-a-half times. True, the market had taken steps to strengthen its position by making additions to inner reserves, but nearly all the houses' resources were committed as margin on collateral security. This was the more significant because the sub-period January 1955–August 1957 was characterised by rising interest rates, with Bank rate successively increased from 3 per cent to $3\frac{1}{2}$ per cent in January 1955, to $4\frac{1}{2}$ per cent in February 1955 and to $5\frac{1}{2}$ per cent in February 1956. The last movement of the period was, however, downward – to 5 per cent in February 1957.

The year 1955 became one to remember for discount-house bond dealers. In the early part of the year some short bond prices fell by as much as 10 per cent and the fall continued for six months after the February increase in Bank rate to $4\frac{1}{2}$ per cent. A depreciation of this magnitude would have roughly equalled the whole of the discount houses' capital and published reserves. In fact the houses were able to mitigate some of the effects of the fall in bond values, but they nevertheless suffered a reduction in published resources of 20 per cent (from £35m to £28m). There were four mitigating factors : (1) inner reserves, which had been strengthened in profitable years, initially provided relief; (2) the clearing banks had, from 1951, followed the example of the Bank of England in varying the rates at which they would lend with the type of security offered (see Chapter 7) : they now unified their rates for money at call, effecting a reduction in the cost of 'basic' money and enabling the houses to increase their running profit; (3) furthermore, some lenders were prepared to reduce the margin of security required against call money, so releasing some of the houses' capital; (4) the final point concerns the manœuvrability of bond dealers. The view of the Bank was that the smaller houses, whose holdings were not large in absolute terms, were able to shorten their books sufficiently to prevent serious loss (expectations had in fact caused them to begin this process before the rise in Bank rate), whereas the larger houses could not sell a comparable proportion of their very much larger holdings of bonds on an already falling market without depressing it unduly.[20]

This view was not, however, everywhere accepted and much would seem to depend upon the expertise of individual dealers and the degree of 'thinness' of dealing.[21] In any case, the Bank admitted that 'nevertheless, in the space of a year the market as a whole reduced its bond holdings by over £110m, or by more than a quarter, from the peak level of September 1954'.

The disasters of 1955 were not repeated in 1956 because the rise in interest rates had been largely discounted in advance. To avoid being forced to borrow from the Bank the houses had pushed the Treasury bill rate closer to Bank rate than had previously been normal. As a consequence bill holdings yielded a substantial return over the cost of borrowed money, whereas selling rates were not increased to the same extent – that is selling *prices* remained healthy. Although Treasury bill holdings fell by about £130 million during 1956, turnover was higher.[22] With regard to commercial bills, restrictions on bank advances because of credit restraint caused an increased demand for commercial bill finance and discount houses' holdings almost doubled during the year.

In the light of the bond classification adopted by Gillett Brothers Discount Co. Ltd at an earlier stage (see above, pp. 153–4), it is interesting to note Gilletts' reaction to the damage caused to bond books by rapidly falling prices during this period.[23] Once it was accepted that falls of up to 10 per cent in short-term bond prices were a possibility, a multiplier as high as eight times published resources could no longer be contemplated because a fall of even 5 per cent would wipe out 40 per cent of (already much reduced) resources. For the future the calculation of the proper size of bond holdings would be modified in two ways : (1) views on acceptable maturities would be shortened : two years would be regarded as an average maturity and anything over three as 'long'; (2) the multiplier would be made more flexible so that it could be adjusted in relation to yields currently obtaining in the bond market – on the theory that the higher the ruling yield the less would be the risk of heavy depreciation. In retrospect the scale of yields adopted looks distinctly low : 3 per cent was to be an average rate and 4 per cent was to be 'high'; but it was reasonable enough given the circumstances in which it was formulated. More important was the principle that the bond multiplier had to be reduced as interest rates fell.

In conclusion, this sub-period of rising interest rates and falling bond prices constituted the most disastrous experience that the discount houses had to face in the twenty years after 1951. In view of what was said earlier about the relative riskiness of various classes of bonds, on the evidence of the Bank (which would, of course, scrutinise houses' accounts), those houses whose books included substantial holdings of low-couponed bonds and bonds at the long end of the five-year range suffered most – as would be predicted.[24]

There was also an example of a change in Bank rate (the increase to 5½ per cent in February 1956) being discounted in advance. Expectations caused those market interest rates which were normally affected by a movement in Bank rate to move close to their predicted *ex-post* positions : examples would be the Treasury bill rate and the yield on bonds. The effect of discounting in advance was evident in the lack of disturbance among the relevant rates following a change in Bank rate. It would, incidentally, be possible to 'over-discount' so that, for example, a 1 per cent change in Bank rate instead of a predicted 2 per cent change would produce a movement in yields in the opposite direction to that anticipated.

Finally, there were some interesting developments in regard to the other two major assets – Treasury bills and commercial bills. If high interest rates were a concomitant of a policy of credit restraint then the expectation would be that discount houses' portfolios would register the following changes : (1) in expectation of a rise in ruling market yields on short bonds the discount houses would shorten the maturity pattern of, and reduce the size of, bond holdings; (2) houses would attempt to raise the Treasury bill rate as close as possible to Bank rate : the net effect on the houses' allocation of bills at the tender would depend upon the view taken by outside tenderers; (3) in the absence of rigid quantitative controls by the Bank the demand for alternative forms of credit in the face of restraint on bank lending would result in an increased flow of commercial-bill business to the discount houses which would provide a substitute for falling holdings of short bonds and possibly Treasury bills.

The next sub-period ran from September 1957 to December 1959. The occasion of a rise in Bank rate by 2 per cent, to 7 per cent in September 1957, provided a classic example of evasive action by discount houses in the face of an expected fall in bond values. Bond dealers seemed to have learnt well the lessons of 1955, for the houses were much better prepared than on earlier occasions.[25] The following action was taken : (1) although by March 1957 bond holdings had been restored almost to the peak reached in 1954, by September they had been reduced again by well over a quarter; (2) furthermore, the market had shortened the average maturity of its holdings and, (3) had switched into bonds bearing higher coupons. For 1957 the year-end figures for bond holdings (£223m) were the lowest since 1951, whereas Treasury bill holdings (£585m) had risen to over twice the level of the seasonal low point earlier in the year.[26]

The extraordinarily high (7 per cent) level of Bank rate was maintained until March 1958, after which it was reduced in a series of small steps to a level of 4 per cent late in November. Taking advantage of the situation in the predicted manner houses rebuilt their books, so that by the end of 1958 holdings, at £321 million, were almost £100 million higher than they were at the end of 1957. The process continued, so that by the middle of 1959 holdings of bonds exceeded holdings of Treasury bills. Significantly at that time, smaller margins on Treasury bill business were making it less profitable. In bidding up at the tender to meet outside competition the L.D.M.A. depressed the Treasury bill rate and were then forced into the Bank to borrow at the penal rate. At the same time the houses were made to pay more for their borrowed funds as the clearing banks moved their rates closer to Bank rate and reduced the proportion of regular money lent to the houses.[27]

In the second half of 1959 a change in expectations caused the process to be reversed. The houses began to substitute Treasury bills for bonds in their portfolios because of rising interest rates abroad which indicated the possibility of a rise in Bank rate. By the end of the year bond holdings had been run down virtually to the level (£322m) of a year earlier. As bond holdings declined so holdings of Treasury bills increased – from about £400 million to £635 million during the last quarter of 1959.

It must be noted that under their new criteria for the bond business (see above) Gilletts fared much better after 1957. Their normal holdings were soon restored to the pre-1955 level and their turnover almost reached £200 million in 1958 and rose far beyond that figure in 1959.[28]

Again, therefore, the houses' portfolio behaviour was as would be predicted in the face of expectations of a rise and a fall in Bank rate, that is the full range of precautionary measures was employed in the time of rising rates (i.e. prior to the 2 per cent jump in Bank rate in September 1957) and then with the decreases in Bank rate during 1958 the houses' tactics became expansionary and bond holdings rose again. The subsequent change in expectations, in 1959, reversed the movement. Noticeable again were the compensatory swings in, especially, Treasury bill holdings as borrowed funds intermittently became available due to the building up and running down of bond books.

The experience was repeated in the remaining sub-periods, January 1960–January 1964 and February 1964–June 1967. The mid-1960s is a convenient juncture at which to leave consideration of the houses' portfolios in terms of their 'traditional' business. After 1965 local

authority bonds began to comprise more than 5 per cent of total portfolio and in 1967 the first entry of certificates of deposit is recorded
(Table 4). In the next chapter the 'new business' of the discount houses,
arising from the development of the 'parallel markets', is examined.

New Business

What could be said to constitute the 'traditional' business of the discount houses would depend to a large extent upon the particular stage of the houses' development at which the enquiry was directed. The bill brokers and later the discount houses first came into being in order to perform the 'equalising function' of the transfer of credit between areas of surplus and deficit funds. At the end of the nineteenth century it was the international 'bill on London' which had come to characterise the business of the discount houses. After the First World War the 'traditional' commercial bill business declined in favour of large-scale dealings in Treasury bills and later in short-term bonds. By the end of the 1950s Treasury bills and short-term bonds had become the staple diet with commercial bills making up only 10 per cent of the whole portfolio. On the eve of the Competition and Credit Control reforms in 1971, although British government Treasury bills were again the biggest single item, such changes had taken place in the composition of the assets portfolio that the Treasury bills, bonds and commercial bills of the 1950s could well be looked back upon as the 'traditional' business.

So far, the analysis has dealt almost exclusively with these major items of the houses' 'traditional' business, and the discussion in Chapter 12, below, of the houses' role in the mechanism of monetary control similarly encompasses only business in Treasury bills, bonds and bills of exchange. During the 1950s, with the exception of the incipient 'temporary money market' in local authority loans (after 1955), the London money market was virtually synonymous with the call-money market centred on the London discount houses. Until 1963, when local authority bonds and stocks were shown separately in the published figures (see Table 4), all items in portfolio other than the major three were combined under 'other assets'. This category, which also included foreign currency bills, short-term non-British government stocks and a small amount of cash in hand and at the banks, never comprised more than 6·7 per cent (the 1957 figure) of the whole portfolio.

By 1971 a much larger variety of assets could, to a greater or lesser degree, be found in a discount house's portfolio, as was reflected in the larger number of categories included in the published figures. In addition to the British government and Northern Ireland Treasury bills and British government (and British government guaranteed) bonds, bank and trade bills of exchange, there would also be British local authority bills and bonds, local authority mortgage notes, promissory notes, dollar and sterling certificates of deposit, preference shares, money lent out, foreign currency bills and interests in subsidiaries and overseas companies and holdings. The developments involved here implied a process of adaptation to changing circumstances and a readiness to seize new opportunities on the part of members of the L.D.M.A. such as had, at several earlier times in their history, saved the houses from emasculation or even extinction.

The changing circumstances and opportunities themselves were connected with important shifts in the structure of the British financial system, in turn brought about by a combination of causes including private-sector initiative in the fact of established practice and rigid convention, changes of regulation introduced by the authorities and strong influences stemming from developments in overseas money markets. The rigid cartelised structure of the British clearing-bank system (including the discount houses as the mechanism of intermediation between the clearing banks) allowed and promoted the development of several so-called 'parallel' markets on which new financial instruments were traded. These new markets developed in conjunction with the 'secondary' banking system, which achieved, over the 1960s, a spectacular rate of growth as compared with that of the deposit banks.

Until the advent of Competition and Credit Control, the traditional and the new markets existed separately, though all the time growing closer together. The effect of the 1971 reforms was to allow the process of integration to advance much more rapidly, so that although a number of separate markets could still properly be distinguished, the old rigid dichotomy between traditional and parallel markets could no longer be sustained. Developments after 1971 are dealt with in Part Three of this book, and for the moment attention is concentrated on matters that properly belong to the late 1950s and the 1960s – namely the nature of the secondary banking system; the emergence of the new markets; the entry of the discount houses into the new business; the inter-connections of traditional and parallel markets; some implications for the control of credit.

THE SECONDARY BANKING SYSTEM

It was a phenomenon of the 1960s that while a small proportion of all banks in Britain (i.e. the deposit banks) continued to constitute the main banking system, a great and assorted collection of non-deposit banks drew together into a secondary banking system within which, despite their diversity, they participated in similar types of banking business.[1] By dint of leaving the provision of a national payments system largely in the hands of the deposit banks, the secondary banks were able to avoid the inhibiting effects of the associated ratios and conventions and to foster instead 'wholesale' banking on a large scale. As wholesale bankers, the secondary banks dealt in fixed-term deposits and loans of large amount and with a high proportion of the business (perhaps 80 per cent) being denominated in foreign currencies and on behalf of foreign clients. Business was transacted on the newly created parallel markets, on which the general level of interest rates was higher than that obtaining on the traditional markets and on which competition was generally fiercer.

Apart from the financial claims in which they dealt and the markets on which they traded, secondary banks differed from deposit banks by way of the principle on which banking was conducted. Just as the principle of prudent deposit banking was *liquidity*, that is keeping a proportion of assets in a form which could readily or fairly readily be turned into cash, so the underlying principle of secondary banking was *matching*, that is comparing assets and liabilities by reference to their maturity and the currency in which they were expressed. This was obviously a necessary strategy in a form of banking in which claims traded were not only for large amounts and at fixed term but also denominated in a variety of currencies; and where no guarantee existed that a matured deposit or loan could be replaced by a similar one. Essential in the matching process were 'inter-bank deposits' – balances with other U.K. banks on the assets side of secondary banks' balance sheets – offset on the liabilities side by comparable amounts of deposits from other U.K. banks. The deposits were lent and borrowed between the banks as a balancing item in the maturity structure of assets and liabilities. Negotiable certificates of deposit subsequently came to perform this function, partially displacing inter-bank deposits. Being marketable, they were found to be more flexible and particularly effective in matching medium-term (i.e. two- to seven-year) loans. The strongly competitive nature of the wholesale markets, with an almost total absence of rate agreements, was a feature of both sterling and non-sterling currencies, the competition in foreign currencies being on a worldwide basis. On the parallel markets in sterling deposits (for example the inter-bank, local authority and finance house markets) interest rates were, therefore, determined much more in accordance with market forces. The floor to the structure was, of course, set by traditional-market rates (described above in Chapter 7) and secondary banks operated to bid funds away from that market by offering more attractive returns and more accommodating maturities. Given the conditions described above, it is likely that secondary banks carried on business on the basis of narrower margins than would be usual in deposit banking, because they would be offering higher rates on deposits but nevertheless having to compete on loans to customers. They were able to do this by avoiding the very high fixed costs incurred by deposit banks on the maintenance of the branch system and in the operation of small individual accounts, and by dealing in the higher-yielding assets traded on the parallel markets.

Designated as secondary banks would be the following: accepting houses; subsidiaries of deposit banks (formed in the mid-1960s to compete in secondary banking); British overseas banks; consortium banks, i.e. groupings of other banks which first appeared in 1964 and expanded rapidly in numbers at the end of the decade; foreign banks, i.e. American and other banks. Of their activities in sterling deposits the Bank of England said in 1969 :[2]

> These banks have played a major rôle in the rapid development of the parallel money markets in London, through which they both extend and take short-term liquid finance. Their sterling funds are largely employed in loans to other banks (the inter-bank market, which these banks were instrumental in creating, provides both a use for and a source of readily available liquid funds. The development of the market has undoubtedly been important in the growth of these banks) and to local authorities, besides advances to private customers; the volume of such loans, particularly those of the local authorities, can be expanded or diminished very rapidly and flexibly by way of switching funds between foreign currency and sterling and there will often be a considerable flow of funds in response to changes in the calculated profit and risk involved in such switches.

It was during the period 1958–60 that the transactions of secondary banks became significant within the banking sector and during the decade after 1961 they were growing much faster than the deposit banks. Because of the nature of credit restrictions in force (e.g. advances control) the secondary banks were able to expand both through their foreign currency business and through loans to local authorities, which were made profitable because of the banks' low overheads.

A comparison of the growth rates of the deposit banks and of the other banks strongly suggests that some sterling funds were switched to the latter as a result of the higher yields offered, for although the absolute increase was very much the same for both groups the percentage increase for the other banks was much faster . . . this trend, which seems to have been in evidence throughout the period 1952–67, but especially since 1960, is probably associated with greater financial sophistication, particularly among company treasurers, and with higher interest rates, which have made depositors more conscious of interest rate differentials.[3]

THE PARALLEL MONEY MARKETS

(a) Euro-currency markets
The parallel money markets, which grew up alongside the secondary banking system and contributed greatly to its development, attained a size greater than that of the discount market within a period of less than twenty years.[4] The joint development of parallel markets and secondary banks can be traced back to 1955, when local authorities were debarred from borrowing at will from the Public Works Loan Board and compelled instead to seek most of their capital requirements from the market. Because of the high level of interest rates at that time local authority treasurers resorted to the device of short-term deposits on a large and growing scale. This move induced secondary banks to bid for deposits at market rates in order to lend them to local authorities as 'temporary money'. The next significant date was 1957, when the use of sterling acceptance credits for financing trade between two third-party non-sterling countries was banned (see Chapter 9). The secondary banks revived a pre-war practice by actively seeking non-sterling deposits so as to be able to finance this trade.

This initiative encouraged a development which had begun about four years earlier whereby dollar balances migrated to Europe and into the hands of secondary banks. Further stimulus arose from the attainment of convertibility of many currencies into dollars in 1958 and, in 1959, from the onset of credit squeeze conditions in the U.S. economy which caused American companies to look overseas for their dollar borrowing. In the 1960s, the development of the Euro-dollar market was encouraged : (a) by the operation of Regulation Q of the Federal Reserve Board whereby American banks were limited in the rates they could offer for deposits, so that dollar depositors tended to seek alternative outlets with 'Euro-banks'; (b) by the fact that short-term interest rates in the United States were generally below rates obtaining abroad; (c) by the inability of American banks to meet the demand for dollar loans, which produced unsatisfied borrowers who were prepared to pay more than the going rate for loans in New York. Estimates of the growth of the Euro-dollar market give its size as : $1 milliard in 1960, $3 milliard in 1961, $10 milliard in 1965, $25 milliard in 1968 and $46 milliard in 1970.[5]

The inter-bank market in Euro-dollar deposits began about 1962 and in later years currencies other than the dollar began to feature on the Euro-currency markets, growing from just over 10 per cent in 1969 to almost 20 per cent in 1971. Furthermore, acceptance credits denominated in U.S. dollars began to appear, and bills drawn on these credits circulated in the market (probably around $250 million at the end of 1971). There also developed in London a market in Euro-dollar 'commercial paper' as a by-product of the great expansion of commercial paper business in New York.[6]

(b) The inter-bank market in sterling deposits
The inter-bank market in sterling deposits, which began about 1964, was mentioned above in connection with 'matching'. The number of participants in the market in 1971 was estimated at 160 banks including clearing bank subsidiaries.[7] As the short-term parallel money markets developed the cash positions of the secondary banks became increasingly liable to disturbance – for example by the receipt of deposits for which there was no conveniently matching loan. In order to achieve a more rapid and flexible means of adjustment than that provided by the fully secured call-money system of the discount houses the inter-bank market was organised for the 'giving' and 'taking' of unsecured sterling deposits – the majority through brokers. In 1971 there were ten active deposit brokers, almost all of whom were members of the Foreign Exchange and Deposit Brokers Association, together with about thirty-five other firms who acted as brokers on a smaller scale. The bulk of the business was transacted by four foreign-exchange brokers. While the amount of direct dealing between banks was probably of significant proportions, it is not likely to have been greater than 25 per cent of the total : the proportion tending to be affected by the size of margins and broker's commission.

The origins of the inter-bank market are obscure, and of various suggested explanations the following seems the most plausible.[8] It is that the market began in an arrangement, at first unofficial, between the foreign exchange dealers of various banks to lend to each other surplus funds, at rates lower than the unrealistically high rates charged by the banks – for book-keeping purposes – on extra funds allocated to their foreign exchange departments for outward arbitrage. The practice later became routine. This would help to explain why the inter-bank sterling market in many cases developed in the banks' foreign exchange departments rather than their money market departments.

The really interesting point about the development of the inter-bank market was that it involved British banks in overcoming their traditional reluctance to borrow from each other. The process was a gradual one, as it had been in the development of inter-bank dealings in Euro-dollar deposits in the late 1950s, which had first established the principle. The inter-bank sterling market grew, in one sense, unnoticed, for it was not until the late 1960s that inter-bank sterling rates enjoyed regular quotation in the financial press. Whatever its beginnings, however, it is most likely that the stimulus for its organisation on a large scale derived from the experience of the Euro-dollar market in London. A widely accepted estimate of the size of the inter-bank market at the end of 1969 was around £2000 million.

For the discount houses, the development of a market that provided non-clearing banks with an alternative to the call-money market, as an employer of surplus funds available for return at very little notice and for a higher rate of interest, necessarily constituted a threat to their business. Nevertheless, the discount houses themselves came to act as principals in the inter-bank market, borrowing funds unsecured in what was christened the 'cloth cap' market.[9] For the house that could provide eligible security for loans, however, the traditional money market remained more attractive: unsecured borrowing and lending in the inter-bank market and the absence of a lender of last resort kept borrowing costs higher. At times rates could be extremely high because institutions which found themselves in the position of *having* to get hold of the money would be prepared to do so even at a very high price. As well as being borrowers in the inter-bank market the discount houses also came to participate to a limited extent as lenders. In 1971 sterling balances with U.K. banks amounted to £27 million (0·9 per cent of total assets).

(c) Negotiable certificates of deposit

Negotiable certificates of deposit (C.D.s) first appeared on the New York market in 1961. Their introduction to the London market was delayed, partly as a result of the operation of the tax laws.[10] C.D.s denominated in dollars were introduced in 1966 by the London branch of an American bank and sterling C.D.s first appeared two years later, in 1968. The return on a C.D. was calculated in a different way from that on Treasury bills and bills of exchange, in that the overwhelming majority of C.D.s bore a rate of interest rather than being issued at a discount. For sterling C.D.s interest was calculated according to English practice, on the basis of a 365-day year, whereas in the case of dollar C.D.s issuers followed American practice, of using a 360-day year.

Banks began to issue C.D.s, as opposed simply to taking term deposits, because of the attractions that C.D.s had for potential depositors. The most important feature was their marketability : a quality conferred by the existence of a well-organised secondary market in C.D.s on which depositors could liquidate their holdings prior to maturity. C.D.s were in this way made similar to bonds. For the issuing bank the marketability of C.D.s meant that they could be issued at rates lower ($\frac{1}{8}$ per cent on average) than for term deposits of the same maturity. It also meant that depositors would be willing to part with liquidity for a longer period.[11] On the other hand, the most serious drawback of C.D.s for both issuers and depositors again stemmed from their similarity to bonds : in expectation of a rise in interest rates C.D.s became difficult to issue and often unsaleable in the secondary market.

The provision of an active and efficient secondary market in both dollar and sterling C.D.s was largely the work of the discount houses, who were the main dealers. During the course of 1971 houses' holdings varied between 80 per cent and 88 per cent of all dollar C.D.s held by dealers and between 89 per cent and 93 per cent of all sterling C.D.s.[12] Other dealers in the sterling C.D. market comprised three accepting houses and in the dollar C.D. market five London branches of U.S. and Canadian securities houses.

For the discount houses, as the main dealers in the secondary markets, C.D. business possessed disadvantages. The status of C.D.s in portfolio was from the start influenced by the fact that they were not recognised at the Bank of England as eligible security against last-resort loans. This, in turn, made C.D.s less popular with the clearing banks as collateral against call money : at least up to the time of Competition and Credit Control their use incurred a higher rate of interest on the call money and thereafter the proportion acceptable in any parcel of security was restricted. The balance of funds needed to finance the sterling C.D. book would be borrowed on the inter-bank sterling market. The dollar C.D. book would, of course, be financed entirely by borrowing on the Euro-dollar market.[13]

Because discount houses operated as dealers in making a secondary market in C.D.s, the tactics they employed in managing the size of their holdings was analogous to that discussed earlier in regard to their bond book. In times of falling rates the houses would attempt to hold a larger book, while in times of rising rates they would endeavour to have a much reduced book. In this way the houses would, as with bonds, stand to earn dealing profits as well as running profit.[14]

Unlike the situation in bonds, however, in time of rising rates when the marketability of C.D.s would be severely limited discount houses would expect that issuing banks would step in to give financial support. In the case of dollar C.D.s formal channels existed for giving help. In line with practice in New York, discount houses would be able to draw on dollar accounts with American and other banks in London. Support for secondary market dealers in sterling C.D.s was less ready and where discretionary help was given by a bank it would take the form of either loans to the houses or the purchase of other banks' issues from their portfolio. The practice developed among discount houses of extending the limits for holdings of C.D.s issued by those banks which had given help.

While the overall growth of the C.D. markets was not rapid, the development of the sterling C.D. market was particularly slow, being checked in its early stages by a period of rising interest rates. Nevertheless, the discount houses' holdings of sterling C.D.s were consistently higher than those of the dollar certificates (see Table 4). First shown separately in 1968, sterling C.D.s were £56m (3·4 per cent of total portfolio) against the corresponding figure for dollar C.D.s of £39m (2·3 per cent); by 1971 the figures were respectively £457m (14·9 per cent) as against £108m (3·5 per cent).

The local authority loans market

The decision by the Chancellor in 1955 to restrict access to the Public Works Loan Board (P.W.L.B.) to local authorities not able to satisfy their capital requirements through the market or other channels, was cited above as the key event which initiated the development of the local authority 'temporary money' market, the parallel market system and the secondary banking system. The time has now come for a closer look at the local authority loans market.

Apart from the Chancellor's decision and the fact that interest rate conditions were favourable to the use of temporary borrowing, restrictions were in force on the issue of stock by local authorities. Consequently, local authorities began to take short-term funds, the majority of which were in the form of deposits. The amount grew rapidly after 1956 and in March 1969 totalled over £2000 million, of which almost three-quarters was repayable within seven days. Deposits were, in fact, taken on a variety of terms – for example overnight or at call; subject to two days' notice or to seven days' notice by either side; for fixed maturities up to 364 days.[15]

The minimum amount taken on deposit was usually £50,000,

though smaller sums were negotiated. Sums of £500,000 and £10 million were normal dealing but sums as high as £25 million were occasionally deposited. Average daily turnover was high and on some days could reach tens of millions of pounds. The deposits were taken against the issue of Deposit Receipts which, because they were not transferable, provided no scope for the establishment of a secondary market.[16]

The market was organised by a number of firms acting as brokers, the majority of business being undertaken by specialists. Contact between brokers, potential lenders and potential borrowers was maintained by telephone. Apart from the secondary banks, lenders included industrial and commercial companies and other, miscellaneous, lenders such as charitable trusts; a significant proportion of the money came from abroad.

The market in which the local authorities operated was very competitive and, to the extent that money coming from abroad was taken, one that was liable to lose funds without warning – especially during times of sterling weakness.[17] In contrast, however, with the situation in the inter-bank market, there was a sort of lender of last resort to guarantee the liquidity of borrowers. The clearing banks would grant overdraft facilities, though this meant that they might have to increase their lending under conditions which were difficult for the banks – and of course for the discount houses. Local authorities in financial difficulties could also turn to the P.W.L.B. Access to the P.W.L.B. was made easier in 1964 and 1967 with the result that the rate of expansion of the market was reduced.

Apart from deposits, local authorities also raised finance through the issue of bills, bonds and stocks. Discount houses carried on business in these securities, to the extent of initiating the introduction of new types of security, encouraging the expansion of established types, and making a greater or lesser proportion of the market in all.

Local authorities obtained their powers to issue bills by means of a special local Act. None was passed for thirty years after 1935, although some authorities were issuing bills during this time under powers previously obtained. Powers of issue were granted to an increasing number of authorities after Manchester Corporation was authorised to increase the maximum amount of its bills in issue, in 1965. The maturity of local authority bills would be expected to be between three and six months after the date of issue. They were negotiable and were usually a bearer security, which discount houses and others would take up on a discount basis. The bills were tendered for on a Friday afternoon, in the first instance by means of the telephone. For the discount houses the increased availability of these bills provided welcome new business, for they were generally eligible for rediscount at the Bank of England and consequently were readily acceptable to the clearing banks as collateral against call money.

In February 1964, as noted earlier, the discount houses played the leading part in introducing local authority negotiable one-year bonds.[18] The first issue amounted to only £500,000 but the houses' holding of these bonds probably approached £50 million in March 1965 and by 1968 the figure was probably nearer £100 million. They were not eligible as security against loans from the Bank so that their usefulness as collateral against call money from the banks was limited. Usually discount houses would obtain yearling bonds through the medium of a broker or in some cases direct from a local authority. Regulations made in 1964 allowed local authorities in England and Wales to issue up to £1·5 million of the bonds so long as they agreed the timing of the issue and its terms with the Bank of England. For the larger local authorities, bigger issues were possible up to a ceiling of £10 million for an authority with an outstanding loan debt of more than £300 million. The quality of immediate negotiability which distinguished yearlings from normal local authority bonds stemmed from the requirement that the office of the registrar for the bonds had to be in the City of London. In general, while they provided a worthwhile yield for investors they were cheaper for local authorities than term loans. From Table 4 it can be seen that local authority securities, including yearlings, were recorded as only £17m (1·3 per cent of the whole portfolio) in 1963, but had grown to £67m (4·6 per cent) in 1965, to £148m (8·9 per cent) in 1968 and £478m (15·6 per cent) in 1971.

THE PARTICIPATION OF THE DISCOUNT HOUSES

The treatment so far has indicated that the parallel markets, as they grew up, differed in their mode of operation almost totally from that of the classical discount market. In the discount market of the 1950s and 1960s personal visits would be made to a high proportion of the banks in London and the money borrowed would be fully secured. Close and continuous supervision of market conditions was maintained by the Bank, which, of course, stood ever ready to act as lender of last resort. In the parallel markets, on the other hand, dealing was done solely through the medium of the telephone and all loans made were unsecured. The authorities made no attempt to manage the market directly and there was no lender of last resort. Nevertheless, although slowly, the distinctions between the markets became increasingly blurred as business came to be done across lines of demarcation : the process was completed by Competition and Credit Control.

It can be argued that there were pressures at work in the 1960s, in regard to discount houses' traditional business, which caused the houses to move towards a broadening of their base of operations. The secular decline in the availability of Treasury bills after 1959, the direct controls placed on commercial-bill business in 1965 and the increased caution on the bond book occasioned by the losses incurred in 1955, 1957 and 1964 are all obvious candidates. More positively, and with varying degrees of alacrity, houses were always ready to exploit new opportunities for profitable business. Certainly, as the houses launched successively into business in local authority bills and bonds and in certificates of deposit and became borrowers and lenders in the interbank markets, they not only broadened and transformed their own portfolios but also made the rigid distinctions between traditional and other markets increasingly irrelevant. So much so, that in addressing himself to the problem of nomenclature thus posed, a commentator in 1969 produced the following useful summation :

> These markets have been variously designated as new, secondary and parallel, but . . . the markets are no longer 'new'. In size they are certainly not secondary and this word is now used – more appropriately – for markets, such as those in certificates of deposit, which deal in paper which has been issued elsewhere. Since so many points of contact with the traditional market are developing, 'parallel' also is becoming a misnomer. But in conjunction with the traditional market they in effect constitute virtually the whole range of outlets for short-term funds, and we propose to call them collectively the 'complementary' markets.[19]

Table 11 is of considerable interest as it summarises houses' activities, at the end of the period, in the various traditional and complementary markets either as direct dealers or as brokers. Until April 1971 discount houses that had affiliations with foreign-currency deposit brokers were debarred from dealing as principals in the markets in dollar C.D.s and foreign-currency acceptances. Thus it was that only a limited number of houses participated directly in the provision, after 1968, of a market in foreign-currency bills of exchange, with portfolios financed by borrowing in the Euro-currency market. Houses with broking interests dealt indirectly through subsidiaries, that is firms of brokers which acted as intermediaries in the relevant markets. The rule did not apply to dealings in sterling C.D.s and all houses acted directly as principals.

Of the eleven houses that comprised the L.D.M.A. in 1970, five took part in broking activities through subsidiaries (see Chapter 15, below). The view has been canvassed[20] that the houses that carried on broking business (in addition to their more traditional dealing) represented the more enterprising and innovative elements among the houses, believing in the utter necessity, in a time of increasingly complex markets, of using a mode of operation that could support large staffs of specialists. On the other hand, houses that held back from broking business could be seen as representing the more conventionally-minded elements, seeing it as being in the nature of a discount house to operate only as a dealer and to enjoy the goodwill that flowed from buying and selling only on behalf of its own account. Given the rapidity of change in the London markets the former group would seem to have possessed a more realistic appreciation of affairs.

THE STRUCTURE OF INTEREST RATES

The question of the differences in interest rate structure that discount houses encountered as they entered the complementary markets has so far only been touched upon. Up to the mid-1960s the base for the rates structure in the non-traditional markets was set by movements in Bank rate or the Treasury bill rate. Thereafter, the old channels of official influence waned in importance and the key rate for sterling markets in London became the inter-bank rate for sterling deposits. Consequently it was in relation to this rate rather than Bank rate that the loan rates of secondary banks and finance houses came to be adjusted.[21]

The market which came to be so important for the determination of interest rate conditions in London was itself marked by great instability, due to the conditions upon which participants traded upon it. Lacking the cartel arrangements and automatic last-resort help at Bank rate of the discount market, and the stand-by accounts with clearing banks of the local authority and finance house markets, the market rate for inter-bank sterling funds was free to fluctuate widely under the full impact of the forces of supply and demand. Particularly in the earlier days of the inter-bank market, when borrowing and lending unsecured was regarded as a less than respectable mode of business, there existed a significant differential between the rate for fully secured 'night' money in the discount market and the rate for unsecured overnight loans on the inter-bank market. The differential became smaller as unsecured borrowing became more familiar and more acceptable, and it virtually disappeared in 1971 with the abolition of rate agreements in the call-money market.

Wholely within the complementary markets, there would be interest rate differentials both between markets and within each individual market according to maturity. On the sterling side, the slope of the yield curve would normally be gently upward from the short to the longer maturities, with the differential between overnight and one-year deposits of about $\frac{1}{2}$ per cent.[22] However, with expectations of falling rates the yield curve would reverse its slope downward towards the longer maturities. Differentials between markets were influenced by technical factors, for example local authority borrowing was affected seasonally with the progress of the financial year, and the finance houses' demand for funds was largely a function of available opportunities for lending. For any given maturity, the normal spread of rates over markets would be $1-1\frac{1}{2}$ per cent, from sterling C.D.s at the bottom end, through deposits from non-bank customers, inter-bank deposits and local authority deposits, to finance house deposits at the top end.[23]

Activities in the Euro-currencies market – namely taking deposits from outside the market, inter-bank deposits, dollar C.D.s, Euro-acceptances and Euro-commercial paper – were international in scope, although a high proportion of the business was transacted in London. Consequently, because the market was used for arbitrage and speculation in foreign currencies, changes in market conditions could quickly be transmitted between currencies and from international markets to domestic markets. The Euro-dollar market – the largest of the Euro-currency markets – was particularly potent in this regard; for example the huge speculative inflows of funds in 1970–1 brought forth action by the Bank in September 1971 in the form of restrictions on flows of overseas funds to the United Kingdom and a reduction in Bank rate.

It has become clear from the previous discussion (see Chapters 5 and 10) that a major and continuing preoccupation of the authorities during the period was with the regulation of short-term interest rates. Prior to the full development of the complementary markets, while Bank rate and the Treasury bill rate still set the rate structure in London, regulation could be a close and continuous process; after the mid-1960s the authorities' powers of control through the accustomed channels were severely reduced and the question arose of the means whereby regulation of the new rate structures might be established.

In choosing their strategy the authorities were guided by the following considerations. The continued development of London as an international financial centre was seen as depending upon the maintenance of market conditions as free as possible from official restrictions, the strength of the complementary markets being seen, rather, as a function of the growing commitment to them of banks of international standing which enjoyed the support of the monetary authorities of their home countries. On the sterling side, non-intervention was considered desirable because it was believed that the operation of the complementary markets had had a beneficial effect on conditions in London by maintaining interest rates at a level lower than would otherwise have been the case. This was a consequence of the widening of portfolio choice for foreigners wishing to invest funds in London at short term to assets other than Treasury bills. It meant that crucial significance no longer attached to the level of the Treasury bill rate, thus giving the authorities greater freedom to set Bank rate at a (lower) level more in line with the needs of the domestic economy.

On these grounds it was decided that influence over conditions on the complementary markets should be indirect rather than direct, that is by establishing links with them through an extension of the activities of the discount houses, as institutions at the centre of the traditional channels of control. It was for this reason that the houses were encouraged to participate in the new areas of business. On a purely technical level, secondary banking involved trade in the deposits of clearing banks, so that the simplest way for the Bank to control trading conditions on the sterling complementary markets was to strike at the source of the deposits in the activities of the clearing banks.[24] Once the discount houses were actively participating in the sterling markets the effects of official action could quickly be diffused through the normal operation of the discount market : (1) to the clearing banks in the classical manner; (2) to the secondary banks which both borrowed and lent on the complementary markets and bought and sold bills in the discount market; (3) through the trading behaviour of the discount houses, which, faced with officially induced changes in monetary conditions in the discount market, would tend to adjust their activities in the complementary markets accordingly.[25]

It was to be an effect of the implementation of Competition and Credit Control to introduce a system of regulation which should be common to all designated banks and other institutions operating in the sterling and non-sterling markets in London.

The Mechanism of
Monetary Control

Ever since the London bill dealers were granted discount accounts at
the Bank of England, in the aftermath of the crisis of 1825, the discount houses have occupied a peculiar and key position in the mechanism through which the Bank might seek to control the private-sector
banking system.[1] In the present chapter this role of the discount houses
is examined in the context of the controversy, which was 'important
for the development of British monetary economics'[2] for a period of
a decade and a half from the mid-1950s, over the question of central
bank control of the level of bank deposits.[3] It has already been shown
(see Chapter 7, above) that the reserve ratios originally adopted volun-
tarily by bankers, as a matter of professional prudence, were later imposed by the monetary authorities as possible means of regulating
bankers' operations in order that they might help to implement, or at
least that they might not frustrate, official policy.

It is not intended to provide a comprehensive survey of the debate
or to examine its wider implications but rather to draw out some main
principles and, in the light of available evidence, to explore the part
played by the discount houses. For reasons which will become clear
later in the chapter it will be useful to begin by examining the relationship between the volume of bank deposits and the amount of bank
cash.

PRINCIPLES OF BANK DEPOSIT CONTROL

In principle, if the banks and the non-bank public hold a constant
proportion of total deposits in the form of cash and the supply of cash
is fixed by the authorities then the volume of bank deposits is determined as some stable multiple of the quantity of cash supplied. The
relationship for a single bank can be expressed as :[4]

$$D = \frac{1}{B} C_b$$

where B is the bank's cash ratio, D is deposits and C_b is the bank's cash. On receipt of an additional cash deposit the banker can increase his loans and thereby his deposits by an amount equal to the increase in cash multiplied by the reciprocal of the cash ratio, giving :

$$\Delta D = \frac{1}{B} \Delta C_b$$

where Δ represents increments in cash and deposits.

The relationship applies equally to the multi-bank system taken as a whole, except that the same multiple increase in deposits comes about as the outcome of a number of steps. In each step the banker, in correspondence with his famous argument that he does not 'create' deposits but only lends monies deposited with him, lends in fact only $1 - \beta$ times any additional cash that he obtains, in order to keep a constant ratio between cash and deposits. The explanation is, of course, that taking all banks together, loans lost at the bank-clearing will be transferred to another bank, in which they will again provide the basis for expansion. At each stage of expansion total deposits increase by a gradually diminishing amount until the limiting value is reached. The process continues until the steadily diminishing amounts of cash held back at each stage sum to the initial increase in cash. Consequently, deposit expansion can be written as :

$$\Delta D = \Delta C_b + (1 - \beta) \, \Delta C_b + (1 - \beta)^2 \, \Delta C_b \ldots + (1 - \beta)^n \Delta C_b$$

which approaches the limit $\dfrac{\Delta C_b}{\beta}$

The principle is, therefore, that if the banks and the non-bank public keep a stable relationship between some asset and total deposits and the authorities have control over that asset then they can bring about a multiple change in the level of bank deposits. Operating on a fixed cash ratio of 8 per cent, a given reduction in banks' cash will bring about a reduction in the total of bank deposits of $\Delta D = 100/8 \Delta C_b$. For a minimum liquidity ratio of 30 per cent the change in total deposits would be equal to $\Delta D = 100/30 \Delta L_b$, where ΔL_b indicates the reduction in specified liquid asset holdings.

The theoretical principles involved here are simple enough to grasp. However, the interesting questions – those which will throw light on the behaviour and role of the discount houses – involve the nature of the transmission mechanism linking contrived changes in cash or liquid asset reserves and the resulting changes in total bank deposits. The authorities apparently made no use of cash-base control of the banks and probably put pressure on liquidity ratios only as a means of influencing the growth of bank advances rather than the level of deposits. Nevertheless, in the theoretical controversy at least, the question of cash-base control must be viewed as the 'standard case'. The debate developed in the following way.

In 1951 the prevailing view was that which had been summarised by the Macmillan Committee in their report of 1931, namely the theory, which came to be known as the 'Old Orthodoxy', whereby the authorities reduced banks' cash through open market operations and achieved a multiple contraction in the level of bank deposits :

> . . . in making an adequately high bill rate effective in the market, the Bank of England varies the amount of its assets, and hence of its deposits, to the necessary extent, which, in turn, has the effect of changing on a much larger scale the quantity of credit made available by the joint-stock banks, since, when the banks' deposits at the Bank of England are increased by a given amount, these banks feel themselves free to increase their own assets by nine or ten times this amount.[5]

In the mid-1950s this position was challenged by an alternative school of thought whose view (the 'New Orthodoxy') claimed that because of changes in the markets for short-term debt and also because of certain market goals pursued by the authorities, namely stability of short-term interest rates, the control mechanism could no longer operate by means of pressure on the cash base. It was argued that the liquidity ratio should be given effect through restriction of the supply of liquid assets. Reaction against the 'New Orthodox' position came in the early to mid-1960s in the form of the 'Neo (Old) Orthodoxy', so named because of the similarity of its view to that of the Macmillan Committee. Again control was to be achieved through pressure exerted on the cash ratio coupled with abandonment of the authorities' stability goal on short-term interest rates.

This last is now the prevailing orthodoxy among an influential section of academic opinion.[6] The view has been summarised as follows :

> If the Central Bank wants to control interest rates, then the money supply will be perfectly elastic at the chosen rates. If the Central Bank wants to control the money supply :
>
> (a) it must abandon interest rate stabilisation; and
> (b) it has a variety of techniques for control at hand.
>
> It could operate on cash, Treasury bills, or any other nominal quantity it chooses. The precision of the control and the size of the multi-

G

plier linking the money stock to the magnitude controlled will depend on the predictability and interest elasticity of the demand functions for those assets. In the present state of knowledge, control of the cash base would give the surest control.[7]

Assuming that the Bank has decided to cause the banks to reduce the level of their deposits by means of a restriction of the supply of cash, the main steps of the process in theory proceed as follows :

(1) The Bank makes open-market sales of securities *to the non-bank public.*[8]
(2) Bank deposits and bank cash both fall by the same amount and the cash base falls belows its fixed 8 per cent level.
(3) To restore the ratio to the new lower level of deposits the banks withdraw call money from the discount houses.
(4) Faced with an overall shortage the discount houses replace the lost call money (i.e. their borrowed funds) by borrowing from the Bank on the security of eligible paper.

Given this situation a number of logical possibilities can follow, the actual course of the process being determined at two key points. The first concerns the terms on which the Bank chooses to lend to the discount houses.[9] To lend at current market rates would merely be to replace funds lost to the banks with new funds at the same rates. In terms of the relationship between the current yield on their assets and the cost of the funds with which the portfolio is financed the discount houses would be faced with no immediate need for action. If on the other hand the houses were forced to borrow at a rate that was penal, in the sense that it was higher than market rate and so involved them in running losses on their bill portfolios, they would thereby be placed in a disequilibrium position.[10] Upon the houses' reactions to this situation would depend whether or not a multiplier contraction of bank deposits would result.

In order to escape the effects of penal-rate borrowing the houses could be presumed either : (1) to replace funds borrowed from the Bank (repay the loan) with funds borrowed from sources other than the Bank of England or the clearing banks; or (2) to attempt to reduce their bill holdings.[11] In either case the banks' cash base would again be reduced below 8 per cent : in the first case because the discount market would be repaying the loan with what would in fact be clearing-bank deposits; in the second case, by failing to replace maturing bills and repaying the loan with the proceeds the discount houses would again be drawing on clearing-bank deposits. To restore their cash the banks would make further withdrawals of call money and the process would, in principle, continue until bank deposits had fallen by an amount equal to twelve-and-a-half (100/8) times the initial cash reduction.[12]

It is logically possible for a decline in the bill holdings of the banking system (clearing banks and discount houses) to come about in the following ways : (a) due to a reduction in the total volume of bills outstanding (a supply solution); (b) by way of a net sale of bills to non-bank holders, either : (i) at the initiative of the banking system in offering lower prices for bills and selling them at lower prices, or (ii) at the initiative of the non-bank public whose demand for bills would rise consequent upon the higher yield obtainable following official action, in selling bills on the open market and/or raising Bank rate.

VERSIONS OF THE TRANSMISSION MECHANISM

Taking the three schools of thought introduced above in turn, the transmission mechanism was in practice seen to operate in the following ways. The Old Orthodoxy of the Macmillan Committee saw a multiple contraction of bank deposits as coming about due to a reduction of bill holdings via a reduction in the total of bills outstanding. In a situation in which the bill of exchange was an important means of short-term finance and an important constituent of discount houses' and banks' portfolios, a rise in short-term rates of interest brought about by restrictive monetary policy would cause traders to discount their bills elsewhere which, in turn, would cause the supply of bills in London to decline. Discount houses would, therefore, have a reduced commitment to take up bills, and the excess of bills sold over bills purchased would provide the houses with the necessary funds to replace borrowing from the Bank which would, in turn, further reduce banks' cash.

There were empirical objections to this scheme, for example that the critical rise in interest rates would not only divert bills from London but would possibly also operate to increase the money supply because of the working of the gold-standard system. Even more pertinent was the observation of Lord Bradbury in his 'Memorandum of Dissent' from the view of the Macmillan Committee, that, with the enormous increase in the supply of Treasury bills, the nature of the bill market had radically changed (compared with 1914).

When the holdings of the market were mainly commercial bills drawn on London on foreign account, a rise in bank rate diminished the supply of these bills. Now that the market holdings are largely Treasury bills and other Government 'floaters', a restriction in the volume of bankers' cash, followed by a reduction of their market money, merely drives the 'market' 'into the Bank', i.e. forces the Bank of England to recreate the credit it has previously withdrawn . . .[13]

It was on this very basis – that the British government Treasury bill had become the dominant constituent of the banking system's bill portfolios – that members of the New Orthodox school of the mid-1950s maintained that there was no longer the possibility that the mechanism could work according to Old Orthodox principles. Because increased rates of interest could not be expected to bring down the amount of government borrowing, a multiple contraction of bank deposits could no longer be brought about via a reduction in the total of bills outstanding.[14]

In evidence to the Radcliffe Committee the Bank of England claimed that because the Bank acted as lender of last resort to the banking system, control via the cash base could not be exercised and that consequently leverage should be exerted on the banks through pressure on the liquidity ratio.[15] The Committee in their conclusions agreed that the liquidity ratio was indeed the correct basis for control – *not*, however, because of the Bank's last-resort function but rather because of the authorities' desire for stability of the Treasury bill rate.[16] This meant that even if a cash reduction was brought about, the banks could always obtain cash by selling their holdings of surplus liquid assets (Treasury bills) to the Bank. The solution clearly lay in control of the total of the banks' liquid assets. Given the dominant position of the Treasury bill in banking system portfolios this meant in practice selling more government debt to the non-bank public, and because it was not considered desirable for the public to become holders of large amounts of short-term liquid assets the technique really implied a policy of funding.[17]

The New Orthodox control technique implied a transmission mechanism which involved a two-part functional relationship between the size of the Floating Debt and the size of the clearing banks' liquid asset holdings. A reduction, for example, in the size of the Floating Debt would bring about a proportionate reduction in the Treasury bill holdings of the banking system and that reduction in Treasury bill holdings would bring about a similar reduction in the banks' total liquid assets. Now if the Floating Debt is taken as being equal to the outstanding volume of market Treasury bills minus 'overseas official' holdings it can be shown that there was a close relationship between changes in the total of bills outstanding and the holdings of the banking system for the years 1951–66. This was not, however, the case with the relationship between the banking system's Treasury bill holdings and liquid asset totals : the series moved closely together between 1951 and 1958 but thereafter there was increasing divergence.[18] The explanation lies in the increased availability of the other categories of liquid assets, namely bills of exchange, following the resurgence of commercial bill finance, plus call money – lent both to the discount houses and to others outside. Thus was New Orthodoxy, as a *logically* valid technique of control, overtaken by changing real-world conditions. The clearing banks came to be able to expand their holdings of liquid assets independently of the supply of Treasury bills.

These criticisms of the New Orthodoxy came from a school of thought whose own view lay close enough to that of the Macmillan Committee for it to be dubbed Neo (Old) Orthodoxy. The cash base was again to be the fulcrum for leverage and the possibility of a multiple contraction of bank deposits hinged on the behaviour of the discount houses following their being forced into the Bank and made to borrow at penal rates. To escape penal borrowing and so set the contractionary process in motion the discount houses would have either to take up fewer bills or sell more bills to non-bank holders, or refinance their portfolios from (cheaper) outside sources.

If attention is concentrated on the first possibility – that the multiple contraction of deposits would be brought about by the discount houses being able to reduce their bill holdings – the second of the two suggested 'key points' in the sequence is reached. The theoretical mechanism contains an assumption concerning the non-bank demand for Treasury bills, namely that it can be represented by a stable curve which shows larger amounts being demanded at lower prices, that is higher discount rates. In the context of the situation at the weekly tender the discount houses could, by lowering their collective bid price (raising the rate) ensure that more bills would be taken up outside the syndicate. In this way, the cash reduction brought about by the Bank's open market operation would result in the banking system reducing holdings of liquid assets as the next stage in the process of multiple reduction of bank assets and liabilities.

ALTERNATIVE MODELS OF THE TREASURY BILL TENDER

The next task, following on the analysis of the Treasury bill market in Chapter 8, is to examine in detail possible events at the weekly Treasury bill tender in an attempt to ascertain whether the houses had the power to reduce their Treasury bill holdings at will. The main groups of institutions that tendered for Treasury bills have already been enumerated and divided between the 'syndicate' on the one hand and the 'outside tender' on the other. Leaving aside the option whereby individual members of the syndicate could dissent to the extent of 15 per cent of their quota, the discount houses tendered at an agreed common price. Consequently, competition for bills was divided between the syndicate bid and other tenderers' bids. It is legitimate to divide the competition in this way because of the fundamental and unique constraint on the L.D.M.A. that they guaranteed to take up if necessary all the bills on offer, at the syndicate price.

Prima facie, it can be argued that the quantity of bills allocated to the L.D.M.A. was a function of : the total of bills on offer; prices bid by outside tenderers; the syndicate bid price; the quantities of bills tendered for by those outside tenderers who bid higher than the discount houses (plus the amounts demanded by those who happened to bid at the same price as the syndicate, but this element will be disregarded). Holding everything else constant, the implications would seem to be that : (*a*) the key determinant was the size and price-effectiveness of the outside tender; (*b*) the L.D.M.A., in the nature of their function of 'covering the tender', took that (residual) amount of bills left over after (outside) tenders at higher prices had been satisfied.

There is support for this view in the statements made in evidence before the Radcliffe Committee :[19]

Q. 3472 (L.D.M.A.) : 'We get a percentage, which varies with the demand from other people; it may vary very considerably.'

Q. 379 (Bank of England) : 'The discount market contrive to offer the lowest price which is accepted and as a result only a portion of their tender is accepted, varying with the amounts tendered for at prices above.'

Q. 387 (Bank of England) : 'I would not say they have a monopoly. They have something much less. The amount of bills they get in the tender each week varies a great deal depending on the size of the outside tender and the relative prices that are offered.'

Q. 388 (Bank of England) : '. . . the important figure is the size of the outside tender, because the percentage that the discount market gets is the percentage of the amount they apply for which is variable.'

Going a stage further, the Bank stated in 1964 :[20]

. . . the proportion varies quite widely from week to week, depending on the total of the bids that have come from other tenderers, and on how accurately they have guessed the price at which the discount houses have tendered. A high proportional allotment at this price may indicate either that the discount houses have outbid all but a few of the other tenderers, or simply that the other tenders are small.

The element of 'guessing' introduced here will be shown to be of central importance for a successful evaluation of the situation at the tender. Also noteworthy is the fact that the syndicate is depicted as competing actively, within the tender-covering constraint, for that amount of bills needed to satisfy portfolio requirements.

Indication of the number of participants and degree of competition involved in the tender can be obtained from the same sources. First the Radcliffe *Minutes* : Sir Oliver Franks (Q. 404) suggested that the element of competition was first of all between the unified tender of the discount houses and the outside tenderers and that it was increased by room for manœuvre between individual houses. That degree of competition, however, took place within a fixed administrative framework laid down by the Bank; it was, in other words, '. . . a little garden of competition with high walls of administrative determination'. The Bank, in reply, thought this to be broadly true except that the degree of competition was perhaps a little greater than would be gathered from that description. Further, the Bank estimated (Q. 379) that : '. . . there might be only one price above, or there might be thirty-five prices above. If you have a movement of Bank rate, nobody knows where he is going to be. There is usually a large difference between various tenders.' Also (Q. 399) : 'Where there is a movement in Bank rate, it is very common for there to be a wide range of prices. I can remember one instance when we had thirty-six different prices.' Further (Q. 400) : [the difference between the highest and lowest price in those circumstances] '. . . could be 2s [10p] per cent. It is quite frequent for the range of prices accepted to vary by 1s [5p] per cent.'

When questioned by the Select Committee on the Nationalised Industries[21] in December 1969 the L.D.M.A. defended the prevailing system, arguing (Q. 1277) that although the tender system was a market in which the competitors were fewer than they would have been without the syndicate in operation, it was justified on the grounds of efficacy in government financing. In any case (Qs 1272, 1273) there was still a healthy degree of competition arising from the strength of the outside tender which fluctuated with changing expectations on interest rates.

Further evidence, given to the Radcliffe Committee at a time when the outside tender was relatively very strong, yields clues as to the extent of information available to competing bidders when fixing their prices. Of influences behind the level of the syndicate's bid the Bank said (Q. 394) :

It depends what the discount market want to do. . . . In some cases they may be influenced by external events, by the movement of the exchanges, and will feel they must pay less for the bills, that is to say, put the rate up. Other weeks they may feel they must have the bills and they bid for them accordingly. That determines whether the outside tenderers get in or not.

On the other hand, as regards information available to the outside tenderers, the Bank said (Q. 395): 'Generally speaking some outside tenderers have a pretty good idea : others do not; in consequence very frequently they make offers substantially but unnecessarily more favourable.' On the state of the discount houses' knowledge of the probable bids of the outside tenderers the Bank said (Q. 396): 'It is not very easy to explain because the outside tenderers are not a readily identifiable body. They may get some impression of what a particular tenderer may do, but it may be very slight and not covering any substantial amount of bills.' As far as the Bank's own tender was concerned the Bank made it clear (Q. 397) that they 'kept it to themselves' when they went into tendering.[22] To the Select Committee in 1969 the Bank said of the demand for Treasury bills from foreign central banks (Q. 507): 'They tender through us to a very substantial extent. Central banks, of course, have to keep their funds liquid, particularly in foreign markets, and Treasury bills are a very important element in their resources.'

The overall impression gained from the evidence is of a very imperfect market moulded by institutional constraints. Because the sale of bills took the form of a sealed-bid auction there was, apart from collusion over price on the part of the L.D.M.A., necessarily a lack of information available to competing bidders as regards the strength of each other's bids. Nevertheless, there was a very real element of competition for bills even though the authorities admitted it to be 'within prescribed limits'.[23] Because of the agreement to cover the tender the L.D.M.A.'s allotment was by definition a residual amount. Of crucial importance for the extent of the residue was the strength of the outside demand – a point repeatedly stressed.

Clearly, any model of the Treasury bill tender which is to provide a real understanding of the factors involved should necessarily contain the following features :

(1) It should distinguish between allocation to the syndicate and to the outside tender.
(2) It should attempt to specify demand functions for Treasury bills for both the syndicate and the outside tender, in a situation in which individual units are bidding to satisfy their own particular needs as they see them at the time.
(3) It should take account of the lack of information available to participants in the tender as regards the likely bids of other com-

petitors, i.e. it should incorporate the element of 'guessing' (uncertainty and expectations), introduced above.

(4) Because of the discount houses' obligation to cover the tender, the model should explain the syndicate's allocation as being a residual amount of the total offer, as a function of the size and strength of outside bids.

Several studies have been made of the pre-1971 Treasury bill tender which attempt to explain the nature of competition at the tender and to show how the syndicate's allocation of bills was determined. Although none of these is completely satisfactory in itself it is possible, in the light of available evidence, to incorporate elements from each of them into a more complete evaluation of the discount houses' ability to effect changes in the size of their Treasury bill holdings. This is done below using three extant models, on the basis of the criteria suggested above.

The first model constituted part of the Neo (Old) Orthodox attack on New Orthodoxy.[24] The purpose of R. L. Crouch's analysis was to refute the New Orthodox assertion that there was a strong positive causal relationship between the supply of Treasury bills and the quantity of bank deposits. He was attacking the empirical validity of the assumptions which underlay New Orthodoxy and specifically the first leg of the implied two-stage linkage – that a change in the size of the Floating Debt would tend to be reflected in a change in the banking system's holdings of Treasury bills. Crouch wished to show that in the face of a cut in the supply of Treasury bills the discount houses and therefore the banks had the power to maintain desired holdings. Note that in the context of the empirical validity of the Neo (Old) Orthodox adjustment process the same principle applies but in the opposite direction, that is that in the face of penal-rate borrowing from the Bank the discount houses would have the power to *reduce* their allotment of bills.

This model satisfies some of the suggested criteria : it distinguishes clearly between the syndicate and outside tenderers and it specifies an outside tenderers' demand function for Treasury bills (see Fig. 3, p. 266). On the other hand the syndicate's demand function is not specified. Furthermore, instead of giving primacy to the size and price-effectiveness of the outside tender the model gives all the initiative to the syndicate, while the outside tenderers are cast as passive buyers with a stable demand curve.[25] The endowment of the syndicate with the knowledge necessary to make precisely the correct bid is justified on the grounds that it merely smooths the adjustment process to the same final equilibrium. The elements of uncertainty and expectations are excluded.

What is crucially absent from this approach is the specification of the syndicate's demand function for Treasury bills. The impression given is that the syndicate would be prepared to bid up to any price to obtain the bills they want. Certainly the outside demand for the bills could be viewed as being a stable function of the price of the bills, but so also could that of the syndicate. If it is to be assumed, for the purposes of the model, that for the outside tenderers tastes and the prices of substitutes and complements remain unchanged, then the same must hold for the discount houses. For all participants in the tender the size and composition of portfolios must be viewed as being determined by the expected pattern of relative rates of return and by the cost of borrowed funds. Treasury bills would then be bid for at a higher price (lower rate of return) only if such a course of action were viewed as being profitable.

A reply and an alternative analysis to that of Crouch appeared in the following year. A. D. Bain[26] first of all demonstrated that the allocation of Treasury bills at the weekly tender did not determine the volume of the bills available as liquid assets to the domestic banks. This was due to the existence of the active secondary (resale) market in Treasury bills, which was described earlier (see above, Chapter 8).[27] Secondly, in place of Crouch's static model, in which the demand for bills was introduced as a stable function of their price, Bain sought to provide a more satisfactory explanation of the real-world situation by means of a dynamic model, in which outside tenderers' bids were mainly determined by what they *expected* the syndicate to bid. In order to examine Crouch's contention that the syndicate could increase their share of the bills allotted by raising their bid, Bain set out to derive a demand curve for Treasury bills and concentrated attention on the outside demand for bills (see Fig. 4, p. 266). A most important empirical finding was that outside tenderers appeared 'on the whole' to pitch their bids slightly above what they anticipated the syndicate bid would be.

Bain's analysis led him to the conclusion that the syndicate *could* increase their allotment in any week by increasing their bid but that in order to be able to maintain a greater share over a given period they would have to raise their syndicate price 'steadily' and 'contrary to expectations' over the length of that period. If their action then produced results contrary to the authorities' wishes in regard to the stability of the Treasury bill rate it would attract corrective action in the form of penal-rate borrowing from the Bank. In other words, due to institutional and policy constraints, the houses were prevented from adjusting their Treasury bill portfolios optimally, so that :

Far from being a cartel which can determine the price or the quantity of the bills it buys, it is a much closer approximation to the truth to regard the syndicate as the residual buyers, who pay a price determined by the authorities and obtain a quantity determined by the total supply of bills and the strength of outside demand.[28]

In terms of its basic approach Bain's model goes much further towards satisfying the criteria : there is a clear distinction between allocation to the syndicate and to the outside tender; attention is concentrated on the demand of the outside tender; the conclusion is that the syndicate took up the residual amount of bills; the chief emphasis of the approach is on the lack of information available to competing bidders, and expectations play a central part. Bain's contribution lies in the provision of an empirically based analysis of the bidding behaviour of outside tenderers in relation to the syndicate bid. Lacking in the model is specification of the demand functions for the participants. This omission leaves the analysis somewhat 'up in the air'.

The next contributor took issue with the conclusion reached by Bain, as representing an extreme statement of what he called the 'conventional' view – that the tender rate on Treasury bills was fixed by the authorities and involved no operation of market forces.[29] B. Griffiths argued that the conventional view derived from the existence of those institutional arrangements (examined in Chapter 3, above) which originated in the 1930s. The view implied that the cost functions of the discount houses affected only their profits and not their bid price. He maintained that the institutional arrangements did not directly fix the Treasury bill rate, for the simple reason that the discount houses had to use their own judgement in arriving at the syndicate price. It followed that normal price theory could be used to explain the determination of the syndicate bid in just the same way as for any other market price that was not explicitly controlled.

In Griffiths' approach, the elements of uncertainty and expectations are dismissed as of little relevance on the grounds that if each participant's bid were assumed to be based on an estimate of the other's bid then the determination of the Treasury bill rate would become a problem in game theory. Wishing to demonstrate that normal price theory could be utilised, Griffiths described the outside tenderer's demand for bills as an increasing function of the interest rate, while the syndicate's behaviour at the tender was cast in terms of factors entering into the familiar marginal conditions, marginal cost = marginal revenue (see Figs. 5, 6, p. 267).[30] This is where the theoretical strength of this approach lies. Its weakness stems from the failure to highlight the lack of information available to competing bidders and in the lack of any attempt to provide an explanation of bidding tactics at the tender.[31]

There are therefore two basically different approaches to be reconciled. While on the one side Griffiths' model can be seen as representing a more complete version of that of Crouch, Bain's approach emphasises the explanation of participants' behaviour under conditions of uncertainty. An attempt at reconciliation is valid because all three models point to the same conclusion, namely, that the syndicate had the power to increase its allocation in any week by increasing its bid. Bain and Griffiths, of course, put constraints upon such behaviour which were, respectively, institutional – in the sense that the Bank would not allow the syndicate persistently to increase its bid and so to readjust the Treasury bill rate contrary to the Bank's wishes – and economic, in so far as the houses would only bid up for bills to the point at which $MC = MR$ on bills. How can Griffiths' theoretical model, with its marginal conditions of standard price theory, be reconciled with the realistic and empirically based analysis of Bain and his finding that on the average outside tenderers pitch their bids at a level just above what they expect the syndicate's bid to be? The explanation might go as follows.

For the discount houses the obligation to 'cover the tender' was a potentially powerful influence on bidding behaviour. It was shown above that when fixing their bid price the L.D.M.A. were mainly concerned with the possible changes in the cost of their borrowed funds during the period for which they would be lending money to the government. In time of a general expectation of a Bank rate increase the syndicate could be expected to make the maximum reduction in their bid price, consistent with not attracting penal-rate borrowing from the Bank, due to the probability of having to take up a large proportion of the bills on offer. With no general expectation of a Bank rate change, the houses would bid for bills taking into account the cost of borrowed funds, the rate of return on alternative assets and the views of the Bank. Fluctuations in outside demand would influence the size of the syndicate's allotment and thereby force possible readjustments in the composition of their total asset portfolio.

For the outside tenderers, Treasury bills were viewed as one alternative form in which temporary surpluses of cash could be held. From the point of view of security and liquidity Treasury bills were always a viable alternative to bank deposit-accounts. The variable that could induce a greater or lesser volume of demand for Treasury bills would be the yield on the bills. For a company treasurer wishing to invest a temporary surplus the greater would be the probability that the surplus would be held in the form of Treasury bills, the higher was the yield on Treasury bills relative to the yield on other assets.

It is important to notice that given the 'yield on other assets' the 'yield on Treasury bills' would really mean the price at which the outside tenderer would make a successful bid at the forthcoming tender.[32] The higher he set his price the more likely he would be to receive allotment in full but the lower would be the yield on the bills taken up. Company and public corporation treasurers would have been encouraged to switch into the bills by observing : (*a*) the general trend of the yield on Treasury bills in the resale market but also (*b*) the results of recent weekly tenders and particularly the lowest price (highest yield) at which tenders had been accepted and the percentage of the offer allotted at that price.

The lowest price accepted would, of course, be the syndicate bid. If the individual outside tenderer's bid fell short of this price he would receive no bills. If, however, he could manage to bid at a price which turned out to be just slightly higher than the syndicate price, he would receive allotment in full and would take up the bills at a relatively very high (compared with the rest of the tender) yield. If the syndicate bid was not expected to change and did not in fact change, the task for the outside tenderer would be quite straightforward. If, however, the syndicate were to lower their bid (i.e. raise the rate) unexpectedly, the individual outside tenderer would still receive allotment in full but would pay an unnecessarily high price. If on the other hand, the syndicate were to increase their bid (i.e. lower the rate) unexpectedly, the outside tenderer would receive few or no bills. Consequently, success for the individual outside tenderer would depend upon correct anticipation of the syndicate's bid at the tender. This is where the element of 'guessing' comes in. In the context of the conditions at the tender, therefore, the theoretical simplicity of standard price theory provides little explanatory aid.

There is support for this view of the nature of the tender in an observation made by the Radcliffe Committee on the subject of restrictive practices in the discount market. There was one practice which they thought to be designed to bolster the existing structure of the discount market rather than to serve the purpose of maintaining the orderly market desired by the authorities.

This is the practice of deliberately manipulating the syndicate bid week by week in order to discourage 'outside' tenders. The operator outside the syndicate is at some disadvantage if he tenders at a price much different from the syndicate bid : either he misses the bills, or he pays much more for them than the principal market operators pay for their bills. During the early months of 1959 (and the phenomenon has been observed on earlier occasions), at a time when official policy required stability, the syndicate appeared to have jumped its bid up and down in an effort to discourage outside operators.[33]

In other words, because of the crucial importance for the outside tender of managing to place their bids just above the price bid by the syndicate, the discount houses would attempt to maintain their holdings ('shaking off' outside demand) by behaving unpredictably ('contrary to expectations'). If the resulting deviation in the Treasury bill rate were to stray outside the tolerances allowed for by the authorities then corrective action would, of course, follow (see appendix).

The important point is that it is not sufficient to regard outside demand for Treasury bills during the relevant period as having been simply a stable function of their price. Empirically it has been found that when the syndicate reduced their bid compared with the previous week, their percentage allotment was more likely to increase rather than decrease and that this was particularly so in times of monetary stringency. For example, between July 1961 and June 1966 the syndicate reduced their bid price compared with the previous week on fifty-six occasions : the percentage of bills allotted at the lowest price accepted fell in twenty-eight weeks, rose in twenty-seven weeks and was unchanged in one week. Because the whole control debate was concerned with periods of restriction, when the analysis was confined to the period October 1964 to June 1966 it was found that of the twenty weeks in which the market reduced its bid, its proportionate allocation fell in six weeks but rose in fourteen weeks. Whatever the limitations of the evidence adduced it presents a *prima facie* case for believing that at least in the period tested there was a '. . . sufficient degree of instability in non-market demand at the tender to make it very difficult for the market to exercise any very close control over its own allotment.'[34]

What of the other avenues through which the Neo (Old) Orthodox mechanism might have operated? Could the houses have escaped penal-rate borrowing by reducing the size of their commercial bill holdings? This route would have involved the houses in reducing the number of bills in the banking system by discounting fewer bills per time period. In view of the discussion in Chapter 9, above, it would again appear that the houses' power was severely limited. Discount rates apart, the most important factor in commercial bill business was goodwill, and houses would have been very wary of going against convention and risking future business by refusing to take bills from accepting houses, banks and traders.

The final route through which the mechanism might have operated involved the discount houses in replacing funds borrowed at penal rates from the Bank with cheaper funds from non-bank sources. The question which arises here is the same as that which would arise in a situation in which houses successfully reduced holdings of Treasury bills which were consequently taken up outside the syndicate – namely, whence would outside tenderers have obtained the necessary funds? In principle they might have run down holdings of money balances or have sold some other interest-bearing asset. Certainly a reduction of money balances would have enabled a multiple reduction of bank deposits to proceed, but empirically this possibility was of little relevance because operators in the Treasury bill market would either not have had sufficient 'idle' or 'active' balances which could be run down, or such a development would have taken too long for the multiplier process to operate.

Could then a rise in the yield on Treasury bills relative to yields on other assets have persuaded holders of other assets to switch to some extent into bills? It is likely that potential Treasury bill holders would have switched from some asset which was a close substitute and which would have had a high cross-elasticity of demand with Treasury bills. During the relevant period this other asset would very likely have been short-term loans to local authorities. Assuming that in the short term, supplies of Treasury bills and local authority debt would have been inelastic with respect to the rate of interest (on the grounds that a given total of the two types of debt must all have been held by someone), a disturbance of the sort envisaged would have initiated a spiral of rate increases which would have continued indefinitely without restoring equilibrium.[35]

Sharply rising short-term interest rates would have tended to deter the authorities from the use of cash-base control of the banking system (*a*) because of the previously mentioned fear of destabilising interest-rate changes moving from the short to the long end of the spectrum and so affecting the gilt-edged market; (*b*) because of the damaging effects they might have had on institutions with 'sticky' interest-rate structures, for example building societies. In fact, in the United States during the credit squeeze of 1968–9 the Federal Reserve was forced to employ direct controls to prevent the banks from highly competitive bidding for small and medium-sized deposits, which experience had shown could seriously embarrass the 'savings and loan associations' (similar to British building societies). In the United Kingdom, spiralling interest rates in 1973 brought political pressure on the government to control the increase in mortgage rates, which they did by means of a subsidy (or 'bridging grant') and later a ceiling on the rates banks could offer for deposits of less than a specified amount (£10,000).[36]

Therefore the same conclusions apply to the alternative routes by which a multiple reduction of bank deposits might have been effected as applied to that of a reduction in discount houses' Treasury bill portfolios. The inference to be drawn is that control techniques which command assent among academic economists because of the soundness of their theoretical structure may be totally impracticable when set in the context of real-world situations.[37] It is significant that at no time since the war have the authorities lost sight of their twin responsibilities of *supporting* financial markets (supporting the liquidity of financial institutions) as well as *controlling* them. At no time have they attempted to influence either the level of bank deposits or the level of bank advances by means of the orthodox technique of squeezing the banking system's cash base.

Appendix: Official Management of the Treasury Bill Rate

Much has been said in the present chapter and in Chapter 8, above, about the arrangements at the Treasury bill tender and the importance of the syndicate in making a market price in the weeks following the tender. Despite the relative decline in the volume of Treasury bills outstanding during the 1960s the authorities continued their policy of maintaining close control over the level of the Treasury bill rate. The question of exactly how the Bank exerted influence on the rate is important not only because the discount houses were centrally involved in the process but also, and more immediately, because the authorities' policy towards the Treasury bill rate acted as an important constraint on the successful operation of the Neo (Old) Orthodox control mechanism. If the houses' bidding behaviour caused the Treasury bill rate to deviate from the level chosen by the authorities then action would be taken to restore the desired situation.[38]

For the authorities, the most direct way of influencing the Treasury bill rate was by means of a change in Bank rate, but because Bank rate movements were invariably too large and too infrequent to maintain fine control, then, given the level of Bank rate, some additional means of influence was necessary. The authorities were of the opinion that this was provided through their day-to-day management of the money position in the market and in particular by the device of forcing the discount houses 'into the Bank' to borrow at Bank rate. In this way, the average cost of the houses' borrowed funds would be raised and consequently the houses would be prompted to raise the rate at which they tendered for Treasury bills.[39]

Referring to data for the period 1960–2 Alford,[40] using least-squares multiple regression techniques to test single equation hypotheses, examined the relationships between: borrowing at Bank rate, the houses' average money rate and the maximum Treasury bill tender rate. The results did not support the orthodox view, that making the discount houses borrow at Bank rate increased their average money rate which in turn caused them to raise the rate at which they tendered for Treasury bills. At least for the period tested the effect on the average money rate of borrowing at Bank rate appears to have been too small to give much credence to this explanation. In addition, it was found that the average money rate was generally worse at explaining the Treasury bill rate than was Bank rate. Attempts to detect any direct influence of borrowing at Bank rate upon the Treasury bill rate were unsuccessful. In general, it was recognised that the market situation under review was a complex one and that expectations appeared to play a very important role.

It was in attempting to explain the processes by which the Bank exercised influence over the Treasury bill tender rate that Griffiths employed his price theory analysis of discount house behaviour at the tender.[41] As with Alford the mechanism for influencing Treasury bill rate involved the authorities in changing either the cash reserves of the clearing banks and/or the level of Bank rate.

In the first case, the enforcement of penal-rate borrowing would not affect the houses' marginal costs, only their profits (so that there was no incentive for them to alter their trading behaviour). Marginal costs could only be increased through two channels : (*a*) as an open-market sale of gilts was taken up by those institutions from which the discount houses borrowed call money, the reduction in supply of call money would increase its marginal cost; (*b*) if by forcing them to borrow at Bank rate the authorities increased the houses' expectations of subsequently being forced into the Bank, their marginal cost function would shift to the left (so that each amount of Treasury bills would be associated with a higher level of interest rates).

Influence could also be exerted via the revenue function. The open-market sales of gilts would reduce their price and raise their yield so that outside holders would substitute gilts for Treasury bills as the yield on gilts rose relative to that on Treasury bills. The outside demand for the bills would decrease and the syndicate's revenue function would be shifted outward. 'Both the effects on the cost and revenue functions facing the syndicate create an excess supply in the bill market, and so produce an increase in the Treasury bill rate.'[42]

In the second case the effect of an increase in the level of Bank rate would *inter alia* automatically increase the rate on bank deposits. As the rate on deposits rose relative to the rate on Treasury bills, deposits would be substituted for bills in portfolios, so that the outside demand for bills would fall and the average revenue function would move to the right. In addition, with a given probability of being forced into the

Bank, an increase in Bank rate would increase the penal rate the houses would have to pay and this would increase their marginal costs. Therefore, the effect of an increase in Bank rate would be to create an excess supply in the Treasury bill market with a consequential increase in the rate.

Part Three

THE MODERN DISCOUNT HOUSES IN OPERATION: II, 1971 AND AFTER

13 Competition and Credit Control

In 1971 the authorities brought about reforms in the British banking system and techniques of monetary control which were of a magnitude and importance unparalleled in all the years since 1945. The substance of the reforms was set out in a series of official documents, statements and speeches and the reforms themselves and the changed conditions they initiated can be referred to collectively as Competition and Credit Control, after the title of the consultative document in which the Bank first published its proposals.[1]

The essence of the reforms was an attempt by the authorities : (1) to introduce a method of control by which monetary influences on the level of economic activity could be regulated without the use of measures which were discriminatory and which distorted the working of market forces; and (2) to introduce into the banking and financial sectors a state of affairs in which competition and the allocation of available funds by market price would prevail.

Taking advantage of economic conditions favourable to the change the Bank published its consultative document in May 1971. The existing restraints on competition between financial institutions were seen to stem from two primary sources :

(1) The methods of control employed by the authorities themselves, namely (a) quantitative limits on certain categories of lending in sterling applied individually to certain banks and finance houses, so that the resulting limitation on competition and innovation had prevented the efficient from growing and helped the less efficient to maintain the level of their business; and (b) the arrangements whereby the London and Scottish clearing banks, but not other banks, agreed with the Bank to observe the familiar cash and liquid-asset ratios against their deposit liabilities.

(2) The London and Scottish clearing bankers' collective agreements

on interest rates whereby rates paid on deposits and the minimum rates set on advances were fixed by those banks in relation to Bank rate.

The document proposed that the existing liquidity and quantitative lending controls imposed upon the banks should be discontinued and that the banks should abandon their interest-rate agreements. Within this more competitive situation monetary control as envisaged would rely more on changes in interest rates, supported by calls for Special Deposits on the basis of a uniform reserve-assets ratio to be enforced across the whole banking system. Similar arrangements would be made for the deposit-taking finance houses and separate provision for the discount houses. Provision was made for safeguards against the possibly damaging effects of increased competition on savings banks and building societies. The authorities would continue to supply to the banks such qualitative guidance as they might deem necessary.

In parallel with these proposals for a system of credit control which would allow greater freedom for competition in the banking system, it was announced that the authorities would subsequently intervene less in the gilt-edged market. Automatic support for the market was withdrawn such that, except in the case of very short-dated stock (one year or less to maturity), the authorities would no longer guarantee to take stock offered to them. They would, however, retain the right to make purchases, exchanges or sales of any stock at their own discretion and initiative.

For the discount houses, which had not been subject to the old Special Deposit or Cash Deposit schemes, separate provision was made with the intention that their operations should not frustrate the new scheme for controlling the banks.[2] Again the purpose of the changes was to promote freedom to compete, between the houses themselves and between the houses and the banks. The abandonment of three restrictive practices was seen as being central to this aim : the agreements between the houses and the clearing banks dealing with the Treasury bill tender and the supply of call money to the discount houses; the agreement between clearing banks and discount houses which restricted competition for non-bank funds; the collusive agreements between the discount houses themselves on interest rates, discounts and competition for Treasury bills at the tender. On the other hand, the Bank wished to continue to operate as before in the short-term money market. As part of this the L.D.M.A. were requested to continue to 'cover' the tender each week : in return the Bank offered to continue to act as lender of last resort through the discount houses alone, by way of discounting or lending on eligible paper. It was intended, however, that as before the Bank would buy and sell Treasury bills directly with the banks in the day-to-day management of the money market and they would continue to accord to money and discount brokers such facilities as they thought appropriate.

Because call money lent to the discount market (i.e. members of the L.D.M.A., Stock Exchange money brokers and certain other specified firms running a money book) was to qualify without limit as a 'reserve asset' for the purposes of the banks' 'reserve assets ratio' the discount houses' key position in the mechanism of monetary control was, in principle at least, reinforced rather than diminished. Three methods of control were envisaged which took account of the houses' enhanced role. As with the banks, the aim was to move away from quantitative controls and to employ a system which would allow the houses freedom to compete. The controls proposed were : (1) that members of the discount market should hold a stated minimum proportion (50 per cent) of their funds in public sector debt (this minimum conforming closely to the current average practice for the market as a whole ; it was based on the annual average, rather than being a finely calculated figure).[3] (2) A firm undertaking by the market not to engage in very short-term transactions which would enable the banks to substitute 'window dressing' arrangements for genuine observance of their minimum reserve-ratio obligation (in support of this undertaking the Bank reserved the right to require members of the market to account fully for the conduct of their portfolios or 'books'). (3) As before the Bank would expect that each house would maintain an acceptable ratio between the size of its total business and the extent of its capital and reserves.[4]

THE CLEARING BANKS AND PRESSURE FOR REFORM

Essentially, the reforms of Competition and Credit Control were aimed at the banks, especially the clearing banks, and other key lenders. The discount houses were, in a sense, affected only incidentally, by virtue of their position intermediate between the Bank of England and the rest of the banking system. For this reason and because it is difficult to obtain a true understanding of the way in which the discount houses have operated without making reference to the operations of the banks, the following analysis of the effects of the 1971 reforms on the discount houses begins with an examination of their effects on the banks.

One aspect of the 1971 reforms involved dismantling the restrictive practices which had been laboriously built up over the years by agreements between banks, between banks and discount houses and between discount houses. A rationale for the development of these practices and for their persistence over such a long period of time has been suggested as follows :

> that the cartel on banks' deposit rates originated as a method of protecting the banks from possible failure, and especially after 1914, public criticism; that the discount houses' collusive agreements were a method of protecting themselves against the consequences of the clearing banks' restrictive practices; and that the Bank of England supported the early developments (pre-1914) and actively initiated later developments (1918–35) because they facilitated the implementation of a monetary policy which was primarily concerned with fixing the price and quantity of credit to the private sector of the economy and with reducing the interest costs of financing the National Debt.[5]

It would seem, therefore, that not only were the discount houses 'incidentally' affected by a policy of reform of the banking system in 1971 but it was the banks' restrictive practices which had initiated systematic collusion in discount houses' operations originally (see Chapter 3 above).

Although no officially initiated reforms were put into effect prior to 1971, there had been much criticism of the system – especially by academic economists – and some official and other suggestions in favour of actual change. In any case, features which were to emerge as characteristic of the new regime were, in fact, already in evidence under the old – for example, the diversification of bank services and greater flexibility in terms of interest rates. It was to be the function of the freer regime to promote the development of several previously existing trends. To the clearing banks themselves the proposals for reform represented a welcome change of heart on the part of the authorities. When, in 1963, a working party of London clearing bankers under the chairmanship of Mr John Thompson, Chairman of Barclays, decided that the whole cartelised rate structure should be dismantled, the then Governor of the Bank, Lord Cromer, agreed. The move was, however, forbidden by the Chancellor of the Exchequer, Reginald Maudling (who heard about the plan quite by accident whilst in Washington), on the grounds that it would lead to higher interest rates. Following this initiative by the bankers themselves the case for increasing price competition was put forward, in 1967, in the Prices and Incomes Board report on bank charges and again, in 1968, in the report on bank mergers of the Monopolies Commission. Further, in 1969 the banks decided to publish their true profits for the first time – notwithstanding exemptions which they enjoyed under the Companies Acts. Such action was indicative of a willingness for greater competition, and conducive to its realisation.

Certainly, by the end of 1970 there were reasons why clearing bankers should wish to see an end to the cartel. Bank rate, the clearers' datum for rate fixing, was because of a number of factors no longer the determinant of the domestic rate structure that it once was. The first was concerned with the rapid growth of secondary financial institutions over the previous ten years operating in both the corporate and personal sectors. The rate structure of these institutions reflected supply and demand factors – foreign as well as domestic – little related to Bank rate. Because the authorities often shrank from simply bringing Bank rate into line with these other rates, for fear of 'demonstration effects' in the home economy or of adversely affecting exchange flows, institutions still directly affected by Bank rate (clearing banks and discount houses) found themselves increasingly isolated from the realities of the interest-rate situation. A visible effect of this had been the relatively slow growth of clearing-bank deposits compared with the deposit growth of the non-clearers (see Chapter 11). The clearers, consequently limited for most ordinary deposits to a deposit rate linked to Bank rate, had been forced to compete at market rates through specially formed subsidiaries for sterling deposits as well as currencies. However, this development must be attributed to *both* major factors operative in the pre-1971 situation, that is not only to the banks' cartelised rate structure but also to the resort by the authorities to quantitative controls on clearing-bank lending. It can be argued that these controls had had the effect of deterring the clearing banks from attempting to attract new deposits on which they were forbidden to lend and which they were disinclined to invest in gilt-edged securities. Moves that introduced competition for deposits while retaining lending controls would possibly lead only to higher prices for credit. Therefore, to assess the benefits of a situation of freedom to compete in banking it was necessary that the authorities should abandon the bludgeon of quantitative controls on lending.

In any case, clearing bankers had come increasingly to regard lending ceilings as discriminatory and inequitable – because they applied principally to the clearing banks and left their competitors' activities unchecked. In this they had the support of academic economists who condemned the authorities' discriminatory controls as much as they criticised the banks' restrictive practices.[6]

The case for greater competition was given added weight by being advanced at a time '. . . when "influential opinion" was gradually abandoning its earlier faith in "indicative planning" in favour of its still earlier (1951–4) attachment to "competition and market processes". The advent of a Conservative administration in the summer of 1970 both reflected and accelerated this shift . . .'[7] By the end of 1970 *The Times* could say :

> With the heavy emphasis on monetary policy that the Government's resistance to any formal incomes policy implies, and with increasing international criticism that Whitehall's present policies are inadequate to stem inflation, new weapons consistent with the theories of economic laissez faire are being urgently sought by the Treasury.[8]

This quotation includes several of the important elements which appeared to be involved in the situation on the eve of the reforms. Certainly, the government of the day had set its face implacably against a formal incomes policy as a way of tackling the prevailing inflation. There were also indications that official favour inclined towards monetarist views on economic control – to the extent that there were pronouncements in high places accepting the importance of paying more attention to the 'broad monetary aggregates'.[9] A target for money supply growth had been set for the United Kingdom by the I.M.F. in 1967, though this was later modified to a target for domestic credit expansion. On outward signs, there had been at least a partial conversion to 'free market monetarism'. Closer analysis, however, reveals that the reforms had been based on an acceptance of Radcliffe monetary theory (see Chapter 14 below).

With regard to the timing of the reforms it was mentioned above that the authorities had taken advantage of favourable economic conditions. Shortly after the publication of the proposals the Governor of the Bank explained the official view as follows :

> We judge the present situation of low, international interest rates, relatively slack demand for loans and a strong balance of payments to be a propitious moment in which to introduce these changes; and we also believe that they are not inconsistent with the United Kingdom's application to join the E.E.C. or out of line with the general movement towards the harmonisation of credit controls which seems likely to take place on the road to monetary union.[10]

On completion of the discussions with interested parties the new arrangements came into operation on 16 September 1971. The features most relevant for present purposes were as follows.

The 8 per cent cash and 28 per cent liquid-assets ratios which had applied only to the London and Scottish clearing banks disappeared and were replaced for all banks designated as such, by a uniform minimum reserve-asset ratio, to be observed on a day-by-day basis, amounting to 12½ per cent of 'eligible liabilities'.[11] The assets chosen for the new reserve ratio were : balances with the Bank of England (other than special deposits); British government and Northern Ireland government Treasury bills; company tax reserve certificates; money at call with the London money market; British government stocks with one year or less to final maturity; local authority bills eligible for rediscount at the Bank and (up to a maximum of 2 per cent of eligible liabilities) commercial bills eligible for rediscount at the Bank.[12]

In this context the money at call with the London money market which the Bank considered eligible was to comprise :

> funds placed with members of the London Discount Market Association, with certain other firms carrying on an essentially similar type of business (the discount brokers and the money trading departments of certain banks traditionally undertaking such business) and with certain firms through whom the banks finance the gilt-edged market, namely the money brokers and jobbers. In order to constitute an eligible reserve asset, funds placed with these firms must be at call (or callable, if not explicitly at call) and must be secured (in the case of the jobbers, on gilt-edged securities).[13]

The special deposits device was retained and was intended to apply as a uniform percentage across the banking system, based on each bank's total eligible liabilities.[14]

The collective agreements on interest rates that London and Scottish clearing bankers were to abandon as a key aspect of the scheme involved both rates paid on deposits and charged on advances. Henceforth, no rates were to be agreed except where two or more banks might come together for consortium lending, for example to nationalised industries.

These new arrangements were in principle to apply to all banks in the United Kingdom except that in the case of Northern Ireland banks special arrangements were envisaged because of conditions peculiar to the region. Also, those finance houses which took deposits but did not seek and obtain full recognition as banks were made subject to a scheme parallel and very similar to that which applied to the banks. The minimum reserve ratio was, however, set at 10 per cent rather than 12½ per cent of eligible liabilities which, in turn, would exclude money borrowed from the banks so as to avoid double counting. Finance houses would be subject to calls for Special Deposits possibly at rates different from the banks.

THE POSITION OF THE DISCOUNT HOUSES

With regard to the London Discount Market Association, as had been envisaged in the July discussion paper, members would continue to apply each week for a total amount of Treasury bills sufficient to cover the amount of bills offered at the tender. However, they would no longer tender for the bills at an agreed price. The Bank would continue to confine to the discount houses access to last-resort lending facilities by means of loans or discounts.[15] Security for last-resort loans would in future have to include a minimum proportion of Treasury bills. The houses would henceforth maintain at least 50 per cent of their funds in specified categories of public-sector debt. The same ratio would also be kept by certain discount brokers and the money trading departments of banks which operated in the discount market (see below).

For the purposes of the public-sector ratio, 'borrowed funds' would comprise : (a) total sterling borrowing (other than capital) from all sources, less any sterling lending to other discount houses, discount brokers, money brokers or the money trading departments of the relevant banks; plus (b) the excess, if any, of liabilities denominated in currencies other than sterling over the total of assets in such currencies. As with the banks' eligible liabilities, no deduction was to be allowed from the total of borrowed funds if other currency assets should exceed other currency liabilities.

Public-sector debt eligible for inclusion in the 50 per cent ratio comprised the following categories : (a) United Kingdom and Northern Ireland Treasury bills; (b) local authority bills eligible for rediscount at the Bank and negotiable bonds; (c) public-sector bills guaranteed by H.M. Government; (d) company tax reserve certificates; (e) British government stocks and stocks of nationalised industries guaranteed by H.M. Government with not more than five years to final maturity; and (f) local authority stocks with not more than five years to final maturity.

The most important point about the effects of the new measures on the discount houses was that the houses were left not only in existence but also largely unscathed. Those aspects which were swept away were those which found a ready parallel in and also stemmed from the reforms of banking practice. The wholly new public-sector debt ratio, in acting as a check on discount house operations, merely reflected the enhanced importance of 'call money' – as a reserve asset for banks. It is surely significant that given the opportunity to remove the discount market from the centre of operations and to change it beyond all recognition, the authorities should have chosen, as in the past, to retain the houses at the heart of the regulatory mechanism, allowing them the opportunity to adapt to new circumstances and new requirements. Speaking to the Institute of Bankers in November 1971 the Chief Cashier of the Bank said that the part of the money market with which the Bank was most directly concerned was that

> which deals in short-term debt of the central government, for here . . . we are concerned both as an issuing house and as an executant of monetary policy. In framing the proposals in *Competition and credit control* it seemed to us that our objectives could be met without structural change because, despite what the critics may say, that structure serves the interested parties very satisfactorily. Thus, although the discount market's agreements among themselves and with the banks on Treasury bill prices and money rates would go, along with the banks' agreements on interest rates, it seemed desirable and possible to maintain the discount market's rôle in underwriting the Treasury bill tender and as the channel through which an influence on short-term rates of interest was exerted.[16]

As a prelude to the analysis (in Chapter 14, below) of the discount houses' operations and role during the years since the implementation of Competition and Credit Control, the following pages will be devoted to an examination of the very changed world in which the houses found themselves late in 1971, dealing in turn with borrowed funds and the asset portfolio.

IMMEDIATE EFFECTS ON THE HOUSES' BUSINESS

(a) Borrowed funds
The abolition of the banks' interest-rate cartel took place on 10 October 1971, three weeks after the abolition of direct-lending controls, on 16 September. Formally, the change involved the abandonment of a uniform minimum overdraft rate and a maximum rate for seven-day deposits – both determined in relation to Bank rate – and gave the right to each bank to quote whatever deposit and overdraft rates it might choose. In fact, the actual change in circumstances was somewhat less than that suggested. In the first place, by 1971 the device of a minimum overdraft rate had lost virtually all significance. Because of rising costs, an increased concern with profitability and the far higher rates charged by other financial institutions, the tendency had been for the banks to increase rather than reduce the differential between deposit rates and overdraft rates. There was no agreement on an upper limit to lending rates. The significant change for the banks was the abolition of lending ceilings by the authorities.

Secondly, the abolition of the maximum deposit rate caused little stir in the money markets because the banks already bid for large, generally fixed-term, deposits at higher market rates through specialist subsidiaries. This could now be done directly. With regard to small deposits, the banks were already excessively liquid because of the prevailing slack demand for overdrafts. For this reason the banks were generally still taking seven-day money on the same terms as before. Thirdly, whereas both deposit and overdraft rates were previously fixed in relation to Bank rate, from 1 October they were fixed in relation to a 'base rate' determined independently by each bank. 'Base rate' was the term adopted for the rate of interest to be set by each bank individually in the light of its assessment of the market situation, to be used as a point of reference in place of Bank rate for the fixing of deposit and overdraft rates.[17]

As noted above, money at call (or at least callable) with the London money market was to qualify without limit for the purposes of the banks' reserve-assets ratio. The new rules were explicitly stated and a full list of eligible institutions provided.[18] The effect of the new arrangements on the discount houses, which comprised the main component of the call-money market, was, however, somewhat more equivocal. On the one hand, the houses' position was strengthened in that by giving call money reserve-asset status, a supply of call money was assured from a wider range of banks. On the other hand, the L.D.M.A. were but one group among several specified with which reserve-asset call money could be kept. Also, that intricate set of arrangements, described in Chapter 7, which guaranteed a flow of funds to the discount houses on acceptable terms, was demolished.

Deprived of the friendly, protective clothing of the cartel arrangements the discount houses' position began to look very exposed. They had henceforth to compete against each other for funds as well as against other named repositories of reserve-asset call money and, indeed, against all other profitable employments for funds.[19] In other words, from the banks' point of view call money was, given the need to maintain $12\frac{1}{2}$ per cent of eligible liabilities in some form of reserve assets, only one way of deploying assets. To meet the new situation, the houses attempted to ensure that non-clearing banks, which hitherto had had to keep no formal ratio, kept a large proportion of their reserve assets in the form of call money and also that the discount houses continued to make the market in those negotiable instruments which were designated as reserve assets.

There were fears that because reserve-asset money could be 'callable, if not explicitly at call', the stability of discount houses' borrowed funds might be jeopardised by a chimera dubbed a 'callable fixture'. The essence of this device would be to give to the banks the right to demand the going rate for a two or three months' fixture with the option to call at any time to meet a liquidity need.[20]

On the other side of the coin, competition did mean that there was no longer a minimum rate that had to be paid to the clearing banks and that competitive rates could be quoted for commercial money even though local authority and industrial treasurers were by that time sufficiently knowledgeable to ensure that such funds, in volume, were no cheaper than call money.

(b) The asset portfolio – public-sector paper
With regard to the discount houses' asset portfolio, the requirement that at least 50 per cent of borrowed funds had at all times to be invested in specified categories of public-sector debt meant that the portfolio tended to be thought of as being in two parts : that is half in public-sector paper to be held primarily as an obligation and half in private-sector paper held for profit. Given the increased volatility of gilts, the need to meet the 50 per cent requirement and at the same time to maintain the overall liquidity of the portfolio generated a strong demand for Treasury and local authority bills.

The situation in Treasury bills was difficult. Due both to the increased demand and to the small size of offers at the weekly tender the minimum price on allotment rose, with a consequent reduction in yield and profitability. Although the syndicated bid had been abolished, the Friday midday meeting was retained both for the transaction of routine business and also for the fixing of an underwriting price for Treasury bills – namely the price at which the L.D.M.A., in accordance with their new undertaking, would be prepared to take up all the bills on offer. The allocation between houses of the total amount was, as before, worked on a pro-rata basis according to the size of the house. Each house submitted a tender for its own proportion of the total and bid at its own price in view of the agreed underwriting price, which was the minimum price (maximum rate) at which they would apply. In the conditions prevailing in the early days of the new regime, with downward pressure on the Treasury bill rate, it is likely that individual houses' bids bore little relation to the underwriting price. However, in times of large amounts of bills on offer and slack demand at the tenders, the underwriting price would tend to be the price at which individual houses would submit bids.

The other short-term public-sector asset increasingly sought after was the local authority bill. While the course of events in the Treasury bill market had been fairly predictable, that in the local authority market needs some further explanation. Despite the fact that there

H

had been no shortage of local authority bills on offer the majority of the bills issued at consecutive tenders were taken up at a lower rate (higher price) than Treasury bills issued on the same day. This pheno-menon is probably explained by reference to two factors. In the first place, because most of the local authority tenders were held on Friday afternoons – after the result of the Treasury bill tender was known – houses which had failed to obtain the Treasury bills they needed for public-sector ratio purposes might decide to compensate by bidding up for local authority bills. Secondly, a similar effect could be pro-duced by houses which had through personal contact and initiative built up business with individual local authorities. These houses might have decided, during the early days of the more competitive con-ditions, to bid up for the bills of 'their' local authorities, which might otherwise have been tempted by more lucrative alternatives to aban-don old loyalties.[21]

Altogether, the demand for eligible reserve assets in the freer market conditions had forced down yields on the public-sector bills to a level which excluded profit. For the discount houses this develop-ment was particularly ominous. Although in easy money conditions with only small issues of Treasury bills the houses could go elsewhere for their public-sector debt, if money became short and Treasury bill issues increased the L.D.M.A. could find themselves 'underwriting' a large part of the tender.[22]

Treasury bills and local authority bills had taken on a new sig-nificance for the discount houses because other public-sector debt (e.g. gilts and local authority bonds) could not be relied upon to provide an acceptable degree of liquidity. Nevertheless, both of these longer-dated instruments continued to feature prominently in discount house busi-ness. They are now dealt with in turn.

The Bank's modification in May 1971 of its mode of operations in the gilt-edged market represented a return towards the position in the market that it had occupied up to about ten years previously. In making the changes the Bank had taken into account three consider-ations : '. . . the effectiveness of monetary policy, the health of the market and the need to preserve the Bank's ability to finance and re-finance the needs of government.'[23]

With regard to the first of these the Bank had stated that it would no longer be prepared to respond to requests to buy stock outright except in the case of stocks with one year or less to run to maturity. The purpose of this move was to limit more effectively fluctuations in the resources of the banking system which arose from official oper-ations in the gilt-edged market. This was in line with an earlier deci-sion that 'the Bank's operations in the gilt-edged market should pay more regard to their quantitative effects on the monetary aggregates and less regard to the behaviour of interest rates.' The Bank had consequently demonstrated greater flexibility, both of techniques employed and of prices at which it would be prepared to deal. Under the old regime, with its policy emphasis on the total of bank lending, these modifications of Bank tactics were sufficient because the operations of the banks in the gilt-edged market were not of critical importance for monetary policy. The new scheme of control, however, did not allow for the freedom of operators in the private sector to buy and sell at their own initiative large amounts of stock at or near market prices : further withdrawal of official support was therefore necessary.[24]

The second objective of the May 1971 reforms was to improve the health of the market. It was hoped that by limiting the extent of the Bank's operations the marketability of gilt-edged securities would be improved. This was partly a reaction against an earlier policy, with the same objective, which had involved *extending* the Bank's operations. In the light of this earlier experiment the new policy was based on three considerations : (1) so long as the Bank was willing to employ substantial resources in maintaining the marketability of the debt there was no incentive for others to do so; (2) particularly once greater flexibility in pricing had been introduced the domination of the market by an operator of the size of the Bank did not present an appealing picture to new investors; (3) it came to be considered that central to the idea of a market was the existence of a variety of views among operators of a similar size. Because of the intimate involvement of the Bank in the market there tended at sensitive times to be only two views, namely that of the Bank and that of everybody else. It was believed that such conditions '. . . gave rise to very large speculative transactions and made the speculative management of portfolios altogether too easy.'[25]

The third objective of the Bank was to maintain its ability to finance and refinance the needs of the central government. Consequently, the familiar operations described earlier continued as before.

These were the publicly declared intentions and motives of the authorities. They represented a shift of opinion which would have been very much to the taste of the Radcliffe Committee. To the non-Bank participants in the gilt-edged market the most immediate and obvious change was that the government broker was no longer always on hand to act as 'jobber of last resort'. The major query in everyone's mind, however, was that although a policy of not giving help to the market on bad days would be quite consistent with the chosen method of control, via a reserve-asset ratio, what would the authorities in fact do if the market were to suffer a very serious fall such that the jobbers

became overloaded with stock? In the early days of the new gilt-
edged market rules there was no opportunity for finding an answer to
this question. The new policy began and continued for the first few
months (the new rules became operative in July not September 1971)
in an atmosphere of market strength induced by a downward trend of
interest rates in easy money conditions.

In fact, the market had shown substantial gains with only isolated
and untypical falls, and in these favourable conditions the authorities
were seen to be operating much as before. The major exception was
that the government broker no longer nursed the market and this
caused a change of tactics among the gilt-edged jobbers who began
to deal much more warily. To ordinary dealers it meant that whereas
formerly they could have sold stock to the government broker and
been pretty certain of getting it back with only small loss if they had
miscalculated market movements, in the new conditions sales to other
dealers could involve the prospects of heavy loss if the market were to
change unexpectedly. In this respect it was anticipated that the gap
between buying and selling prices would in any case widen and that
prices would change more abruptly so tending to limit the amount
of stock sold.

For the institutions participant in the gilt-edged market, the new
dealing conditions were bound to induce a reappraisal of policy. Apart
from the Bank's declared intention of withdrawing close support from
the market, gilts were to qualify as reserve assets for the banks only up
to one year to final maturity, while for the discount houses' public-
sector ratio they were to be eligible up to five years to final maturity.
In view of the loss of liquidity on their other-than-one-year gilts, the
banks could well find it prudent to restrict the bulk of their holdings
to stocks within five years to maturity and to take on longer maturities
only to take advantage of favourable investment opportunities.

Similarly with the discount houses : apart from purchases made in
order to satisfy the requirements of the public-sector ratio, there
was the feeling in some quarters that, deprived of the customary
support of the government broker, houses would no longer be so ready
to take in stock on a falling market. Nevertheless, there were also
suggestions that positive advantage might be gained from the new
conditions for houses prepared to be active dealers, quoting two-way
prices in competition with the jobbers. It is very doubtful, however,
whether this ever materialised, and certainly the resources of the discount market would have proved inadequate for them to fulfil this
function in the climate that subsequently prevailed.

The other longer-dated public-sector security – local authority
bonds – found official recognition under the new arrangements only

as an eligible asset for the purposes of the discount houses' public-sector ratio. In this role they could present themselves as an attractive proposition. They could produce satisfactory returns and were generally eligible as security on borrowed funds. They did, however, possess disadvantages. While in normal times the bonds could easily be turned over, the absence of a substantial market in this debt outside the discount houses could result in a liquidity crisis in times of stringency, if houses in general had come to rely too heavily on the bonds to satisfy ratio requirements. Also, they were vulnerable to capital loss, either on valuation or realisation, at a time of rising rates.

(c) The asset portfolio – private-sector paper
So far, attention has been directed to the 'bread-and-butter' half of the discount houses' portfolio. It was on the other, private-sector, half that the houses had to rely for whatever 'jam' they could get.

Because they had in the past been instrumental in allowing the clearing banks to escape from official control through pressure on their liquid-assets ratios, commercial bills – or more specifically the bank bills favoured by the banks as security on call money – received special attention under the new regulations. The discount houses' public-sector ratio obviously excluded them and they could be counted as a reserve asset for all banks only up to a maximum of 2 per cent of eligible liabilities. Furthermore, to be acceptable for inclusion as reserve assets commercial bills had to be eligible for rediscount at the Bank of England. In general, eligibility was confined to '. . . bank bills payable in the United Kingdom, accepted by certain British and Commonwealth banks.' The 'eligible' banks were specified to comprise '. . . the members of the Accepting Houses Committee, the London and Scottish clearing banks, the larger British overseas banks and those Commonwealth banks which have had branches in London for many years, together with certain other banks and some Bank of England customers of long standing.'[26]

There was, of course, nothing new in the notion of eligibility for rediscount at the Bank : what was new, was that for the first time the Bank was prepared to allow access to a definitive list of eligible acceptors, kept at the Discount Office. Furthermore, whereas under the old system bills might command the agreed fine bank-bill rate whether they were eligible or not, in making eligibility for rediscount at the Bank explicit and synonymous with eligibility as a reserve asset, the new rules gave rise to a discount rate differential in favour of eligible bills. Although the distinction between eligible and ineligible bills, both in terms of reserve-asset status and, in the prevailing conditions, in terms of rate, was theoretically entirely logical from the point of view of liquidity, there were those in the discount market who found the measure arbitrary and against the spirit of Competition and Credit Control. In particular, it was seen as usurping the traditional function of a discount house because : 'In the past it has been possible when determining a rate for a bank acceptance to treat undoubted status on a par with rediscountability, and indeed when selling parcels of Bank Bills we have made no distinction in rate on this score.'[27]

It was explained in an earlier chapter that prior to 1971 the L.D.M.A. fixed a 'fine' discount rate for the best quality bank acceptances. This was abandoned early in August of that year, before the new rules came into force. The effect of competition was to force down the rate for eligible bank acceptances, not to the same degree as for the public-sector paper but sufficiently to make the cost of bill finance competitive with that of bank lending. With the use of bank acceptances in a reserve capacity so closely circumscribed and trade bills having no eligibility whatsoever, it was likely that the market would in future look for a rate of return which would compensate. Late in 1971, however, the rate on eligible acceptances was little different from the cost of call money and therefore provided only a very small return, approximately equal to the yield differential between the rate of *interest* on borrowed funds and the rate of *discount* on the bills. For the future, the higher returns offered by trade bill business indicated a possible line of development for the private-sector half of the portfolio.

One market into which gloom and despondency had not crept for discount houses was the active and growing market in sterling certificates of deposit. In the years immediately prior to 1971 this market had grown from nothing to around £2000 million, had a turnover approaching that in the short-bond market and, like its American counterpart, provided the opportunity for making profits on the size of turnover alone. With other asset markets in the doldrums the discount houses felt constrained to exploit fully the opportunities available in the C.D. market, as Table 4 indicates.[28] They were further encouraged by the size of the market itself and the high level of activity which made for great ease of dealing and, consequently, liquidity of the instruments themselves. Experience had not yet shown, however, just how robust the market would prove to be in a crisis.

CONCLUSION

This survey of the principal changes brought about by the reforms of September 1971 and their impact on the discount houses and those most intimately connected with them can be concluded with the reiteration of a few key points. The most fundamental is that the authorities held the services provided by the discount houses in sufficiently high regard for the houses to be retained intact in the new scheme, with a role of enhanced importance in the control process. On the other hand, it was obviously intended that there should be no more cosy agreements to keep out the cold winds of inter-house competition. The conventions that were retained in discount house operations were those intended directly to aid the authorities in financing Exchequer requirements and in the achievement of a desired pattern of interest rates.

The houses had now to compete for a supply of borrowed funds in a situation in which call money was regarded by the banks as only one way of holding reserve assets. Conditions in late 1971 gave the impression that the existence of reserve-asset and public-sector requirements could mean little or no return on short-term public-sector debt. To compensate for this, activity would have to be correspondingly greater on the private-sector side with increased turnover of C.D.s, and central government and local authority bonds. Perhaps the biggest unanswered question at this time was concerned with what action, if any, the authorities might take in the face of extreme weakness in the gilt-edged market.

14 Working under the New Rules

The rules of Competition and Credit Control which were applied to the discount houses in 1971 remained in operation unchanged until July 1973, at which time they were radically revised. It was in the authorities' attempts to work the new policy in the solution of economic problems during this two-year period, that the discount houses and others were to find answers to some of their most disturbing questions.

FAVOURABLE TRADING CONDITIONS, 1971–2

The Governor of the Bank has already been quoted as saying that the new measures were deliberately introduced at what was judged to be a propitious moment, when the balance of payments was strong, international interest rates were low and at home the demand for loans was slack. During the ensuing year the authorities were fortunate in that with economic circumstances either favourable or not strongly adverse, their new policy was given an easy 'running in' period free of any sharp test. For the discount houses and other institutions feeling their way into the new conditions, the lack of stress was equally welcome.

During the financial year 1971–2 external economic conditions were shaped by the consequences of the measures taken by the U.S. government to deal with the dollar crisis. In August 1971 the U.S. government took urgent steps to relieve pressure on the dollar which had been building up over the previous months. These included temporary suspension of dollar convertibility into gold and other reserve assets. At the same time major currencies were given freedom to find their own exchange levels. The disruption of international monetary arrangements brought on by the uncertainty surrounding the health of the key currency led to the Group of Ten meeting in Washington in December. As a result of the 'Smithsonian Agreement', which included proposals for a raising of the official dollar price of gold, currency realignments produced a sterling revaluation of almost 9 per cent against the dollar and a small appreciation in value overall. Sterling remained strong throughout the year, reflecting the sound balance of payments and reserves position.

At home the economy was characterised by stagnancy of production and rising unemployment. In March the Chancellor had brought in a virtually neutral budget but expansionary measures were taken in July. Monetary conditions became progressively easier as the financial year advanced : Bank rate, which had been reduced from 7 per cent to 6 per cent on 1 April, was reduced again to 5 per cent on 2 September. Under the programme for the introduction of the new scheme of credit control the authorities first eased and then removed restrictions on bank lending while the clearing banks for their part dismantled their 'cartel'. Of more immediate concern for the discount houses, interest rates moved in their favour — tending generally to fall throughout the period. The clearing banks' base rates were initially set at 5 per cent — the level of Bank rate — but were then further reduced to $4\frac{1}{2}$ per cent, and the finance houses' base rate fell $2\frac{1}{2}$ per cent in five stages during the half-year to December. Other rates, with exceptions, moved in the same direction.

In spite of the uncertainties surrounding the houses' operations in the more competitive conditions after September 1971 they enjoyed a good year. In the first place, the imposition of the common reserve-assets ratio induced many of the non-clearing banks to switch funds to the discount houses which previously they had placed elsewhere. This was a short-term gain (see Table 3) but it did mean that in the twelve months to December 1971 total borrowed funds rose by about £700 million to stand at almost £3000 million. Concomitantly, the proportion of total funds coming from the clearing banks fell over the year from more than 62 per cent to 42 per cent (from 53 per cent to 42 per cent during the final quarter). The accepting houses, overseas banks and other banks increased their share, from about 23 per cent to almost 38 per cent (from 30 per cent to 38 per cent during the final quarter).

The downward trend in interest rates brought about a corresponding decline in the cost of borrowed funds : standing at $5\frac{3}{8}-6\frac{7}{8}$ per cent at the beginning of the financial year, the rates for call money fell to $1-4\frac{3}{4}$ per cent at the end of November, though subsequently there was some tendency for rates to rise.[1] However, the fall in the cost of borrowing was matched by the sharp falls in the yields on Treasury, commercial and local authority bills (see previous chapter), brought about by the removal of the agreements on rates, new reserve requirements, easy money conditions and in the case of Treasury bills, a reduction in supply. The removal of quantitative restrictions on commercial bills allowed the houses to compensate to some extent for the reduced margins with a substantially increased turnover in these assets. Because of the increased demand for Treasury bills from the banks, discount house holdings were lower than in the previous year, despite the fact that of the extra £800 million of borrowed funds that the houses took in the three months to the end of January 1972 they invested almost £500 million in Treasury bills.[2]

Most of the balance of the funds went into other sterling bills and sterling C.D.s Over the twelve months from December 1970 holdings of sterling C.D.s rose from £268 million to £457 million.[3] The growth of this market continued : at the end of December 1971 £2372 million were outstanding compared with £1089 million a year earlier. The introduction of the new regulations in September 1971 was the signal for several of the London and Scottish clearing banks to begin the issue of certificates of deposit directly rather than through subsidiaries as had been the practice previously.

ADVERSITY UNDER THE NEW RULES, 1972–3

(a) Interest rates
For the discount houses, 1970–1 and 1971–2 were golden years, with profits in the latter at a record level. Public-sector ratios presented no real problems as they conformed closely to the houses' traditional practice, in terms of portfolio mix, and with interest rates generally on a downward trend capital appreciation of gilts, certificates of deposit and so on was virtually guaranteed. Subsequently, conditions were somewhat less friendly, giving the houses their first taste of adversity under the new regime.

The overall economic picture for 1972–3 differed sharply from that for 1971–2. There was a marked expansion of the economy at home accompanied by a rapid fall in unemployment, but the previously strong balance of payments position weakened, with the current account only just in balance as compared with a surplus of £1000 million for 1971 together with a substantial outflow of capital following the even greater inflow of the previous year. The government set their sights firmly on the goal of a higher rate of economic growth and tailored the rest of their economic policy to ensure its achievement. In order to avoid the imposition of restraints on the expanding economy the sterling parity set only six months before in Washington was ruthlessly abandoned when the currency came under pressure in June. Similarly, having ruled out fiscal or monetary measures to dampen the growing inflation, the government introduced statutory means of control over prices and incomes.

In line with growth in the real economy monetary expansion developed apace. In his March 1972 Budget speech the Chancellor announced that the fast growth of output at which he was aiming would entail a growth in the money stock that was high by the standards of past years, the rate of expansion being geared to the needs of the situation.

Overall, 1972–3 turned out to be a year of unprecedentedly high monetary growth and this growth was accompanied by a rapidly rising level of interest rates. In the June quarter the rise in rates was associated with growing activity in the home economy, and it became very pronounced as the balance of payments position deteriorated and pressure on sterling led to an acute shortage of domestic funds. In mid-June the Treasury bill rate rose above Bank rate which was then restored to its normal position above Treasury bill rate with a rise from 5 per cent to 6 per cent. The outflow of funds which caused the banks' liquidity position to tighten led to a rise in short-term rates on the inter-bank market and after the ensuing sterling crisis was resolved with the decision to float, the rates rose at one point to an equivalent of well over 200 per cent per annum.[4] The banks' base rates, which had already been raised from $4\frac{1}{2}$ per cent to 5 per cent early in June, were further raised to 6 per cent late in June and again to 7 per cent late in July, at which level they remained until December.

The significance of Bank rate had been uncertain for some time. Under the new arrangements Bank rate was of less importance as a conventional datum for rate fixing. In addition, the interest rate flexibility that the freer regime envisaged made necessary the introduction of a last-resort lending rate that could be kept easily in step with movements in the market rates and at the same time be free of traditional policy implications. Early in the autumn the Treasury bill rate was again above Bank rate, depriving it of its customary potency. The authorities allowed this situation to continue for several weeks but then abolished the Bank rate after 270 years of existence and instituted a 'minimum lending rate' on 13 October 1972.

As its name implied the rate was intended to be the minimum level at which the Bank would lend at last resort to the discount houses. However, unlike Bank rate, minimum lending rate was to be determined automatically in relation to the Treasury bill rate by a known formula : the average rate of discount at the most recent tender plus $\frac{1}{2}$ per cent, rounded up to the nearest $\frac{1}{4}$ per cent, to come into effect on the Monday following the tender. In this way the inherently arbitrary aspect of Bank rate was removed together with the reflationary/contractionary demonstration effects that followed a change in its level. Further, the change would resolve any possible conflict between, say, the need for a high Bank rate for external monetary considerations with that of a need to maintain an unchanged or reduced level of Bank rate for internal reasons. Notwithstanding these reforms the Bank made provision for exceptional circumstances by reserving to itself powers to make discretionary changes.[5]

In practice the banking system found that minimum lending rate was not intended merely to follow market rates. The Special Deposit requirements imposed on the banks, in order to curb the growth of their lending, were supplemented by the repeated enforcement on the discount houses of last-resort borrowing at minimum lending rate for seven days. This, together with larger offers at the tender, brought a rise in the Treasury bill rate and with it a rise in minimum lending rate, from $7\frac{1}{4}$ per cent on 13 October to 9 per cent at the 22 December tender.

In January and February forces were at work to bring the rates down again. While money rates rose because of money shortage consequent upon tax payments to the Exchequer, the average rate of discount at the Treasury bill tenders and therefore minimum lending rate fell, due both to the high level of demand for reserve and public-sector assets and the small amounts of bills on offer.[6] Despite moderating influences in the form of seven-day penal lending and Special Deposit payments the minimum lending rate fell at the 19 January tender to $8\frac{3}{4}$ per cent. A further influence arose from expectations among investors[7] that government borrowing rates would fall and the consequent heavy purchasing of gilts brought about an acute cash shortage. The 'very heavy' open market purchases of bills by the authorities in relief of this shortage made Treasury bills scarce in relation to demand and led the discount houses to bid up at the tenders. The fall in the Treasury bill rate was subsequently steadied by the Bank forcing the houses into seven-day borrowing at minimum lending rate.

Conditions in the inter-bank and other wholesale sterling markets, with interest rates rising steeply, reflected the extent of direct competition for funds by the clearing banks. Because the parallel markets had come to provide a significant proportion of the banks' total resources base rates tended to move in step with movements in interest rates on those markets.[8] In consequence, base rates were moved upward from 7 to $7\frac{1}{2}$ per cent in mid-December and then in steps to $9\frac{1}{2}$ per cent in mid-February 1973. After a further upward jump following the Budget in March wholesale rates fell quite steeply and base rates were cut to 9 per cent early in April.

Because freedom of interest-rate movement was considered to be central to the working of Competition and Credit Control, rates were not frozen under the provisions of the statutory prices and incomes policy introduced in November 1972. On the contrary, the authorities were at that time actively promoting the increase. Over the quarter to April 1973 the general level of interest rates 'peaked' and fell back slightly. Nevertheless, in April the government took action, by means of a subsidy, to prevent building societies from raising their mortgage rates to unacceptable levels.[9] By the end of April 1973, when rates had been tending to fall for several weeks, the minimum lending rate stood at $8\frac{1}{4}$ per cent and the clearing banks' base rates at 9 per cent. Although originally the banks' deposit rates for seven-day money were generally changed at the same time as base rates and by the same amount, from July 1972 the margin was reduced from 2 to $1\frac{3}{4}$ per cent due to the banks having to bid up for deposits to maintain lending.

Rates on short-dated local-authority bonds began the year at about 5 per cent but climbed to 9 per cent in December and over 10 per cent in March 1973. Local authority deposits carried interest rates broadly in line with other short-term rates and yields on three months Euro-dollar deposits, which were above domestic rates during the first half of 1972, averaged around $5\frac{1}{2}$–6 per cent during the second half before climbing to $9\frac{1}{2}$ per cent during the first quarter of 1973, followed by a slight fall during April.

(b) Borrowed funds

These were the relevant economic conditions under which the discount houses had to operate during 1972–3. For the houses it was a period, compared with the previous year, largely free of major structural alterations : the only one of importance being the transformation of Bank rate (for so long a key consideration in discount houses' affairs) into minimum lending rate. Rather, the houses experienced a year of operations under the new rules during which interest rates were generally rising rather than falling.

Borrowed funds fell slightly in total over the year, from £2578 million at 19 April 1972 to £2413 million at 18 April 1973.[10] By source, loans from the London and Scottish clearing banks increased by 14 per cent at the expense of all other sources, excluding the Bank.[11] Borrowed funds were also dearer, with the cost of borrowing rising steeply from less than 5 per cent in April 1972 to around 9 per cent early in 1973, with a subsequent fall to around 7 per cent late in April. In the day-to-day round of money getting, the fears the houses experienced in the early days of Competition and Credit Control – of the introduction of disadvantageous lending practices by the banks –

were to be proved groundless. Practical considerations caused the banks and discount houses to make arrangements for call money to their mutual advantage. Specifically, the so-called 'callable fixture' referred to earlier proved to be less a device employed by the banks to exploit the position of the discount houses and more a natural outcome of the new situation. It became a well-established practice that large amounts of money would be lent for stated periods, but whereas the banks' initial expectation was that the funds should be placed with the discount houses at rates prevailing in the inter-bank market they were later willing to accept much lower rates. This was because the houses could always argue that the rate for callable fixtures should be related to the rate for a Treasury bill of the same tenor – in so far as the latter was the only alternative reserve asset. Also, of course, there would be little point in paying up for callable fixtures unless they could show a reasonable profit on securities held by the houses : though this would be less true at a time of rising rates.

Acceptance of the notion of a 'callable fixture' sprang from two sources. First, 'fixtures' combined stability for a portion of borrowed funds for the discount houses, with freedom from the rate agreements for the lending banks. Under the new rules, however, money had to be at least callable if not explicitly at call in order to count as a reserve asset. Consequently, although all funds would be ultimately callable, it was intended that the device of a callable fixture would combine advantages of both call money and the traditional fixture. Money at call plus callable fixtures together made up 'reserve-asset money' for the banks. Notwithstanding the enhanced popularity of fixture money, however, the majority of funds was still lent to the discount houses in the traditional manner, at call.

Another effect of the new arrangements was to relieve the 'unhealthy' situation brought about by the excessive dependence of the discount houses on the clearing banks for call money. Between 31 December 1970 and 31 December 1973, the proportion of call money derived from the clearing banks fell from 62·3 per cent to 45·9 per cent. Having satisfied reserve-asset requirements the practice was to employ surplus funds, very profitably, in the inter-bank market, so that banks were lenders in that market as well as borrowers. It was because of the higher rates obtaining on the inter-bank market and local authority market that the discount houses tended not to be the first choice for non-bank lenders : though badly needed funds could always be bid out from the commercial and manufacturing companies which would normally place funds elsewhere. Discount houses themselves, of course, took some funds unsecured from the inter-bank market. In addition they were, to a very limited extent, lenders on that market. It could happen that a house would take reserve-asset money from a bank and, confident that as reserve-asset money it would probably not be called, lend it out secured on the inter-bank market. The same money could thus be borrowed by a subsidiary of the original lending bank, or even by the bank itself.

The annual pattern of shortage and plenty in borrowed funds was much as before but, weekly, the tax days on Tuesday, Wednesday and Friday produced relative scarcity, though the Tuesday situation was mitigated by government disbursements. On the fifteenth day of each month the payment of oil royalties removed funds from the market. The characteristic daily rounds of the London banks by each house's representatives were now much reduced in number. With about 250 banks in London a house might visit only about ninety. The chief cause of this was that borrowed funds now possessed a much greater element of 'stickiness', that is the tendency of banks to leave money with individual houses. The impression obtained is that it could be a struggle for houses to gain reserve-asset money but that once they had it they tended to keep it. Banks would expect them to move the rates on the money up when there was a general rise, with the implied threat that the money would be called and re-lent elsewhere if the houses failed to comply. This posed no great problem as the houses themselves had become much more 'rate conscious' since September 1971.

(c) *Public-sector assets*

On the assets side and dealing with public-sector assets first, the discount houses' holdings of Treasury bills fell by a total of £109 million, from £399 million at 19 April 1972 to £290 million at 18 April 1973. Prior to September 1971 Treasury bills had been a discount house's most liquid asset and afterwards they became a reserve asset for both discount houses and banks. In the early days of Competition and Credit Control competition for Treasury bills had been very fierce, with rates forced down below the average cost of money. This situation continued into 1972 because of the small amounts of bills on offer at the weekly tenders.[12] During the period of falling interest rates the houses could take this in their stride because of the record profits they were earning elsewhere. The interesting point to emerge was that even in the subsequent, more stringent, times there was no tendency among the houses to return to the use of a syndicated bid although there may have been occasional *ad hoc* agreements between individual houses to tender at a certain price. The following statement may be regarded as a useful summation of discount house attitudes to the situation.

I think in practice we have found as a market that the necessity of obtaining a good allotment of Treasury bills did not in fact exist. We have learned to go without for weeks on end, relying on the fact that occasionally we would have the opportunity of buying from the Government broker on the odd days when money was in surplus . . . houses have only tendered seriously when their ratios were so low that they had to have Treasury bills. Otherwise they have submitted realistic bids only for their absolutely minimum requirements and retreated in price for the bulk of their quotas. Thus . . . different houses at different times have made the running at the tender.[13]

For the discount houses, operating conditions in the gilt-edged market were fundamentally influenced during 1972–3 on the one hand by generally rising interest rates and on the other by the authorities' policy of withdrawal from active management of market conditions.

The overall trend of the market, as measured by the *Financial Times* index of government security prices, was downward. The index fell from over 80 in April 1972 to around 71 in the middle of June and then recovered slightly to hover at around 72 until the end of the year. There was a further sharp fall to 69 in March 1973 (following the Budget) followed by a rise to 70, at which level it stayed until the end of April.[14] For discount-house bond operations the implications of these movements were predictable. From a position in the past in which gilts had been the houses' chief profit earner, by the end of 1972 they had become the smallest traditional item in portfolio. Favourable conditions had led to holdings rising to a peak of £453 million at 19 April 1972, whereafter they fell steeply to the very exceptionally low level of £95 million at 13 December. There was a recovery during the first quarter of 1973 but it was sufficient only to carry holdings to a level of £253 million at 18 April – little more than half that of a year previously.

The chief interest point of the year lay in the effects on the bond market of the sterling crisis of midsummer 1972 and the action taken by the Bank when extreme weakness of the market threatened. Not only was some clue given as to how far the authorities would be prepared to let the market go, but also it provided a sharp lesson for the discount houses that fundamentally affected their attitude towards their role in the bond market.

The end of the rising market in fixed interest securities was indicated by the Smithsonian Agreement of December 1971 (see above, p. 218). Prices fell steadily from the end of January 1972, but it was not until May that the market became really weak. There were reverses for the government in the working of its incomes policy, an end to the fall in overseas rates, a deficit on the balance of trade and indications in the Budget of the probability of a large borrowing requirement. Against this background the serious falls in the price of gilts were brought on by the government's need to sell stock at the end of April. The authorities had been supplying stock through the long tap at a price above the market level and potential sellers had held back in the fear that if the decision to sell should prove wrong they might have to buy the stock back from the authorities at a loss (higher price). However, when the authorities announced that bids for the long tap would be accepted at about the market level and that two additional issues, a medium and a long, would be made, inhibitions vanished and large-scale selling took place.[15]

With the gilt-edged market in disarray the stage was set for the drama over the sterling crisis in June. Whatever the immediate cause of the run on sterling (it is said to have been a speech by the Shadow Chancellor of the Exchequer to the effect that sterling would have to be devalued within a month or two) the feeling had been growing that the unrealistically high parity set for sterling in Washington could not for long be maintained within the close limits agreed under the European Economic Community 'snake in the tunnel' currency arrangements.[16] To end the drain on the reserves and to solve the problems of an impossible parity, sterling was floated on 23 June and Britain withdrew from the E.E.C. intervention arrangements. The London foreign-exchange market was reopened on 27 June and on the following day in the gilt-edged market the events took place which were to prove so controversial. After having allowed the market to fall unimpeded over several weeks prior to the float, the authorities suddenly took action to steady the market. It was the fact of intervention itself that incensed discount-house bond dealers. Having watched their gilt-holdings fall in value over a period of time, they were prevented by the official intervention from taking advantage of the recovery phase of the market to make good their losses.

The situation to which the authorities controversially reacted was that of sharply falling reserve-asset ratios of the banks. The view existed in the market that the banks would have to make substantial sales of gilts so as to correct the position. With the possibility of the banks unloading some £350 million of stock on to an already weak market, operators took the view that it might be better to sell in anticipation of such a move and the further price falls that it would certainly engender. This would have seemed a wise course of action to take, in view of the policy pronouncement by the authorities that with the exception of stock with less than a year to maturity they would no longer be prepared to take stock up at the instance of the market. Nevertheless, the authorities had reserved to themselves discretionary powers of intervention, namely to make purchases of stock of any maturity entirely at their own discretion and initiative. It was in accordance with this provision that the Bank acted to relieve the situation by means of an arrangement whereby stock would be purchased from the banks and resold to them after a short time. In the event the banks were able to restore their reserve positions sufficiently to be able to buy back the stock in mid-July.[17]

As a result of the Bank's action the gilt-edged market ultimately became more steady but the immediate confusion it caused may have been a contributory factor in the decision to withdraw from the market of three firms of stockjobbers within the space of three weeks. None of the firms was bankrupted but of the first two firms to go, Smith Brothers and Pike and Bryant, Smith Brothers lost nearly £400,000. There was alarm in the City when they were followed by Francis and Praed who had been trading in the government bond market for about eighty-five years. The withdrawals inevitably meant a reduction in the degree of competition in stockjobbing, with the result that most institutional business had to go to one of the two major jobbers : Wedd Durlacher Mordaunt and Akroyd and Smithers, who between them handled 75 per cent of the business.[18]

For the discount houses, the Bank had been put to the test in the gilt-edged market and had been found wanting in resolution and in consistency in its behaviour. In the light of the apparent pressure on the banks' reserve-asset ratios the houses had 'gone bears' and waited for the banks to sell their gilts. The Bank's intervention had prevented them from buying new lower-priced stock to replace that which they had sold. In the past they had been large traders and holders of short gilts, providing a valuable service for the authorities (as indicated in earlier chapters) safe in the knowledge that the government broker would implement the Bank's role of jobber of last resort. Now, discount houses' confidence in bond business had been severely shaken, as was shown by the change in the extent of their bond holdings over the course of the year under review.

The decline in the houses' holdings of Treasury bills made it difficult for them, at times, to maintain their public-sector lending ratio above the 50 per cent minimum, despite a net increase of over £100 million in their holdings of local authority bonds.[19] Each month holdings of the bonds reached new record levels, rising from £380 million at the start of the year (about 75 per cent of the total issue) to £527 million towards the end of the year (about 88 per cent of the total issue) : an increase of almost £150 million. It was noted earlier that because of their position as a reserve asset for the discount houses only, and because of the close relationships which had been cultivated between individual houses and local authorities, the local authority bond offered certain advantages and disadvantages that a year's experience under the new rules tended to confirm. On the one hand they provided a stable and intermittently profitable constituent of the public-sector portfolio and one over which the houses had a certain measure of influence. On the other hand, because the discount houses made such a large part of the market in this paper there was, in a sense, no proper market and the dangers that therefore stemmed from large-scale trading in the paper became more pronounced as time went by.

(d) Private-sector assets

In the 'private-sector portfolio', it was noted above that competition in the early days of the new regime had sharply reduced the rate on eligible bank acceptances – not to the same extent as on Treasury bills but sufficiently to make them competitive with the prime overdraft rates of most of the major banks. In addition, because the banks would readily take the bills as security against borrowed funds and would, to a limited extent, buy them outright, bank bills remained popular with the discount houses. Indeed, over the last three-quarters of 1972 commercial bills were the houses' only consistent profit earner. However, by the end of 1972 there was reason to believe that these happy circumstances would not continue and that in the future the houses would have to look to good-quality trade bills, which commanded higher discounts. By that time the rate on fine bank bills plus the usual one per cent acceptance commission gave a cost of financing by this method significantly greater than the clearing banks' prime lending rate of base rate plus one. Also, because of the easy availability of short-term money in the market the acceptance credit was not being employed by borrowers of the highest standing, and generally new users were confined to small and medium-sized finance houses anxious to increase their lending base.[20]

As a result of the ease with which bank advances could be obtained and of the existence of the inter-company market for business financing, the demand for trade bill finance by the top-class borrowers – including traditional users in the timber and pulp trades – fell away during 1972. There was conviction, however, that a general tightening of alternative sources of credit would quickly bring a revival. One development of some promise was the facility officially given to the nationalised industries to pay their suppliers by means of bills of exchange. Although the bills could not be included by the houses in their public-sector ratios, experience had shown that the bills could be discounted at competitive rates.[21]

Whereas in the early days of Competition and Credit Control the discount houses' faith and confidence in the strength of the sterling C.D. market had known few bounds, there had crept into the houses' dealings, after another year of experience, a certain reserve and caution. True, the market had weathered the storms of June 1972 extremely well and doggedly continued to expand in the succeeding months. Nevertheless, innovations in dealing and communications that made the market less imperfect, together with the operations of the clearing banks in the market, had made rates much more sensitive. Consequently it was no longer possible, for example, to undertake large-scale selling without risk of causing disruption. The price the discount houses paid in acquiring their more careful attitude in the C.D. market was the experience of taking significant losses in the second half of 1972 : losses probably even heavier than those on the gilt-edged market. On the *forward* C.D. market, profitable expectations had been such as to lead the houses into trading without properly covering their positions, with resulting painful carrying losses when money rates rose unexpectedly. Although these experiences did not bring about any serious reduction in turnover on the C.D. market, the tendency was for portfolios to be kept shorter; also the forward market dwindled in size.

Over the year in question discount houses' holdings of sterling C.D.s fell from £488 million at 19 April 1972 to £455 million at 17 May. Holdings then rose to a peak of £601 million at 16 August, after which they fell steadily to £363 million at 15 November. Thereafter the trend was upward, to finish the year at £524 million at 18 April 1973.[22] Apart from the disquiet aroused by the June crisis the size of holdings was influenced in the second half of 1972 both by the need to observe the public-sector lending ratio and also by the rising trend of interest rates which made longer-term assets a risky proposition.

These events must be seen against a background of enormously expanded C.D. issues. There was remarkable growth in the value of outstanding sterling C.D.s issued by the banking sector as a whole, from less than £2800 million in March 1972 to more than £5300 million in March 1973. Of the March 1973 figure nearly one-third was accounted for by the London clearing banks. Apparently, in order to secure funds in anticipation of an expected increase in demand for advances the clearing banks resorted to massive issues of sterling C.D.s. After the first bout of these tactics the secondary markets became more resistant to the banks' issues, the bulk of which were probably placed either with other banks or with the banks' own customers. In April 1972, of about £3000m of sterling C.D.s issued for all banks, £1775m were also held by banks. By March 1973, of just over £5300m issued for all banks, £3265m were also held by banks. The corresponding figures for the clearing banks alone were £431m issued and £326m held, rising to £1722m issued but only £390m held (the figures for October 1971 were : £83m issued and £77m held).[23] For the secondary market made by the discount houses, the entry into the C.D. market of an influence as powerful as that represented by the clearing banks could be a cause for concern. As a protection against increases in the rate structure, secondary market dealers could be expected to raise their quotations for large issues of a particular usance.

THE THEORETICAL BASIS OF MONETARY CONTROL

The Competition and Credit Control scheme, together with the reasons put forward for its introduction, was examined in the previous chapter in some detail. It is beyond the scope of the present work to make an overall assessment of this approach to monetary control but a few general observations will be in order as an introduction to an analysis of implications for the discount houses' role.

It was indicated earlier that because of official statements made at the time of the introduction of the new scheme and because of pressures known to have been exerted by the I.M.F., the view was taken by some commentators that the authorities had, to some extent at least, embraced the principles of 'monetarism'. Others, however, saw in the prominence given to the structure of interest rates in the control process a new flowering of the rival 'credit' approach to monetary policy, and close parallels were drawn with the position adopted twelve years earlier by the Radcliffe Committee. Still others noted elements from both schools and concluded that the ambiguity present in official explanations of the scheme's theoretical basis indicated a desire on the authorities' part to reserve to themselves maximum room for manœuvre. In fact, the introduction of Competition and Credit Control was a move that represented two aspects of official thinking : (1) it demonstrated the acceptance by the authorities of Radcliffe monetary theory, with the implication that the *availability* of credit to the economy would be regulated through manipulation of the structure of interest rates; (2) it recognised the importance of ending discriminatory and economically inefficient forms of monetary control.

That Radcliffe was indeed the basis of the new scheme, despite appearances to the contrary, can be argued as follows.[24] First, empirical evidence for Britain did not indicate to the authorities that the conditions necessary for the implementation of monetarist policy, that is in terms of the exogeneity of the money supply, and the stability of money supply multipliers and money demand functions, did in fact exist. Secondly, evidence pointed to the superiority of changes in bank lending rather than money supply in explaining changes in aggregate demand. These empirical findings reflected the existence of market imperfections in the British financial system and caused the authorities to recognise the importance of availability effects in the transmission process.

It will be recalled from Chapter 5 (above), that the Radcliffe Committee argued for control via action on the whole liquidity position by means of changes in the structure of interest rates. These would regulate the availability of credit through influence on lenders (notably the banks) either through changes in capital values of assets held or through the relative stickiness of the rates offered by some intermediaries. The Competition and Credit Control scheme differed in that the concept of liquidity involved was the narrower and more precise one of the liquidity of all designated banks (and finance houses). It was intended that banks' liquidity would be influenced by changes in the structure of interest rates induced by calls for Special Deposits acting upon a common minimum reserve-assets ratio. In turn, changes in banks' liquidity would influence the availability of funds to the economy.

Support is given to this interpretation of the 1971 reforms by the following statement by the Governor of the Bank :

> Rather the intention is to use our control over liquidity, which these instruments [minimum reserve-assets ratio and Special Deposits] will reinforce, to influence the structure of interest rates. The resulting changes in relative rates of return will then induce shifts in the asset portfolios of both the public and the banks. . . . Special Deposits can be used not only to mop up any abnormal excess liquidity, but also to oblige the banking system to seek to dispose of assets not eligible for the liquidity ratio . . . in this way we shall be able to exert, when appropriate, upward pressure on interest rates – not only rates in the interbank market but also rates in the local authority market and yields on short-term gilt-edged stock.[25]

The 1971 changes in the structure of banking in Britain were also important in the related context of the debate over the relationship between banks and non-bank financial intermediaries. In this debate the 'New View' of money, advanced by J. G. Gurley, E. S. Shaw and J. Tobin, saw all financial intermediaries, including banks, as fundamentally similar credit creating institutions, each producing its own distinctive form of financial asset; the apparent differences between banks and non-bank financial intermediaries (N.B.F.I.) arising only from the controls to which the banks alone were subject.[26] It was in their attack on this position that J. H. Gutentag and R. Lindsay attempted to re-establish the uniqueness of commercial banks on the grounds that the liabilities of banks alone constituted means of payment. Because N.B.F.I. held their reserves in the form of bank deposits their credit creating capacity, though qualitatively similar to that of the banks, was necessarily quantitatively such smaller. Banks and N.B.F.I. thus operated on different credit tiers.[27]

In the context of the British financial system between, say, 1951 and 1971, when only the clearing banks operated subject to lending ceilings and the interest-rate cartel, N.B.F.I. were able, by charging realistically high rates on loans and offering realistically high rates on deposits, to cause holders of bank deposits to switch into assets provided by N.B.F.I.[28] While the change of ownership of bank deposits would not reduce the nominal stock, it would do two things : (1) increase N.B.F.I. reserves, N.B.F.I. credit and therefore total credit and aggregate demand; (2) the resulting increase in the price level would reduce the real value of bank deposits in line with the demand. Consequently, in order to preclude this inflationary influence it was necessary that the clearing banks should be made more competitive by the removal of discriminatory controls and the abolition of restrictive practices. The 1971 scheme of control was accordingly common to a very wide range of designated banks and finance houses. The incentive for the clearing banks themselves to be competitive and thus to maintain public demand for their deposits lay in the need to prevent the reduction through inflation of the real value of bank deposits and, by the same token, of banks' assets and therefore profits.[29]

THE DISCOUNT HOUSES' ROLE IN THE CONTROL MECHANISM

The way in which the discount houses were affected by the introduction of the new scheme had both a 'competition' aspect and a 'control' aspect, as noted earlier. It was the authorities' intention that while the houses should have maximum freedom to compete, their operations should not, through the enhanced importance of the call-money market, be allowed to undermine the authorities' arrangements for the control of the banking system.

The most obvious change was that cartel and convention in discount houses' operations were abandoned in parallel with reforms taking place elsewhere. Nevertheless, because of the importance attached to the maintenance of this key channel for monetary influence, the houses were to continue their accustomed activities in Treasury bills and money, while the Bank would continue to lend at last resort to the banking system only through members of the L.D.M.A.[30]

The development of the Bank's lending policy towards the discount houses was traced in some detail in Chapter 7. There was a further step forward in October 1971 when the Bank began to make available to the houses limited borrowing facilities which the houses, in the light of their individual competitive positions, could exercise at their discretion. The use of the facilities and the rate of interest charged to the houses were to be regarded as confidential as between the Bank and the house concerned. It was not intended that the introduction of these facilities should in any way inhibit the Bank's ability to require the houses to borrow in the traditional manner, either as an act of monetary policy or as a technical smoothing operation in money market management.[31]

Following the replacement of Bank rate by a minimum lending rate which was determined by a formula that related it to the Treasury bill rate, the operations of the houses at the weekly tender assumed a new importance. It was noted in the appendix to Chapter 12 that in Bank of England orthodoxy a rise in Treasury bill rate would be brought about by forcing the discount houses to borrow at last resort at a penal rate. After the introduction of the new rules the Bank was free to determine, day by day, prices at which it would be prepared to deal in Treasury bills. In September 1972 the Bank made known its use of a technique whereby an increase in its mid-week dealing rates for Treasury bills was to be interpreted as a definite signal to the houses that a higher pattern of interest rates was officially desired.[32] Such a signal had first been made in June 1972 and it is likely that the sharp rise in the Treasury bill rate in September was the direct result of another deliberate signal. In addition to this indirect way of influencing the Treasury bill rate and thereby the minimum lending rate after October 1972, the Bank retained powers to make arbitrary changes in minimum lending rate according to the needs of the situation (an example of this was given above).

Because money at call, or at least callable, with members of the discount market was to qualify without limit as a reserve asset for banks, the discount houses were involved in the creation of reserve assets. It was in an attempt to avoid the difficulties potentially raised that the authorities imposed the 50 per cent public-sector ratio and sought undertakings from the houses with regard to the 'window dressing' of banks' balance sheets.

The importance of the discount houses as creators of reserve assets was compounded in that the houses' public-sector ratio differed in size and composition from the reserve ratio of the banks. In principle, where reserve ratios of different sizes are in operation extra credit-creating capacity can be generated by the transfer of reserves to the institutions with the lower reserve ratios. Where ratios differ in composition a similar result can be obtained by switching assets between institutions until they are optimally placed. Even if, after 1971, discount houses had been required to maintain the same *kind* of reserve assets as the banks, it would have been possible to create excess reserves by means of transactions which, for example, led to the houses holding more gilts with less than a year to maturity and the banks an equivalent amount of extra call money. Because only half of the houses' extra gilts would have to be kept as reserves against call money the rest would constitute excess reserves. In addition, however, the discount houses were allowed a *wider range* of reserve assets than the banks, for example gilts with up to five years to maturity. In this case the houses could take the gilts from the banks in exchange for assets which were eligible as reserves with the banks. Any such transactions would result in excess reserves being created. The houses would, however, be inhibited from taking the process too far because of the dangers involved in increasing their holdings of longer-dated debt, during periods of rising interest rates.

In general, and within their public-sector ratio constraint, the houses were enabled to take call money from the banks and by investing it in assets which though they were not eligible reserve assets could be used as security on loans, to convert those assets from non-reserve into reserve assets. Examples of such assets, apart from the gilts mentioned above, would be C.D.s, commercial bills not eligible at the Bank (some bank bills and all trade bills) and local authority bonds and stocks. The high level of the houses' activity in these assets after September 1971 was noted earlier.

Under the 'control' aspect of Competition and Credit Control it was intended that as the relevant institutions began to press upon their reserve ratios they would take appropriate action to curb the growth of the supply of credit. Consequently the next step will be to trace out the implications of a situation in which both the discount houses and the banks found themselves under pressure from their respective ratios.

Logically the pressure could be relieved by the institutions either increasing their holdings of assets eligible for the reserve ratios or by reducing their holdings of non-reserve assets.[33] For the discount houses the latter would be the more likely course because of the problems involved in acquiring additional public-sector assets, for example the situation of excess demand for Treasury bills, and the inadvisability of taking on two-to-five-year gilts at a time of stringency when the generality of dealers would be selling. The houses could instead reduce the extent of their non-reserve asset holdings, for example by running off or selling in the secondary market C.D.s and commercial bills. Because this action would reduce the overall size of portfolios, call money would have to be repaid to the banks. Consequently a reduction in reserve assets for the banks would be involved, just at a time when their own reserve ratios would be under pressure.

For their own part the banks as a whole would seek to relieve the pressure in a manner which would not involve : (*a*) a reduction in their profitable advances business (though this would be the solution looked for by the authorities); (*b*) large gilt-edged sales, which would bring capital losses on a falling market. Rather they would attempt to increase both their eligible liabilities and reserve-asset holdings. If the new deposits for the banks were to provide the corresponding reserve assets, the funds would have to come ultimately from the public sector or the overseas sector.[34] Otherwise, and leaving aside the option of inter-bank sales of C.D.s, which would increase deposits but drive down reserve ratios, the funds would come from the discount houses. By selling C.D.s to the houses and returning the funds as call money, banks could increase both deposits and reserve assets. The conflict between discount houses and banks would arise because banks would be attempting to increase call money, and thereby worsen the houses' public-sector ratio, just at a time when houses would be trying to escape the squeeze by reducing call money.[35] The houses could thus be forced into reducing their holdings of C.D.s in a situation in which banks would be issuing new C.D.s. The effect would be to increase the rate of interest on C.D.s and to reduce the rate on call money, thus discouraging the banks from holding call money. In parallel, the houses would have to bid up for Treasury bills in order to force down the yield and thus make them less attractive to the banks.

The yield differentials thus produced by the conflict could bring about a perverse reaction from the point of view of credit control. First, unless banks were to increase their rate on advances as fast as the rate on C.D.s, the broader (M3) version of the money supply and the quantity of bank lending would grow as funds were borrowed to be re-invested profitably in C.D.s – as, for example, took place during June and July 1972. To minimise this effect the authorities would have to ensure, by means of changes in minimum lending rate, that banks' base rates were increased as necessary. Second, upward pressure on the money supply would also occur as the yield differential opened up between private-sector paper (C.D.s) and public-sector assets (Treasury bills, local authority bills, local authority bonds and stocks). The extent of the transfer of funds by arbitrage from the public to the private sector, and therefore the effect on M3, would depend upon the extent to which the assets were held by non-bank private-sector holders. In this respect, transfers out of local authority paper would tend to be more important than transfers out of Treasury bills, as the eligibility rules seemed to recognise.

The above analysis is given added significance by the fact that the authorities were ultimately to recognise the inadequacies of the public-sector ratio, as a check on the activities of the discount houses in the new scheme of control, by abolishing it in July 1973.[36] The effects of this move will be examined in the next chapter.

15   The Changing Discount Market

INTRODUCTION

The authorities operated Competition and Credit Control unchanged for barely two years before the introduction, in 1973–4, of significant modifications to the mechanism of control. For the discount houses the changes involved abandonment of their 50 per cent public-sector ratio, while for the banks a supplementary credit-control scheme was devised whereby pressure would be exerted on the liabilities, rather than the assets, side of their balance sheets.

CHANGES IN ARRANGEMENTS
FOR CONTROLLING THE DISCOUNT MARKET

With effect from 19 July 1973 the authorities dropped the public-sector ratio requirement for the discount houses and replaced it with :

> a control which limits aggregate holdings of certain assets by each house to a maximum of twenty times its capital and reserves. These are all assets other than those defined as public sector assets for the purpose of the discarded 50 per cent ratio. Allied to this limit there is the continuing requirement that the size of each house's total business should bear an appropriate relationship to its capital and reserves. This overall limit reinforces the twenty times multiplier in restricting the creation of reserve assets through the discount market.[1]

The reasons given by the Bank for the removal of the 50 per cent requirement lend significance to the critical analysis of this method of control advanced in Chapter 14 (above). For the Bank it '. . . tended to complicate the Bank's task of securing adequate influence over credit extended by the discount market, and produced distortions in short-term money markets.' The crux of the problem lay in the practical disadvantages which arose from the dichotomy drawn between eligible and non-eligible assets for the houses' ratio. Where a house had no significant margin over its reserve requirement it could take on additional non-public-sector paper only if it could acquire an almost equal amount of eligible public-sector assets. The Bank came to recognise that, as argued in the previous chapter, public-sector assets were thereby put at a premium and the rates for them driven down relative to rates on other assets. Further, the yield gap between public-sector and non-public-sector paper was forced open even wider at times when the Bank relieved a cash shortage in the market by purchasing quantities of Treasury or local authority bills. Pressing close upon their ratios the houses would either dispose of other assets, so further raising their yield, or would bid up for public-sector assets so further reducing their yield. Falling rates on public-sector assets would bring downward pressure on the Treasury bill rate, minimum lending rate and banks' base rates, just at a time, possibly, when other (for example C.D.) rates could be rising. The implications of the yield differentials thus produced were analysed in the final part of Chapter 14 above.[2]

Other practical disadvantages had been found. Certainly, the status of call money as a reserve asset meant that the Bank needed to maintain control over the size of the houses' private-sector portfolio : but control by means of the 50 per cent ratio had proved to be too severe. Fluctuations in the extent of the government's need to finance its borrowing requirement at short term could put the houses' liquidity under unduly heavy pressure. For example, houses under pressure from their ratios and having to respond to market-smoothing purchases of Treasury bills by the Bank, might be forced into greater illiquidity by having to sell off bank bills (private-sector assets, but eligible as collateral for last-resort loans) or to purchase other types of public-sector paper which would not be eligible for last-resort borrowing. In order to avoid such situations the Bank had at times been inhibited from giving 'direct help' to the market by further purchases of Treasury and local authority bills and had completed operations by buying eligible bank bills instead.

It was intended that problems such as these should be precluded by the substitution of the twenty-times multiplier, which gave houses much greater flexibility to meet temporary changes in circumstances. At the same time it was not intended that there should be any easing of credit control, as (*a*) the multiplier in respect of 'non-defined' assets was to be regarded as a maximum rather than as a norm; (*b*) the Bank would watch carefully the relationship between houses' total business and their capital and reserves;[3] (*c*) the normal operation of the market would ensure that houses would maintain a substantial proportion of 'public-sector-ratio assets' in their portfolio[4] and the eligibility rules for last-resort borrowing (against mainly public-sector assets, with a minimum proportion of Treasury bills) would continue to apply.

ADVERSE TRADING CONDITIONS, 1973–4

During the financial year 1973–4 the discount houses again encountered adverse economic conditions, with interest rates rising steeply in a time of rapid monetary expansion. Compared with the position twelve months earlier, the broader version of the money supply, M3, was rising by (equivalent per annum, rounded) 27 per cent in March, 24 per cent in June, 28 per cent in September and December, and falling to 23 per cent in March 1974. In taking action to deal with this high rate of monetary growth the authorities produced large increases in interest rates from July 1973 onwards. The Bank's minimum lending rate fell slightly between January and July 1973, from $8\frac{3}{4}$ per cent to $7\frac{1}{2}$ per cent. It rose to 9 per cent on 20 July and to $11\frac{1}{2}$ per cent on 27 July, at which level it stayed until the third week in October. After a very slight dip over the following month the rate rose dramatically on 13 November as the authorities used their discretionary powers and set it at 13 per cent. There minimum lending rate stayed until the end of 1973, after which it declined steadily to end the financial year at 12 per cent.

The changes in the control arrangements for the discount houses coincided with the July upsurge in interest rates.[5] This sharp increase, brought about by further calls for Special Deposits from the banks, was apparently intended by the authorities as an offset to rising interest rates abroad. Minimum lending rate increased by 4 per cent in the space of two weeks and, as stock exchange yields rose in line, the prices of government stocks fell sharply. The results for the discount houses were disastrous. As noted earlier, the houses had been caught by rising rates in 1972 and had taken action to reduce their book. Whereas at 19 April 1972 the houses had held £453 million of British government stocks, by 13 December holdings had fallen to only £95 million. Nevertheless, during 1973 the houses had substantially rebuilt their books so that by 20 June they stood at £313 million. The latest price falls, therefore, compounded by the scramble to sell off these no-longer-required public sector assets, brought losses which hastened on the general movement out of government stocks. By 12 December 1973 holdings had fallen to a mere £25 million. Throughout 1974 and into 1975 holdings of government stocks remained at a very low level.[6]

There was a parallel movement by the houses out of local authority securities, and holdings of this paper fell from £651 million at 18 July 1973 to £387 million at 12 December, remaining at around this level throughout 1974. In compensation, houses increased aggregate holdings of sterling C.D.s : from £524 million at 18 April 1973 to a peak of £962 million at 21 November, after which holdings fell to the original level by August 1974. Also, the trend in commercial bill holdings was sustainedly upward after October 1973, rising from £514 million to £873 million at 17 April 1974 and £1182 million by 11 December. As the houses substituted private for public-sector assets their new 'undefined assets multiple' rose, from 13·8 at 15 August 1973 to 19·1 at 20 March 1974. Thereafter, it fluctuated at a high level, with a peak of 19·5 at 20 November.[7]

A SUPPLEMENTARY SCHEME FOR CREDIT CONTROL

The changes of July 1973, though of importance in giving the houses greater freedom in the management of their business, involved no significant revision of the scheme of Competition and Credit Control. Similarly, the qualitative guidance advanced by the authorities on bank lending and the protection given to the building societies by the imposition of ceilings on rates for bank deposits (see Chapters 13 and 14), had been provided for from the outset.[8] However, changes of greater substance were introduced in December 1973, when the authorities introduced their supplementary scheme for credit control.[9]

The supplementary scheme was announced on 17 December 1973 and immediately put into operation. It was intended as a standing scheme which the Bank could from time to time withdraw and reintroduce as necessary, to provide control over the operations of banks and deposit-taking finance houses. Control was to be applied on the liabilities side of the banks' balance sheets, to the rate of growth of the interest-bearing part of banks' eligible liabilities. If the banks were to allow interest-bearing eligible liabilities (IBELS) to grow at a rate faster than that officially specified, they would incur a penalty in the form of calls to place non-interest-bearing Supplementary Deposits with the Bank. For the first six months of the scheme the permitted rate of growth for IBELS was 8 per cent, while the amount of Supplementary Deposits was to be calculated by reference to a three months' moving average (for April, May and June 1974) of the growth of a bank's IBELS above their average for the make-up dates of October, November and December 1973. The rate at which Supplementary Deposits would be callable on any excess growth of IBELS was steeply progressive, up to a ceiling of 50 per cent.[10]

The authorities intended that the scheme should act as a restraint on monetary expansion, including the growth of bank lending, without the need : (*a*) for short-term interest rates and bank lending rates to rise to unacceptably high levels; (*b*) to sacrifice the greater freedom enjoyed by the banking system since 1971, by the reintroduction of advances ceilings and interest-rate controls. Although there would be a limit on competition for business, in that each bank would be constrained within roughly the same rate of overall growth, bankers would enjoy the relative freedom to conduct their own business within that constraint.

Also, the whole approach offered greater flexibility for bankers than, for example, a similar scheme in operation in France. There, bankers incurred a penalty if their lending to the private sector exceeded some permissible rate. The British scheme, on the other hand, by imposing control on the rate of growth of interest-bearing eligible *liabilities* allowed bankers greater freedom in arranging their asset portfolios and did not involve an arbitrary distinction between public and private-sector paper. Further, the Bank was free to specify, as circumstances changed, appropriate rates of growth for both IBELS and supplementary deposits. With regard to bank lending, one of the main objects of the scheme was to '. . . encourage banks to relate their lending commitments to a prudent view of the likely availability of funds; and, at times when the scheme is in abeyance, the possibility of its activation should impose some check upon the extension of facilities.'[11]

Because restraint was imposed upon banks in bidding for funds it was hoped to avoid the situation in which money market rates rose steeply relative to banks' lending rates, and borrowing was encouraged for the purpose of arbitrage. Similarly the banks themselves, in a move to discourage arbitrage operations, had decided to gear overdraft rates to market rates rather than to base rates.

In regulating the growth of their IBELS the banks would tend to concentrate on that part of them which consisted of the large deposits bid for on the wholesale sterling markets : this being the more volatile element of interest-bearing deposits. The funds would have come to the banks either on deposit or against the issue of a C.D. and to the extent that they derived from another bank they could be netted out between banks for the purposes of calculating eligible liabilities. This meant, however, that if individual banks were to attempt to reduce their IBELS by running off such funds as they became due for repayment, the banks being repaid would find that the amount of their inter-bank lending which could be used as an offset to their own borrowing would decrease, so that their IBELS would *increase*. Consequently, all banks taken together could not in this way reduce the total of IBELS, though their efforts to do so would bring about some redistribution of holdings and would depress interest rates on the inter-bank market.

Nevertheless a reduction in IBELS could be induced indirectly as, for example, inter-bank rates fell relative to rates offered by local authorities. This would bring about a switch of funds by non-bank lenders away from banks and in favour of local authorities, who would therefore demand less from the banks through the wholesale markets : as bank borrowing and lending fell so would the total of IBELS.

Similarly, in a situation in which banks held excess reserve assets, they could reduce IBELS by taking advantage of the netting-out arrangement for eligible liabilities, either by increasing their lending to banks through the inter-bank market or by attempting to purchase C.D.s from the large holdings in the secondary market, that is from the discount houses and others, even though this could drive down the rate on C.D.s and therefore affect their profitability. The second alter-native could be the more successful from the banks' point of view in that the discount market's large C.D. holdings could accommodate demand from many banks, whereas an attempt by all the banks to increase inter-bank lending would be self-defeating. On the other hand, in paying for the C.D.s with call money the banks would be reducing both the liabilities and assets sides of the discount houses' balance sheet and could therefore meet with resistance from the houses, who would be reluctant to sell.[12]

In fact, in reporting in the June 1974 *Quarterly Bulletin* that the banks had successfully moderated the growth of their IBELS, the Bank considered that this had been achieved by a judicious pruning of the banks' lending to the private sector. In addition, it may well have been that the releases of special deposits by the Bank in antici-pation of large demands for bank loans from industry, in the event un-realised, left the banks with less need to increase their IBELS. Overall, with the exception of a few small banks which from time to time exceeded the permitted IBELS growth rate and were called to make supplementary deposits, banks were generally able to stay inside the limit, which was increased by the authorities, after the second quarter of 1974, at the rate of $1\frac{1}{2}$ per cent per month.

CURRENT DISCOUNT HOUSE OPERATIONS

A visitor to a discount house early in 1975 would find much in the house's activities that would have been familiar in 1965 and 1955. The house would be borrowing and repaying money,[18] mostly on a secured basis, and acting as dealer or broker in a range of private- and

I

public-sector assets, though the number of departments of the house would have multiplied to take account of the ever-increasing variety of business. Business done over the telephone would have increased compared to business done through personal contact and the telephone system itself would have become more advanced in terms of efficiency and ease of use for the dealers. Though now calling on a smaller number of banks, the house's representatives would be making their morning rounds ('walks') as before, wearing the traditional silk hat. Beneath their City suits, however, the representatives might now be sporting a light-weight harness bearing a two-way short-wave radio, by means of which the latest nuances of market movements would be instantly communicated between houses and representatives.[14]

Of the present-day discount houses' more 'traditional' business, that in Treasury bills (apart from the abandonment of collective tendering) is carried on as before, while for bills of exchange houses continue to judge quality, quote rates of discount and assume liability on parcels sold to customers. On the gilt-edged book dealing will currently tend to be on an in-and-out basis for quick jobbing profits, with holding kept to a minimum. Of the assets traded on the complementary markets, enough has been said in earlier chapters about local authority bills and bonds but a few further points can be made about operations in C.D.s (see Table 4).

Houses do not issue C.D.s but they play a crucial role in making a secondary market, establishing the negotiability of C.D.s by standing ready to quote buying and selling rates. In this, they enjoy the support of the Bank and are encouraged by the issuing banks, with whom stand-by agreements have been concluded so as to ensure continued marketability of C.D.s during times of market weakness. Apart from quoting 'two-way' rates for buyers and sellers of C.D.s, houses will take a view on rates and deal for their own portfolios. Finally, if an investor of liquid funds does not wish to approach an issuing bank directly, in the primary market, he will buy in the secondary market – either from or through a discount house. If the house has suitable C.D.s in portfolio it will act as a dealer, selling direct to the client. On the other hand the house could act as a broker, approaching an issuing bank on behalf of a client who wishes to remain anonymous or who does not himself wish to contact all the issuing banks with a view to obtaining the best quotation.[15]

Discount houses undertake the same sort of operations in dollar C.D.s except that they finance their portfolio with U.S. dollars borrowed in the Euro-dollar market. Again they are encouraged by the issuing banks, for whom the houses can tap a multitude of sources of funds for investment in C.D.s. At the beginning of 1974 more than

130 banks in London were issuing dollar C.D.s,[16] and C.D.s outstanding amounted to about 10 per cent of the estimated size of the Euro-dollar market, or more than $9000 million. The secondary market in dollar C.D.s consists of the thirteen members – of which discount houses form nine[17] – of the International C.D. Market Association (I.C.D.M.A.), plus a number of other dealers. Membership of the I.C.D.M.A., which was formed in 1967, involves a number of obligations – in particular to make firm buying and selling prices to customers, on a net basis without brokerage.

CHANGES IN DISCOUNT MARKET STRUCTURE

As a complement to the increasing range of business undertaken over the years, the discount market underwent a number of changes in its structure. Looking back to the early 1930s, for purposes of comparison, the market was composed of the following firms :[18]

Public limited companies

Founded
1810   Alexanders Discount Co. Ltd
1856   National Discount Co. Ltd
1885   Union Discount Company of London Ltd

Private limited companies
1908   Cater and Co. Ltd
1925   Fairfax and Co. (Ltd from 1930)
1867   Gillett Bros Discount Co. Ltd
1859   Reeves, Witburn and Co. Ltd
1891   Smith St Aubyn and Co. (Ltd from 1931)

Private companies with unlimited liability
or partnerships
1888   Allen, Harvey and Ross and Co.
1895   William P. Bonbright and Co.
1860   Brightwen and Co.
1924   Brocklebank, Hoare and Brown
1819   Roger Cunliffe, Sons and Co.
1913   Daniell Cazenove and Co.
1820   Hohler and Co.
1922   Jessel Toynbee and Co.
1914   Jones and Brown
1886   King and Shaxson
1866   Lyon and Tucker

1903   Ryder Parker and Co.
1922   Seccombe, Marshall and Campion
1901   Henry Sherwood and Co.

The effects of the economic problems of the 1930s and of the war years (see above, Chapters 3 and 4) wrought considerable changes in the structure of the discount market. By 1945 eleven houses with discount accounts at the Bank remained, of which five were public companies, five were private companies and one was a partnership :

The public companies
Alexanders Discount Co. Ltd
Jessel, Toynbee and Co. Ltd
National Discount Co. Ltd
Smith St Aubyn and Co. Ltd
Union Discount Company of London Ltd

The private companies
Allen, Harvey and Ross Ltd
Cater Brightwen and Co. Ltd
Gillett Brothers Discount Co. Ltd
King and Shaxson Ltd
Ryders Discount Co. Ltd

The partnership
Seccombe, Marshall and Campion

In 1946 a new house, Clive Discount Co. Ltd, was formed as a private company. Discount facilities were obtained at the Bank and trading was commenced in 1947. Seccombe, Marshall and Campion, who had traded as a partnership since their foundation in 1922, became a private limited company in 1947. The existing private companies, apart from Ryders Discount Co. Ltd, became public companies. Ryders became public in 1954 as did Seccombe, Marshall and Campion in 1956 and Clive Discount in 1959.[19]

The number of houses in the market increased from twelve to thirteen when Gerrard and Reid Ltd, a private company that had been operating as a running broker and had recently substantially increased its capital, was granted a discount account at the Bank early in 1960. However, the number was shortly afterwards reduced to twelve again when Cater Brightwen and Co. Ltd and Ryders Discount Co. Ltd merged to form Cater Ryder and Co. Ltd, one of the largest houses in the market. In 1962 the L.D.M.A. became an association composed entirely of public companies when Gerrard and Reid, the last private company, achieved public status.

In 1969 the takeover of Gerrard and Reid by National Discount reduced membership of the L.D.M.A. to eleven. There, it was widely supposed, matters would stand but in September 1972 the Bank granted a discount account to Norman and Bennet who thus became members of the Association. Norman and Bennet, a partnership trading as a running broker, made their membership of the L.D.M.A. possible by increasing their capital to £1 million – the minimum capital required by the Bank.

This they did by bringing in an outside backer in the shape of an investment holding company, Wood Hall Trust. This company owned 70 per cent of Norman and Bennet – a situation which raised queries about outsider control as, broadly speaking, the unwritten rule had been that discount houses could not be owned by outsiders. Only a few weeks before, Clive Discount had decided to merge with an eastern trading company, Sime Darby. There was, however, no formal notification that the Bank's policy in this matter had changed. In July 1974 Norman and Bennet merged with Jessel, Toynbee and Co. Ltd.

It was shown in Chapter 11 that as the discount houses extended their activities into the parallel money markets, some of them did so through subsidiaries. Clive Discount obtained controlling interests in both Guy Butler and Co. Ltd, a firm of brokers in the inter-bank and currency deposit markets, at the end of 1965, and Long, Till and Colvin Ltd, brokers in the local authority market. Gerrard and Reid took a small interest in P. Murray-Jones Ltd, a firm broking in the inter-bank, local authority and foreign exchange markets.

With the appearance of dollar certificates of deposit in London in 1966 one house, Cater Ryder, decided not to deal as principals in C.D.s[20] Instead, in February 1967 they took over a firm of brokers in foreign exchange and currency deposits, M. W. Marshall and Co., and shortly afterwards spread their activities into the local authority, finance house and inter-bank markets through the formation of a wholly-owned subsidiary Cater (Brokers) Ltd.

Other examples of houses which chose to engage in broking through subsidiaries included : Union Discount, who took a controlling interest in Roberts Union Co. Ltd, brokers in the local authority, inter-bank and foreign currency deposit markets; Jessel, Toynbee, who acquired a substantial interest in Charles Fulton and Co. Ltd, brokers in the inter-bank deposit and currency deposit markets; and Packshaw Associates, brokers in the local authority markets. Some houses also acquired interests abroad. The most striking example is Cater Ryder, with subsidiaries in the United States, Canada, Australia and Europe. A fuller picture of discount houses' activities both as traders and brokers acting through subsidiaries in the various London short-term markets is given in Table 11.

IN JUSTIFICATION OF THE DISCOUNT HOUSES

It has become customary when writing about the discount houses to include a few paragraphs in justification of the houses' continued existence.[21] Apart from a summary of the functions performed by the houses, writers have tended to rely ultimately on the idea that although the houses are not indispensable, they perform their functions cheaply and efficiently and that in their absence the functions would have to be performed by other institutions. Frequently couched in rather defensive and apologetic terms, these arguments in support have generally failed to identify, or at least to emphasise, the nature of the forces responsible for the situation they seek to justify.

Justification of the customary kind can, indeed, be found in the present volume, the layout of which is designed to provide an analysis of the discount houses' operations and role in each of the various markets and to give prominence to the part they play in the monetary control process. In addition, however, it has been argued in previous chapters that, over the years, the position occupied by the discount houses in the financial system, their business and the manner in which they have performed it, have all to a large extent been determined by the cartelised nature of the British banking system. The restrictive practices of the clearing banks, condoned and encouraged by the Bank of England in pursuit of its own public goals, were the original cause of the houses entering into restrictive agreements, both between themselves and with the clearing banks (see above, Chapters 3 and 13). Any evaluation of the 'usefulness' of the discount houses' functions must, therefore, start from this premise.

Further, a distinction must be drawn between : (1) the discount houses, i.e. profit-making limited liability companies, operating on commercial principles; (2) the discount market, which represents a fusion of the London markets for money, bills and short-term bonds in the activities of the discount houses. The discount market is now known as the traditional market, in contrast to the newer complementary markets. The key point is, however, that there would have been no separate 'parallel' or 'complementary' system if the clearing banks and the discount houses had not been subject to such close regulation and restriction. The discount market would instead have developed and grown freely, as the discount houses sought new business and adapted their services to meet changing needs and to encompass innovation.

Doubtless the pressures of competition would have caused houses to amalgamate more readily or even to withdraw from business, but it is arguable that the discount market as a whole would have been a more dynamic, responsive and efficient institution. Instead, the Bank of England, at whose bronze doors the ultimate responsibility must be laid, chose to sacrifice free market development in order to ensure that its own public responsibilities were discharged. The contentious points upon which the Bank based its choice, for example the shape and stability of the demand curves for Treasury bills and gilt-edged securities, have already been dealt with.

For the thirty years prior to 1971 the houses were to some extent feather-bedded by the nature of the system in which they had to operate. Inter-house competition was at a minimum and the only major shocks came from unanticipated increases in Bank rate. The advent of Competition and Credit Control, although it guaranteed the continued existence of the discount houses in their familiar form, was important not only because it speeded the reunification of markets, traditional and complementary, which need never have grown apart; but also because it dispelled the idea that the discount houses were inherently cosy and traditionalist institutions the existence of which commentators felt the need to justify.

TABLES AND FIGURES

TABLE 1 Items from discount companies' summary balance sheets, selected years, 1890–1966 (£ millions) (Alexanders, National and Union Discount Companies)

Year ending 31 Dec	Capital and reserves	Bills rediscounted	Total liabilities	Bills discounted		Investments	
				Total	Treasury bills	Total	Brit. govt and govt-guaranteed
1890	2·8	13·0	38·6	31·2	–	3·8	2
1900	3·0	9·2	40·9	30·7	4	5·0	2
1913	3·4	16·0	66·8	58·3	3	4·9	2
1918	3·8	15·1	79·3	64·0	32	8·7	4
1930	7·0	40·5	147·3	125·6	89	17·2	14
1935	7·0	25·5	147·5	101·8	63	37·7	33
1938	7·9	19·4	152·6	123·7	73	21·3	18
1945	9·5	8·4	311·6	240·2	204	64·0	60
1951	16·5	65·7	566·6	342·3	311	214·3	203
1954	23·4	59·0	656·2	365·9	340	264·2	254
1957	18·4	55·2	553·8	365·1	319	158·4	148
1961	22·3	58·3	676·5	409·3	303	245·8	241
1966	24·5	67·4	729·6	389·9	253	306·3	198

Notes:

(1) Figures taken from Table (A) 1.13 in D. K. Sheppard, *The Growth and Role of U.K. Financial Institutions, 1880–1962* (London, 1971), pp. 138–9.

(2) Due to changes in accounting procedures the figures for total liabilities no longer include certain items (bills rediscounted and rebates) from 1943.

(3) All figures for Treasury bills and government-guaranteed holdings are estimates.

TABLE 2   Bill circulation, 1922–37 (estimated yearly averages)

Financial year	Commercial bills		Treasury bills (issued by tender)	Total	Average Treasury bill rate %
	Inland drawn	Foreign drawn			
1922–3	188	241	490	919	2·3
1923–4	199	281	466	946	2·9
1924–5	218	365	456	1039	3·6
1925–6	218	415	466	1099	4·3
1926–7	191	302	501	994	4·5
1927–8	193	315	502	1010	4·2
1928–9	198	365	505	1068	4·3
1929–30	202	317	512	1031	5·0
1930–1	172	268	467	907	2·3
1931–2	142	186	485	813	4·0
1932–3	111	136	571	818	0·9
1933–4	111	134	558	803	0·6
1934–5	119	134	443	696	0·6
1935–6	121	138	505	764	0·6
1936–7	133	143	580	856	0·6

Source: T. Balogh, *Studies in Financial Organisation* (Cambridge, 1950) p. 202.

TABLE 3   Sources of discount houses' borrowed funds, 1951–74 (excluding capital and reserves)

Year ending 31 Dec	Total	Bank of England Banking Dept		London clearing banks		Scottish banks		Overseas and foreign banks / Other deposit banks		Other sources / Accepting houses, overseas, other banks		Other U.K. residents		Overseas residents		Currency U.K. banks		Currency Other		A Total assets held	B Total assets minus borrowed funds	B expressed as percentage of A
	£m	£m	%	£m	%	£m	%	£m	%	£m	%	£m	%	£m	%	£m	%	£m	%	£m	£m	%
1951	992	5	0·5	555	55·9	69	7·0	247	24·9	116	11·7									1031	39	3·8
1952	1028	5	0·5	495	48·2	77	7·5	340	35·1	111	10·8									1067	39	3·7
1953	1043	–	–	459	43·8	80	7·6	395	37·7	114	10·9									1085	37	3·4
1954	1051	50	4·8	452	43·0	74	7·0	345	32·8	131	12·5									1090	39	3·6
1955	1014	58	5·7	459	45·3	80	7·9	257	25·3	160	15·8									1068	54	5·1
1956	909	34	3·7	454	49·9	78	8·6	212	23·3	132	14·5									954	45	4·7
1957	903	11	1·2	474	52·5	75	8·3	201	22·3	142	15·7									956	53	5·5
1958	1007	8	0·8	519	51·5	85	8·4	263	26·1	131	13·0									1053	46	4·4
1959	1077	28	2·6	544	50·5	87	8·1	256	23·8	162	15·0									1130	53	4·7
1960	1139	34	3·0	631	55·4	90	7·9	244	21·4	140	12·3									1197	58	4·8
1961	1153	28	2·4	675	58·5	89	7·7	232	20·1	130	11·3									1216	63	5·2
1962	1186	8	0·7	706	59·5	97	8·2	234	19·7	140	11·8									1251	65	5·2
1963	1232	4	0·3	688	55·8	100	8·1	14	1·1	265	21·5	162	13·1							1305	73	5·6
1964	1205	25	2·1	705	58·5	87	7·2	17	1·4	240	19·9	132	11·0							1283	78	6·1
1965	1381	34	2·5	849	61·5	124	9·0	21	1·5	242	17·5	111	8·0							1455	74	5·1
1966	1484	82	5·5	978	65·9	94	6·3	11	0·7	201	13·5	119	8·0							1565	81	5·2
1967	1662	116	7·0	1076	64·7	102	6·1	21	1·3	218	13·1	130	7·8							1747	85	4·9
1968	1573	–	–	1132	72·0	100	6·4	15	0·9	204	13·0	121	7·7							1663	90	5·4
1969	1725	–	–	1304	75·6	98	5·7	12	0·7	202	11·7	109	6·3							1817	92	5·1
1970	2259	–	–	1407	62·3	108	4·8	29	1·3	510	22·6	204	9·0							2352	93	4·0
1971	2961	76	2·6	1241	41·9	88	3·0	43	1·5	1116	37·7	346	11·7	51	1·7	92	3·6	38	1·5	3066	104	3·4
1972	2530	–	–	1020	40·3	130	5·1	57	2·3	936	37·0	305	12·1	81	3·2	72	2·5	23	0·8	2618	88	3·4
1973	2567	–	–	1179	46·0	178	7·0	63	2·5	861	33·5	135	5·3	22	0·9					2621	54	2·1
1974	2916	–	–	1220	41·8	164	5·6	97	3·3	1135	38·9	177	6·1	28	1·0					3026	110	3·6

Source: computed from *Bank of England Statistical Abstract*, no. 1 (1970) and *Bank of England Quarterly Bulletin* (1971–5).

Notes:
(1) Figures for borrowed funds exclude capital and reserves, which are calculated at the right-hand side of the table as a percentage of the total portfolio.
(2) 'Overseas and foreign banks' are the offices in the United Kingdom of banks whose main business is conducted abroad. Figures after 1958 differ slightly in coverage from those for earlier years; this difference is also reflected in the figures for other sources.
(3) One new contributor is included from 18 October 1972.
(4) Before August 1973, currency borrowing was included in sterling borrowing. Other currency borrowing is almost wholly from overseas residents.
(5) 'Other deposit banks' include Northern Ireland banks and the National Giro.
(6) Broken line between rows indicates figures above and below not strictly comparable.

TABLE 4 Assets of the London discount houses as a percentage of total resources employed (borrowed funds plus capital resources 1951–74)

End of year	Total	British gov stocks £m	%	British gov Treasury bills £m	%	Other sterling bills £m	%	Local authority securities £m	%	Negotiable certificates of deposit £ £m	%	Negotiable certificates of deposit $ £m	%	Other £m	%
1951	1031	314	30·5	624	60·5	63	6·1							31	3·0
1952	1067	291	27·3	702	65·8	42	3·9							32	3·0
1953	1085	383	35·3	606	55·9	49	4·5							47	4·3
1954	1090	373	34·2	618	56·7	47	4·3							53	4·9
1955	1068	307	28·7	652	61·0	45	4·2							63	5·9
1956	954	294	30·8	523	54·8	85	9·0							53	5·6
1957	956	223	23·3	585	61·2	84	8·8							64	6·7
1958	1053	321	30·5	594	56·4	70	6·6							68	6·5
1959	1130	322	28·5	635	56·2	118	10·4							56	4·9
1960	1197	440	36·8	574	48·0	117	9·8							67	5·6
1961	1216	449	36·9	533	43·9	183	15·0							52	4·3
1962	1251	488	39·0	502	40·1	189	15·1							72	5·8
1963	1305	442	33·9	529	40·5	249	19·1	17	1·3					67	5·1
1964	1283	438	34·1	453	35·3	302	23·5	39	3·0					51	4·0
1965	1455	500	34·4	484	33·3	339	23·3	67	4·6					65	4·5
1966	1565	542	34·6	424	27·1	404	25·8	101	6·5					95	6·1
1967	1747	544	31·1	548	31·4	437	25·0	115	6·6			14	0·8	89	5·1
1968	1663	306	18·4	471	28·3	560	33·7	148	8·9	56	3·4	39	2·3	83	5·0
1969	1817	364	20·0	399	22·0	629	34·6	192	10·6	97	5·3	31	1·7	104	5·7
1970	2352	160	6·8	876	37·2	697	29·6	224	9·5	268	11·4	39	1·7	88	3·7

End of year	Total	British gov stocks £m	%	British gov Treasury bills £m	%	Other public sector bills £m	%	Other sterling bills £m	%	Local authority securities £m	%	Sterling C.D.s £m	%	Sterling balances with U.K. banks £m	%	Other sterling assets £m	%	U.S. dollar C.D.s £m	%	Other currency assets £m	%
1971	3066	391	12·8	871	28·4	120	3·9	466	15·2	478	15·6	457	14·9	27	0·9	148	4·8	108	3·5	„	
1972	2618	112	4·3	475	18·1	116	4·4	449	17·2	636	24·3	458	17·5	70	2·7	149	5·7	153	5·8	„	
1973	2621	48	1·8	321	12·2	94	3·6	590	22·5	379	14·5	922	35·2	59	2·3	80	3·1	113	4·3	16	0·6
1974	3026	10	0·3	729	24·1	181	6·0	1189	39·3	344	11·4	395	13·1	15	0·5	68	2·2	86	2·8	9	0·3

Source: computed from *Bank of England Statistical Abstract*, no. 1 (1970) and *Bank of England Quarterly Bulletin* (1971–5).

Notes:
(1) Negotiable certificates of deposit: U.S. Dollar C.D.s first issued May 1966; sterling C.D.s, October 1968.
(2) 'Other sterling bills' consist mainly of commercial bills drawn on banks and firms resident in the U.K., and on the London offices of overseas banks. The maximum maturity is not ordinarily longer than six months. Treasury bills of the Northern Ireland government and bills issued by local authorities are also included.
(3) British government stocks are shown at nominal value and are mostly within five years of their final date of maturity.
(4) 'Other assets' include foreign currency bills and a small amount of cash in hand and at the banks; before June 1963 local authority securities were also included here.
(5) Before August 1973 other currency assets were included in sterling balances with U.K. banks or other sterling assets.
(6) The figures include a new contributor from 18 October 1972.

TABLE 5 Bank of England intervention in the money market: January 1 1951 to June 20 1973

	FREQUENCY OF INTERVENTION				AMOUNT OF INTERVENTION ($£$ m.)			
		Assistance given					Assistance given	
Year	No intervention	At or above Bank rate	Other	Surpluses absorbed by sales of Treasury bills	Advances at or above Bank rate	Other advances	Purchases of Treasury bills	Surpluses absorbed by sales of Treasury bills
1951	137	–	133	28	–	21·4	1410·3	222·0
1952	101	–	192	16	–	127·8	2023·7	144·0
1953	95	–	168	43	–	24·3	2008·6	403·0
1954	135	17	144	21	96·8	–	1566·2	226·2
1955	117	93	143	17	508·4	–	1562·9	158·4
1956	128	64	131	24	310·4	–	1579·7	284·9
1957	131	77	148	6	337·4	–	1772·9	70·8
1958	106	92	172	11	413·3	–	2320·8	158·8
1959	108	48	156	18	177·3	–	1696·3	195·5
1960	93	53	179	24	248·4	–	2428·0	310·2
1961	83	66	169	40	484·9	–	3204·0	489·5
1962	74	63	182	36	445·7	–	3720·5	450·7
1963	61	50	188	42	398·5	–	3899·1	470·4
1964	65	7	220	24	57·5	–	5030·4	300·9
1965	72	49	180	41	560·9	–	4591·9	768·4
1966	43	45	201	49	574·9	691·8	4468·2	893·9

(continued overleaf)

TABLE 5 (*continued from overleaf*)

Year	FREQUENCY OF INTERVENTION				AMOUNT OF INTERVENTION (£ m.)				
	No intervention	Assistance given — At or above Bank rate	Other	Surpluses absorbed by sales of Treasury bills	Advances at or above Bank rate	Assistance given — Other advances	Assistance given — Purchases of Treasury bills		Surpluses absorbed by sales of Treasury bills
							Treasury bills	Other bills	
1967	24	56	256	18	1297·8	5709·3	6376·9		506·3
1968	26	—	249	28	—	6477·0	5167·5		457·8
1969	53	—	149	81	—	183·0	3302·7	279·5	1475·3
1970						—			
1971	42	23 (*Last resort lending*)	181	68	966·2 (*Last resort lending*)	—	5750·4	403·6	2417·5
1972	52	23	140	54	938·0	—	5162·8	620·0	1708·3
1973	16	37	87	17	1424·6	—	2916·9	1022·7	623·8

Source: Bank of England Quarterly Bulletin.

Notes:

(1) The frequency of intervention refers to the number of working days on which intervention of one kind or another took place in the period. The total of days shown will not necessarily add to the number of working days in a given period, as more than one kind of intervention may have occurred on a particular day, e.g. the Bank may have both purchased Treasury bills from the market and lent at Bank rate.

(2) Assistance given 'At or above Bank rate' or 'At last resort' includes, where applicable, bills purchased from the discount market at other than normal market rates.

(3) 'Other' assistance given is by advances or purchases of bills at market rates.

(4) Advances are shown in gross terms without taking account of repayments.

(5) The Table was discontinued as from 20 June 1973 due to the fact that 'changes in the nature of the Bank's intervention in the money market in recent years have made it difficult to show these operations helpfully in tabular form'. BEQB (Dec 1973) 482.

TABLE 6 Short-term rates, selected years, 1945–74

End of year	Bank rate	Treasury bills		Commercial bills		Call money	Inter-bank overnight lending	Local authority loans (3 months)	Sterling C.D.s (3 months)
		Average allotment rate	Syndicate tender rate	Prime bank bills	Trade bills				
		(DISCOUNT RATES)				(INTEREST RATES)			
1945	2	0·5022	$\frac{1}{2}$	$1\frac{7}{32}$	$1\text{–}1\frac{1}{2}$	$\frac{1}{2}\text{–}\frac{3}{4}$	–	–	–
1951	$2\frac{1}{2}$	0·9669	$\frac{3}{32}$	$1\frac{1}{2}$	$2\frac{1}{2}\text{–}3\frac{1}{2}$	$\frac{3}{4}\text{–}1\frac{1}{4}$	–	–	–
1955	$4\frac{1}{2}$	4·0725	$4\frac{1}{16}$	$4\frac{3}{16}$	$5\text{–}5\frac{3}{4}$	$2\frac{3}{4}\text{–}4$	–	–	–
1957	7	6·3746	$6\frac{3}{8}$	$6\frac{1}{2}$	$7\frac{1}{4}\text{–}8$	$5\frac{1}{4}\text{–}5\frac{3}{4}$	–	7	–
1960	5	4·3491	$4\frac{3}{8}$	$4\frac{1}{2}$	$5\frac{3}{8}\text{–}6$	$3\frac{3}{8}\text{–}4\frac{5}{8}$	–	$5\frac{1}{8}\text{–}5\frac{1}{4}$	–
1965	6	5·5212	$5\frac{17}{32}$	$5\frac{7}{8}$	$7\text{–}7\frac{1}{2}$	$4\frac{7}{8}\text{–}5\frac{5}{8}$	$5\frac{5}{8}\text{–}5\frac{7}{8}$	$6\frac{3}{8}$	–
1969	8	7·6500	$7\frac{81}{32}$	$8\frac{3}{4}$	$9\frac{1}{4}\text{–}9\frac{3}{4}$	$6\frac{3}{4}\text{–}7\frac{5}{8}$	$2\text{–}7\frac{1}{2}$	$9\text{–}9\frac{1}{16}$	–
Minimum lending rate									
1973	13	12·42	–	14	15	2–13	$12\frac{1}{2}\text{–}35$	$16\frac{1}{16}$	$15\frac{7}{8}$
1974	$11\frac{1}{2}$	10·99	–	$12\frac{25}{32}$	$13\frac{1}{4}$	$2\text{–}9\frac{1}{2}$	$2\text{–}9\frac{1}{2}$	$13\frac{1}{4}$	$12\frac{11}{16}$

Source: Bank of England Quarterly Bulletin.

TABLE 7 Acceptances of accepting houses, overseas banks and other banks in the United Kingdom, 1951–69

End of year	Total (£m)	U.K. residents	Overseas residents
1951	209·0	90·7	109·3
1952	123·2	64·4	54·2
1953	131·4	66·8	59·9
1954	170·0	82·3	82·2
1955	157·6	82·2	70·8
1956	155·2	82·0	71·6
1957	205·8	96·7	106·5
1958	187·5	92·2	93·5
1959	208·5	118·2	89·5
1960	199·7	123·2	76·5
1961	288·1	187·1	101·0
1962	354·2	224·8	129·4
1963	448·8	282·2	166·6
1964	536·1	353·2	182·9
1965	658·1	443·7	214·4
1966	609·1	402·5	206·7
1967	668·8	458·3	210·6
1968	747·8	467·7	280·1
1969	858·0	489·7	368·3

Source: Bank of England Statistical Abstract, no. 1 (1970) Table 10 (1).

Notes:
(1) Totals up to end of December 1959 include acceptances not allocated between U.K. and overseas residents.
(2) Figures for December 1951 are incomplete but the deficiency is unlikely to be substantial.
(3) New contributors are included from 1964 and 1967. Foreign currency items at December 1967 are affected by devaluation of sterling on 18 November 1967.

TABLE 8   Acceptances of Accepting Houses Committee and their banking subsidiaries, 1951–69

End of year	Total (£m)	U.K. residents	Overseas residents
1951	92·7	69·2	23·5
1952	73·0	54·8	18·2
1953	78·7	58·7	20·0
1954	94·6	70·9	23·7
1955	96·5	74·1	22·4
1956	95·7	71·9	23·8
1957	119·4	81·3	38·1
1958	120·6	81·1	39·5
1959	130·6	96·8	33·8
1960	131·8	99·4	32·4
1961	175·7	145·9	29·8
1962	185·9	148·3	37·6
1963	194·2	152·1	42·1
1964	230·8	189·1	41·7
1965	279·1	235·0	44·1
1966	271·2	220·7	50·5
1967	291·1	231·1	60·0
1968	328·5	260·6	67·9
1969	339·8	275·1	64·7

Source: Bank of England Statistical Abstract, no. 1 (1970) Table 10 (2).

TABLE 9   Quotations on the London Stock Exchange
(all securities officially quoted at 31 March 1967)

	Number of securities	Nominal amount (£m)	Market valuation (£m)
1. British government and government-guaranteed	71	21,775	17,786
2. Local authority and public boards	572	1654	1464
3. Commonwealth governments, provincial and municipal	161	863	709
4. Foreign stocks, bonds and corporation stocks	333	1728	851
5. Loan capital	2084	3693	3186
6. Preference and preferred	2382	1646	1272
7. Ordinary and deferred	3983	12,260	56,763

Source: Stock Exchange, London (quoted in D. Hamilton, *Stock Broking Today,* London, 1968).

TABLE 10   Transactions in short-dated stocks (0–5 years) on the London Stock Exchange

Holder	1967		1968		1969	
	Holdings—End March	Turnover	Holdings—End March	Turnover	Holdings—End March	Turnover
Official holders	1650 (26%)	3746 (23%)	1328 (19%)	3349 (23%)	1906 (28%)	2531 (22%)
Banks	1235 (20%)	980 (6%)	1431 (20%)	815 (6%)	1175 (18%)	610 (5%)
Discount market	627 (10%)	6115 (37%)	556 (8%)	5671 (39%)	252 (4%)	4492 (39%)
Other financial institutions	579 (9%)	1404 (8%)	806 (11%)	1207 (8%)	703 (10%)	1191 (10%)
Other holders	2170 (35%)	4279 (26%)	2920 (41%)	3460 (24%)	2664 (40%)	2797 (24%)

Source: Bank of England Statistical Abstract, no. 1 (1970) Table 14.

Notes:

(1) Official holders include the Issue and Banking Departments of the Bank, the National Debt Commissioners and government departments.

(2) Discount market turnover figures relate to stocks of all maturities; dealings in over 5-year stocks are very small.

TABLE 11 Discount houses: activity in traditional and complementary markets

		Union	Smith St Aubyn	Seccombes	King and Shaxson	Jessel Toynbee	Gilletts	Gerrard and National	Clive	Cater Ryder	Allen Harvey	Alexanders
TRADERS (direct)	U.K. Treasury bills	✓	✓	✓	✓	✓	✓	✓	✓	✓	✓	✓
	£ bank and trade bills	✓	✓	✓	✓	✓	✓	✓	✓	✓	✓	✓
	Local authority bills	✓	✓	✓	✓	✓	✓	✓	✓	✓	✓	✓
	U.K. govt short-term bonds	✓	✓	✓	✓	✓	✓	✓	✓	✓	✓	✓
	£ C.D.s	✓	✓	✓	✓	✓	✓	✓	✓	✓	✓	✓
	Local authority bonds	✓	✓	✓	✓	✓	✓	✓	✓	✓	✓	✓
	$ and other Eurocurrency	✓	✓	✓	✓	✓	✓	✓	✓		✓	✓
	$ C.D.s	✓	✓	✓	✓	✓	✓		✓		✓	✓
BROKERS (through subsidiaries)	Inter bank £ deposits	Roberts Union				Charles Fulton	Kirkland Whittaker	P. Murray Jones	Guy Butler	Cater Brokers	Interfico	
	Local authority deposits	"				Packshaw Associates	"	"	Long Till and Colvin			
	$ and currency deposits	"				Charles Fulton	"	"	Guy Butler	M. W. Marshall	Interfico	
	Foreign exchange	"				"	"	Astley and Pierce	"	"		

Source: *Euromoney* (1970).

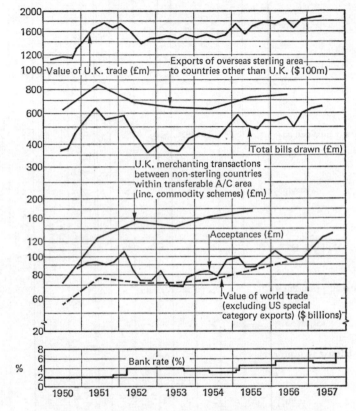

FIG. 1 Bills drawn, trade, acceptances and bank rate.
Source: Accepting Houses Committee, Memorandum of Evidence to the Radcliffe Committee, 1957. Published in Committee on the Working of the Monetary System, *Principal Memoranda of Evidence* (1960).

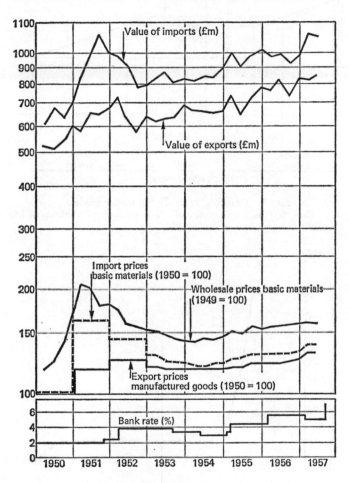

FIG. 2   Bank rate, United Kingdom trade and prices.
Source: As Fig. 1.

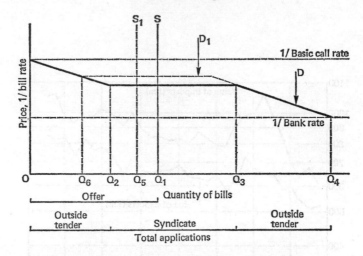

FIG. 3   Crouch's Treasury bill tender model.
Source: R. L. Crouch, 'The Inadequacy of "New Orthodox" Methods of Monetary Control', *Economic Journal* (1964) 918.

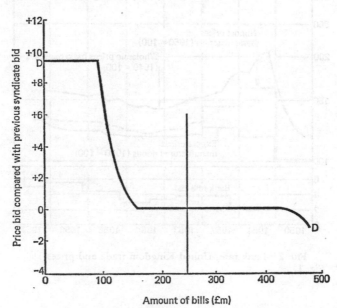

FIG. 4   Bain's typical demand curve for Treasury bills.
Source: A. D. Bain, 'The Treasury Bill Tender in the United Kingdom', *Journal of Economic Studies* (1965) 68.

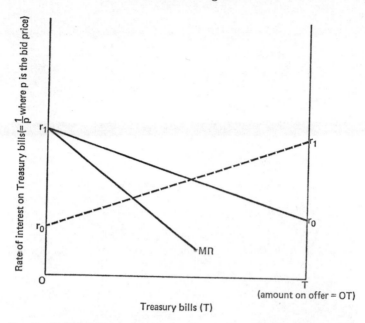

Fig. 5   Griffiths' discount houses' estimate of outside demand for bills.
Source: B. Griffiths, 'The Determination of the Treasury Bill Tender Rate',
Economica (1971) 185.

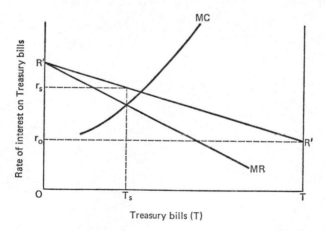

Fig. 6   Griffiths' determination of the discount houses' bid price.
Source: B. Griffiths, op. cit., p. 186.

Notes

PART ONE

Chapter 1

1   W. T. C. King, *History of the London Discount Market* (London 1936) p. xviii (italics added).
2   For many years the law sought to restrict the use of the bill to transactions between merchants. Third parties who discounted bills were denied the full legal rights of a party to the bill and may even have been penalised as holders.
3   London private bankers had their origins in the goldsmiths whereas country banking activities began with merchants and tradespeople of many kinds.
4   L. S. Pressnell, *Country Banking in the Industrial Revolution* (Oxford, 1956) p. 91.
5   The London bill became a standard means of payment between country towns and London and in some areas, remote from the Bank of England and supplies of coin, bills of exchange attained the status of currency.
6   The *Bankers' and Merchants' Almanack* of 1813 listed nineteen bill-broking firms.
7   Pressnell, *Country Banking*, pp. 101–2.
8   King has pointed out that R. Overend and Co. and other bill brokers did a 'jobbing' business in money as a side-line to their major operations.
9   Pressnell, *Country Banking*, pp. 101–2.
10   King, *History of the London Discount Market*, p. 102.
11   Ibid., p. 35.
12   An account of the Bank's measures is given by Pressnell, *Country Banking*, pp. 489–91.
13   It has been pointed out that some authorities, e.g. J. W. Gilbart, *The Logic of Banking* (London, 1859) pp. 572–3, and King, *History of the London Discount Market*, pp. 35–8, lay considerably more emphasis on 1825 as a turning point than others, e.g. Sir John Clapham, *The Bank of England*, vol. ii, p. 136. It can be seen rather as the acceleration of a trend. See M. J. Artis, *Foundations of British Monetary Policy* (Oxford, 1965) p. 49.
14   A contemporary estimated that the discount business of London had doubled in the five years to 1836. See King, *History of the London Discount Market*, p. 43.
15   The attraction of deposits was, for private bankers, only a secondary consideration. Many joint stock banks which began with note issues ceased the practice after a few years. Because of the Bank's monopoly London joint stock banks were exclusively deposit banks.

16 See, for example, Sir A. Feavearyear, *The Pound Sterling*, 2nd ed., rev. E. V. Morgan (Oxford, 1963) ch. 10.
17 King, *History of the London Discount Market*, p. 128.
18 W. T. C. King, 'The Extent of the London Discount Market', *Economica* (1935).

Chapter 2

1   King, *History of the London Discount Market*, 177.
2   In evidence given by the Governor to the 1858 Committee (Select Committee on the Operation of the Bank Act of 1844 (7 and 8 Vict., c.32)). Quoted in King, *History of the London Discount Market*, p. 200.
3   Because consols and Exchequer bills were generally not eligible as security on borrowed funds only those houses with large capital and some proportion of unsecured borrowing could afford to hold them to any extent.
4   With the extension of the principle of limited liability to banking in 1858 there were many bank flotations and by 1862 there was a general mania for company status. King, *History of the London Discount Market*, p. 217.
5   The flotations after 1863 involved the acquisition of existing private businesses.
6   King, *History of the London Discount Market*, p. 237.
7   Credit companies, similar to modern finance companies, appeared in 1863. They dealt in securities beyond the legitimate scope of the banks and discount houses.
8   From £22·5m. to £46·6m. See Table 1.
9   The sensitiveness of world markets to foreign conditions was heightened by the practice of making simultaneous issues of loans in different centres.
10 S. Nishimura, *The Decline of Inland Bills of Exchange in the London Money Market 1855–1913* (Cambridge, 1971).
11 The number of branch banks increased by about 35 per cent during the nine years to 1881 and then by a further 40 per cent in the following decade. While banks were largely indifferent as between discounting and granting loans or advances, for the customer overdrafts had definite attractions compared to bill finance.
12 A complication arises in that the distinction between inland bills and foreign bills was largely legal. Inland bills were commonly drawn to finance British exports. Also, not all foreign bills were instruments for the finance of trade; some were drawn to effect the international movement of short-term capital.
13 Nishimura, *Decline of Inland Bills*, p. 65.
14 The exceptional case was the crisis of 1866 when Gurneys were refused accommodation. For an interpretation see King, *History of the London Discount Market*, pp. 212–14, 242.
15 R. S. Sayers, *Central Banking after Bagehot* (Oxford, 1957) p. 11.
16 L. S. Pressnell, 'Gold Reserves, Banking Reserves, and the Baring Crisis of 1890', *Essays in Money and Banking in Honour of R. S. Sayers*, ed. C. R. Whittlesey and J. S. G. Wilson (Oxford, 1968) p. 170.
17 Ibid., p. 180.
18 For an account see King, *History of the London Discount Market*, p. 289.
19 Apart from seeking harmony with the actions of the Treasury, which controlled the disposition of the national debt and worked closely with the national debt commissioners, he attracted to the Bank deposits from local authorities which would otherwise have been made available to com-

mercial banks, and ensured that the deployment of India Council funds did not disturb market stability. See Pressnell, 'Gold Reserves', pp. 191–2.

Chapter 3

1 *The Economist*, 24 October 1914, quoted in W. M. Scammell, *The London Discount Market* (London, 1968) p. 195.

2 See E. V. Morgan, *Studies in British Financial Policy, 1914–25* (London, 1952) pp. 99–105.

3 R. S. Sayers, *Gilletts in the London Money Market 1867–1967* (Oxford, 1968) p. 69.

4 Contrasts between the approaches to a strategy of war finance during 1914–18 and 1939–45 are drawn in the following chapter.

5 The *First Interim Report*, Cd. 9182 of the Committee on Currency and Foreign Exchanges after the War, under the chairmanship of Lord Cunliffe, the Governor of the Bank, was made public in November 1918.

6 See D. E. Moggridge, *The Return to Gold, 1925: The Formulation of Economic Policy and its Critics*, University of Cambridge, Department of Applied Economics, Occasional Papers, 19 (Cambridge, 1969) pp. 12–17.

7 Currency notes were legal tender notes issued through the Bank of England under the authority of the Treasury. Notes were taken up by commercial banks for their customers and paid for by a transfer from 'banker's balances' to the Currency Notes Redemption Account, the proceeds being on-lent to the government.

8 Moggridge, *Return to Gold*, p. 23.

9 In D. E. Moggridge, *British Monetary Policy 1924–1931: The Norman Conquest of $4.86* (Cambridge, 1972).

10 The announcement that the gold standard was to be restored at the old parity of $4.86656 was made by the Chancellor, Winston Churchill, in his budget speech.

11 The total availability of bills between the wars is shown in Table 2.

12 On the other side of the coin it could be argued that in handling homogeneous government paper the houses were losing the justification for their existence, i.e. of selecting suitable bills for customers from a heterogeneous input.

13 Discussed further below, pp. 45–51.

14 Collective bids were apparently arranged through the small firm of Jones and Brown. Sayers, *Gilletts*, pp. 81–2.

15 It has been estimated that roughly half of the discount houses' money was affected in this way. Furthermore, the 'sticky' seven-day rate influenced average rates for day-to-day money. Ibid., p. 83.

16 Short-term loans to discount houses with a specified term.

17 The relevance for the discount houses of restrictive practices and collusion in the money markets is discussed below.

18 The pound was probably over-valued by at least 10 per cent as a result of restoration at the pre-war parity. See Moggridge, *Return to Gold*, pp. 71–80, 81.

19 This rise in Bank rate was blamed for the withdrawal of funds from New York and the start of the slide that led to the Wall Street crash.

20 There was a higher proportion of non-selfliquidating paper, similar to 'finance' paper, and of short-term credits 'renewed' for longer periods. Lower quality bills were accepted for rediscount at the Bank.

21 The Standstill Agreement of 17 September imposed a virtual moratorium on all German overseas liabilities.

22 Feavearyear, *The Pound Sterling*, p. 369. There was also a desire to attract foreign money to London with which to repay outstanding credits from France and America.

23 See Tables 1 and 2. Throughout the inter-war period growth of the supply of Treasury bills was regarded as inimical to the authorities' ability to control the level of bank credit. The fear persisted that by allowing their bill holdings to run off the banks could force the Bank of England to create additional cash by means of inflationary Ways and Means Advances.

24 The houses were, of course, still discounting commercial bills and they took on increasing amounts of bonds; Treasury bills were now, however, the mainstay of their portfolios.

25 R. J. Truptil, *British Banks and the London Money Market* (London, 1936) p. 312.

26 B. Griffiths, 'The Determination of the Treasury Bill Tender Rate', *Economica* (1971) 181–4.

27 A few provincial banks continued to pay interest on current accounts until the Second World War when all banks agreed not to compete for deposits by increasing interest rate payments. B. Griffiths, 'The Development of Restrictive Practices in the U.K. Monetary System', *Manchester School* (Mar 1973) 3–16.

28 Griffiths, *Manchester School*, 8.

29 On the second occasion the guidance amounted to an instruction.

30 The authorities' supportive role, i.e. that of keeping banks strong so as to avoid failures, has been an important feature of official support for restrictive practices. Moves towards concentration or restrictive agreement have generally been preceded by economic or financial crisis.

31 On the grounds that it was not subject to sudden depreciation in value. Interestingly, support was denied by one of the 'Big Five' on the grounds that the agreement would force up the cost of government borrowing on Treasury bills above free market levels.

32 In this way the banks officially admitted for the first time that they would take bonds as security. It is interesting to note that at this time it was possible to obtain regular money from outside lenders at $\frac{1}{2}$ per cent against all types of security and overnight money reasonably plentifully at $\frac{1}{4}$ per cent.

33 Sir Henry Clay, *Lord Norman* (London, 1957) pp. 465–6.

Chapter 4

1 The revival of commercial bill business was a dream which really came to fulfilment only after the mid-1950s, and the increased volume of business in both bonds and Treasury bills provided a life-saving diet during the intervening years.

2 R. S. Sayers, *Financial Policy 1939–1945*, History of the Second World War: United Kingdom Civil Series (London, 1956) p. 6.

3 In particular, sales of bonds of all types to the banks can be maximised if the authorities take care to allow the banks to maintain their conventional ratios of shorter- to longer-dated assets recognisably intact. In the case of Treasury bills, the discount houses can be expected to take up an

increased amount, selling some on to the banks and holding the remainder against additional call money from the banks, so long as the authorities provide the necessary supplement to the cash base of the system.

4 The trend of the yield on old consols was upward after 1935 and during the first three quarters of 1939 the progressive worsening of the international political situation caused it to rise in a series of steps to just over 4 per cent. It was only later realised that apart from political considerations and a higher level of economic activity, the rising trend in rates was being encouraged by the operations of clearing banks which, faced with rising demand for advances and having a shortage of money market assets, sold securities.

5 It was assumed, for example, that in the case of financial institutions, banks would in general be able to work on the basis of a lower set of rates than would insurance companies.

6 Statutory recognition came eleven months later when the rate on Ways and Means borrowing was limited to 3 per cent.

7 Sayers, *Financial Policy*, p. 143.

8 The Report, 'Defence Expenditure and the Economic and Financial Problems Connected Therewith', of the Standing Committee of the Economic Advisory Council, 20 July 1939. Influential in the formulation of the Committee's final position, Keynes rejected the use of the interest-rate weapon on the grounds that: (1) it could do little to regulate the demand for real resources; (2) it would nevertheless make government borrowing more expensive and perhaps more difficult.

9 When buying up stock during the annual savings drives and towards the end of each tap's run the institutions sold off shorter-dated bonds in substantial amounts.

10 See W. T. C. King, 'The Changing Discount Market', *Banker* (Mar 1947) 176.

11 Due to the death of Hohler's senior partner on active service.

12 The practice was for the houses to finance most of their bill portfolio through the clearing banks (at 1 per cent until October 1945 and at ½ per cent thereafter) but hardly any of their bond portfolio, which could be financed more cheaply through the outside banks—most of which worked to a standard rate of 1⅛ per cent (⅝ per cent by 1947) for loans against bonds, with 1 per cent for mixed parcels of bills and bonds and sometimes even less than that for marginal night money against bonds.

13 King, *Banker*, 178–9.

14 United Dominions Trust in Ryder and Co.

15 The exception was Seccombe, Marshall and Campion which, as special buyer for the Bank, was not subject to the same conditions.

16 No details of capital were available from the one partnership left in the market and three of the private companies gave no figures for reserves; there were also, for all the houses, substantial inner reserves.

17 Considered to be a particularly inflationary form of finance, i.e. borrowing from the Bank of England which had the effect of an equal addition to the cash base of the banking system.

18 That amount that could not be met from taxation revenue and sales of gilt-edged securities.

19 Sayers, *Financial Policy*, pp. 218–19.

20 This would occur, *ceteris paribus*, whenever net T.D.R. borrowing, i.e. new issues of T.D.R.s minus repayments either on maturity or for pur-

chases of bonds, was greater than the fall in the public's demand for bank advances.

21 In addition, of course, the Treasury were perennially in favour of minimising the cost of servicing the National Debt.

22 H.C. Deb 15 April 1947, pp. 61–4. Quoted in J. C. R. Dow, *The Management of the British Economy 1945–60* (Cambridge, 1964) p. 224.

23 See J. M. Keynes, *The General Theory of Employment, Interest and Money* (London, 1936) p. 203. In view of the outcome of Dalton's experiment, this reference is particularly apposite.

24 C. N. Ward-Perkins, 'Banking Developments', *The British Economy 1945–50*, ed. G. D. N. Worswick and P. H. Ady (Oxford, 1952) pp. 214–15.

25 They collected on their own books the very short maturities that were unpopular with other holders. See Chapter 10.

26 Only five of the eleven houses published their true bond position. The only one of the Big Three among the disclosers – Union – revealed a bond ratio of over thirteen to one. At the nearest comparable dates available – mostly in 1946 – the other four showed ratios of about twelve to one, though they commanded a smaller amount of hidden reserves. See King, *Banker*, 178.

27 W. T. C. King, 'The Market's Changing Role', *The London Discount Market Today*, 3rd ed. (London, 1969) p. 10.

28 There were corresponding moves among rates for small savings, e.g. Defence Bonds and Saving Certificates, and on rates at which the government lent money, e.g. lending through the Local Loans Board.

29 £305m was in exchange for Local Loans Stock called in and £177m was for cash.

30 For example, nationalisation issues and devaluation.

31 For 1950 the total of tender bills in issue was about £12,500m. The last of the T.D.R.s were run off in February 1952.

32 See Chapter 9.

33 The banks continued to provide part of the bond money at 1 per cent and the rest at no more than 1¼ per cent. By the end of the cheap money period in 1951 the discount houses' combined portfolio stood at record level: nearly £1200m, of which £885m were bills (including £75m commercial and municipal bills) and just over £300m, bonds.

34 Sayers, *Gilletts*, p. 152.

PART TWO

Chapter 5

1 Except for the financial year 1956–7.

2 The Bank believed that circumstances in the gilt-edged market could quickly affect the situation in the foreign exchange market (balance of payments problems were perennial). Also large-scale bond sales by the private sector would have resulted in increases in the banks' cash reserves.

3 See D. C. Rowan, 'The Monetary System in the '50's and '60's, *Manchester School* (Mar 1973) 23–5.

4 *Management of the British Economy*, p. 230.

5 A. R. Nobay, 'The Bank of England, Monetary Policy and Monetary Theory in the United Kingdom, 1951–1971', *Manchester School* (Mar

1973) 48. Previously, between 1945 and 1951, funding policy had been inhibited by the policy of low interest rates and in any case the Bank was preoccupied with the recurrent convertibility and exchange rate crises (especially 1947, 1949 and 1951).

6 For a discussion of the role of the liquidity ratio see J. E. Wadsworth, 'The Nature and Uses of Bank Liquidity', *Monetary Theory and Monetary Policy in the 1970s*, ed. G. Clayton, J. C. Gilbert and R. Sedgwick (London, 1971) pp. 195–217.

7 *Bank of England Quarterly Bulletin* (Mar 1963).

8 Rowan, *Manchester School*, 24.

9 *Report of the Committee on the Working of the Monetary System*, Cmnd. 827 (the *Radcliffe Report*) para. 434.

10 See Dow, *Management of the British Economy*, pp. 252–61, including the table of Bank rate changes.

11 For example: (*a*) to attract external capital, by interest incentive or declaration of intention; (*b*) to work via effects on internal demand.

12 *Radcliffe Report* (1959) para. 5.

13 The Committee's view on the efficacy of monetary measures was summarised in paras 382–97 of the Report.

14 *Not Unanimous*, ed. A. Seldon (London, 1960).

15 *Radcliffe Report*, para. 397.

16 The effect could be envisaged to operate on both firms in the private sector and bodies in the public sector and also on households' saving and borrowing decisions.

17 *Radcliffe Report*, paras 392–3.

18 The inadvisability of direct controls was seen to stem not so much from difficulty-of-administration considerations as from the belief that further growth of new intermediaries would be encouraged outside the range of the controls.

19 Rowan, *Manchester School*, 26.

20 *Radcliffe Report*, paras 514, 519.

21 If the use of these were to become prolonged, consideration would have to be given to the possibility of imposition of comparable restraints on other groups of lenders. *Radcliffe Report*, paras 506–11.

22 See 'The Operation of Monetary Policy Since Radcliffe', *BEQB* (1969) 453.

23 J. H. Kareken, 'Monetary Policy', *Britain's Economic Prospects*, ed. R. E. Caves (London, 1968) pp. 78–89.

24 The authorities point out, however, that even at such times they are vulnerable because of the need to refinance maturing debt.

25 Special Deposits were designed to impinge on liquidity ratios rather than cash ratios so banks would realise liquid assets to meet a call in cash. The resulting interest-rate movements, because they were part of a calculable response, were considered manageable.

26 *BEQB* (1969) 456.

27 The extension of direct controls to non-deposit bank intermediaries reflected increased awareness of their growing relative importance. As a parallel to the Special Deposits scheme the authorities devised the Cash Deposits scheme as a restraint on the intermediaries in more normal times (it was never used).

28 A requirement of the authorities based on their beliefs about demand conditions in the Treasury bill market. See Chapters 8 and 12.

K

Chapter 6

1   See Chapter 15.
2   All money borrowed from the clearing banks was secured. The same principles apply today.
3   During the period the banks closed at 3 p.m.
4   Some items made their first appearance in the money book only late on in the period and the relative importance of various items changed from time to time, as the following chapters make clear. Not shown are items denominated in foreign currencies, which were financed by borrowing in the appropriate currency.
5   See below, Chapter 8.
6   To the dealers 'the task appears as a composite task of selling bills and borrowing money: the more bills sold, the less money has to be borrowed'. Sayers, *Gilletts*, p. 152.
7   Allen, Harvey and Ross Ltd, *This is Bill Broking* (London, 1968) p. 18.
8   Representatives of the discount houses and the discount brokers wore this distinctive head-gear whenever they were out in the City on business. The tradition continues up to the time of writing.
9   See however Chapters 13 and 14, on the effects of Competition and Credit Control on this practice.
10   C. W. Linton, 'The Commercial Banks and the London Discount Market', *The London Discount Market Today*, 3rd ed. (London, 1969) p. 54.
11   These matters are examined more closely in the next chapter.
12   Allen, Harvey and Ross, *This is Bill Broking*, p. 22.

Chapter 7

1   See Table 3.
2   Linton, 'Commercial Banks', 1965 ed., p. 39; 1969 ed., p. 46.
3   Bankers' Deposits at the Bank are equivalent to cash and constitute the mechanism through which indebtedness between the clearing banks is discharged.
4   Linton, 'Commercial Banks', 1965, p. 41; 1969, p. 47.
5   After 1962 refinanceable export credits were included in the liquid assets ratio, being that part of finance for exports, backed by E.C.G.D. guarantees, which was rediscountable at the Bank.
6   Linton, 'Commercial Banks'.
7   Cash would flow out at the end of the week in wage payments and household spending and flow back as traders banked their takings.
8   Committee on the Working of the Monetary System, *Minutes of Evidence* (1960) Questions 3485–94.
9   The expectation in the discount market would be that if a bank had to call off its regular money it would be pressing close on its liquidity ratio.
10   See the notes to the table. Examples of individual banks in each category can be found in the *Bank of England Statistical Abstract*, no. 1 (1970) pp. 49, 66–7, and in subsequent issues of the *Bank of England Quarterly Bulletin*.
11   This had been a regular practice before the war with the larger discount houses and the merchant banks. Sayers, *Gilletts*, p. 158.
12   See H. F. Goodson, 'The Functioning of the London Discount Houses', *The London Discount Market Today* (London, 1969) pp. 30–5.

13   Prior to February 1955 the deposit rate was fixed in relation to Bank rate through discussion between bankers.
14   See Table 6.
15   Sayers, *Gilletts*, p. 156.
16   Periods of sixty-three and ninety-one days became usual for fixtures with the clearing banks. Occasionally fixtures to cover particular circumstances might be agreed with merchant and other banks.
17   For example, with a gilt-edged security standing at 95 a loan of £100,000 would require as collateral a parcel of security totalling £110,000.
18   Goodson, 'Functioning of the London Discount Houses', p. 30.
19   The Bank, of course, performs the same functions today.
20   For a full account see : 'The Management of Money Day by Day', *BEQB* (Mar 1963) 15–21.
21   These are monetary economists' terms and would not be regarded as common parlance in the discount market.
22   In the summer of 1974 the Discount Office, as a separate entity, was abolished and its former activities were divided into the two closely related functions of the supervision of the banking system and the day-to-day management of the money market, each performed by a new division within the Chief Cashier's Department.
23   Far more difficult problems of supervision were posed by the proliferation of foreign banks in London.
24   For many years before the war and previously in the nineteenth century advances were generally at a margin above Bank rate. Before 1926 and particularly around the turn of the century this margin varied; thereafter it was nearly always ½ per cent.
25   'The Functions and Organisation of the Bank of England', *BEQB*, revised offprint (Dec 1970) 6.
26   The situation, common in the sixties, in which neither banks nor discount houses held sufficient bills and which was relieved by overnight lending at market rates were described above.

Chapter 8

1   The Treasury bill was created and introduced to provide the Exchequer with a short-term marketable borrowing instrument which would supersede the inflexible and unpopular Exchequer bill. The occasion was the need, in the mid-1870s, for the government greatly to expand the size of the Floating Debt. Walter Bagehot, approached through Lord Welby by the Chancellor of the Exchequer, advised that the English Treasury should fully exploit its unrivalled credit standing by borrowing from the market on a security that resembled as closely as possible the familiar commercial bill of exchange.
2   For an account of the use of sixty-three day bills, a technically successful though unpopular and consequently expensive form of borrowing, see *BEQB* (Sep 1964) 187.
3   See J. Q. Hollom (the then Chief Cashier of the Bank of England), 'The Bank of England Today', *Journal of the Institute of Bankers* (June 1964) 176–8.
4   'The Treasury Bill', *BEQB* (Sep 1964) 192.

5 The figures are taken from the *Radcliffe Report* (1959) Table 35, and from *Financial Statistics* (H.M.S.O., various issues) Table 19.

6 During the 1960s the central government's borrowing requirement rose from £375m in the financial year 1963–4 (with a slight dip to £313m in 1964–5) to a massive £1335m in 1967–8. In 1968–9 there was a surplus of £273m which rose to £1116m in 1969–70. *Bank of England Statistical Abstract*, no. 1 (1970) Table 1.

7 See C. D. Cohen, *British Economic Policy 1960–1969* (London, 1971) pp. 114–19.

8 For a 'realistic' analysis of the way in which portfolio inflows of foreign funds will tend to be prevented from having strong effects on domestic liquidity and interest rates because of the matching of demands and supplies in the Treasury bill market, see A. B. Cramp, *Monetary Management: Principles and Practice* (London, 1971) pp. 88–90.

9 See Table 4.

10 Since 1925 the fixed rate bills – the tap issue – have in general only been issued to government departments and to the Issue Department of the Bank. The Bank has, however, frequently included these among the bills sold periodically in the market to mop up surplus funds. Tap bills would be distinguishable only by the fact that their maturity could be for a period other than the normal ninety-one days.

11 The framework of the tender remained unchanged up to the time of writing.

12 Since decimalisation, of course, the price has been expressed in £p to the nearest ½p, e.g. £97.50, representing a discount of 2¼ per cent for 91 days or 10·03 per cent per annum : equivalent to a yield of 10·30 per cent per annum.

13 The houses tended to take up their bills in a spread covering the whole working week.

14 In calculating bid prices due allowance was made for bills that matured on public holidays. These would not run for exactly ninety-one days so that the rate of discount at any particular bid price was affected. Successful tenderers were sent Letters of Acceptance by post which were, together with payment, exchanged for the bills on the day appointed.

15 'The rate of discount at which the bills are issued through the tap is unknown and is irrelevant to the discount market.' R. S. Sayers, *Modern Banking* (Oxford, 1967) p. 55. In its *Quarterly Bulletin* (Sep 1964) 188, the Bank stated that the tap rate was 'currently at a fraction below the published average rate on tender bills'. Those departments which took up bills were thus treated as if they had made a successful bid at the tender.

16 The Bank's participation in the tender was sometimes identified as a third group – the inside tender. It was invariably the rule that the Bank was able to meet its needs in this way prior to 1971, though this was not always the case in the changed conditions after 1971.

17 Between 1914 and 1944 inter-house business was carried on through the Discount Houses' Committee, which served also as the formal channel through which the authorities communicated their wishes to the houses, for example during wartime. The more formal L.D.M.A. was set up in 1944.

18 See Radcliffe Committee on the Working of the Monetary System, *Minutes of Evidence* (1960) Qs 3351, 3364, 3369. Bank orthodoxy was that if the discount houses tendered at too low a rate the position could be corrected subsequently by forcing them to borrow at penal rates. If the

rate were considered to be too high the Bank could put it right the following week by putting in tenders itself and under-allotting to the market. The validity of this orthodoxy is examined in the appendix to Chapter 12.

19   Ibid., Qs 3366–9.
20   Ibid., Q. 1755.
21   Or for sixty-three days, as was the case between 1955 and 1962.
22   See Goodson, 'Functioning of the London Discount Houses', p. 35.
23   Houses could have special 'commitments', e.g. '. . . running into money for orders, bills due, or it may be a question of making up balance sheets'. Radcliffe, *Minutes*, Q. 3342.
24   'Hot Treasury bills' or 'hots' are terms applying to Treasury bills on their day of issue.
25   Sayers, *Gilletts*, p. 132.
26   'The Treasury Bill', *BEQB* (Sep 1964) 191. In fact part of the totals related to overseas holdings other than those held by central monetary institutions, although at March 1964 such holdings were relatively few – some £50 million.
27   Due to the operation of the tax laws, payment to the inland revenue was not made until nine months or more after the relevant profits had been earned
28   Radcliffe, *Minutes*.

Chapter 9

1   *Radcliffe Report*, para. 584.
2   The frequently quoted legal definition given in the Bills of Exchange Act, 1882, Section 3 (1), is : '. . . an unconditional order in writing, addressed by one person to another, signed by the person giving it, requiring the person to whom it is addressed to pay on demand or at a fixed or determinable future time a sum certain in money to or to the order of a specified person, or to bearer.'
3   Hence 'discount houses', which buy and sell the bills.
4   The discount is expressed as a percentage per annum and computed for the number of days the bill has to run to maturity.
5   See Gillett Brothers Discount Co. Ltd, *The Bill on London*, 3rd ed. (London, 1964) pp. 16–23.
6   Although a bill is judged on the name of the acceptor, the name of the drawer will also be taken into account.
7   The nature of the bills limits the amount that can be marketed on the strength of any one name of drawer or acceptor.
8   See also Chapter 13 for the effects of the reforms of 1971 on the notion of 'eligibility' of bills.
9   Although no maximum rate was set, competition for bills ensured that rates quoted were narrowly contained. Assuming a change of Bank rate at its customary time of midday on Thursday, houses would be able to bid at any price for bank bills until the announcement of the fine rate at 1 p.m. on Friday.
10   The willingness of the banks to take as security various types of paper acted as a powerful influence on the houses' buying policy. From the banks' point of view the acceptability of any particular variety would depend upon the availability of other liquid assets.

11 High rates on bills could be explained by reference to two factors: partly a risk insurance premium and partly an indication of the restricted availability of certain bills. Goodson, 'Functioning of the London Discount Houses', p. 39.

12 J. Grahame-Parker, 'Revival of the Commercial Bill', *Banker* (Mar 1948) 185–6.

13 Despite the unpropitious circumstances of external finance, e.g. exchange control.

14 Grahame-Parker, *Banker*, 187. There had been similar resistance to attempts to stimulate traditional-type bill finance in the 1930s.

15 Note that whereas the rates for good average trade bills (not necessarily the finest) were 3–$3\frac{1}{2}$ per cent at 28 January 1955 as against $2\frac{3}{8}$ per cent for prime bank bills, by 29 January 1965 the rates were $7\frac{3}{4}$–8 per cent as against $6\frac{3}{4}$ per cent. See *Bank of England Statistical Abstract*, no. 1 (1970) Table 29.

16 Ibid., Table 9 (1).

17 R. Law, 'The Resurgence of the Commercial Bill', *Bankers Magazine* (1965) 344.

18 When voyages on world routes took longer, bills tended to be drawn for longer periods and before 1914 longer-dated bills formed a considerable proportion of bills in the market.

19 *BEQB* (Dec 1961) 30. The quantitative restrictions imposed on commercial paper by the Bank are dealt with below in the consideration of supply conditions.

20 Law, *Bankers Magazine*, 343.

21 'Trade bill rates, with certain possible exceptions, should not be firmly based on the rates for bank bills. They are best related to Bank rate or, better still, to the current rates for advances or overdrafts from the clearing banks.' Goodson, 'Functioning of the London Discount Houses', p. 35. Note that only the larger houses with sufficient staff dealt to any significant extent in small trade bills, both because of the cost of checking the credit-worthiness of a large number of small traders and because of the amount of clerical work necessary for only small sums of money.

22 Radcliffe, *Minutes* (1960) Q. 3399. This evidence was given in January 1958 after two consecutive years, 1956 and 1957, in which houses' holdings of other sterling bills had been almost twice as high as in the four preceding years.

23 Law, *Bankers Magazine*, 341–2. For years prior to 1961, when the *ad valorem* stamp on bills of exchange was abolished, the calculations were based on receipts from stamp duty. They could not take into account sight drafts and bills that were executed but not discounted.

24 De Zoete and Gorton, *The London Discount Market* (London, 1969) p. 11. R. S. Sayers calculated that in 1961 Gillett Bros bought trade bills to the extent of $8\frac{1}{4}$ per cent of total commercial bills bought; in 1965 the figure was much higher. *Gilletts*, p. 141.

25 G. K. Young, *Merchant Banking: Practice and Prospects* (London, 1966) p. 36. Drawers of trade bills could secure an acceptance credit by depositing the bill as collateral with a merchant bank.

26 Accepting Houses Committee, *Memorandum of Evidence* (1957) para. 20; Radcliffe, *Minutes*, Q. 5851.

27 On the definition used for the purposes of the credit squeeze, internal finance was very small.

28 The Radcliffe Committee queried the correlation on the grounds that bills outstanding represented only a small fraction (about one-third) of British trade and that acceptances of the accepting houses were in turn a very limited fraction of those bills; also some fraction of total bills drawn would represent trade between foreign countries. Nevertheless, the Accepting Houses Committee maintained that the proportion of British trade financed by bills was relatively constant and that the proportion of bills drawn which represented trade between 'third party' countries was relatively small (Q. 5910).

29 *Monthly Digest of Statistics* (H.M.S.O.) various issues.

30 Radcliffe, *Minutes*, 5843.

31 See Table 4 and *BEQB* (June 1967) 151–2.

32 There are no published figures.

33 Sayers, *Gilletts*, p. 139.

34 *BEQB* (June 1967) 151.

35 To a level not higher than 105 per cent of the March 1965 figures.

36 Or rather, a moderation of its increase relative to the cost of alternatives.

37 *BEQB* (June 1967) 152.

38 Law, *Bankers Magazine*, 345.

39 Young, *Merchant Banking*, p. 30.

40 The book went through three editions during the period 1952–71. It advised potential customers on the use of bill finance.

41 For example Allen, Harvey and Ross's *This is Bill Broking*, which went through five editions between May 1966 and January 1972.

42 *Minutes*, Qs 205, 207, 208, 211, 212.

Chapter 10

1 Reference throughout is to the London Stock Exchange. Some indication of the volume and range of business transacted in fixed interest securities on the Exchange is given in Tables 9 and 10.

2 See Chapter 11.

3 'Shorts', 'mediums', 'longs', 'undated'.

4 J. D. Hamilton, *Stockbroking Today* (London, 1968) p. 138. On very large amounts it could be half that figure.

5 The houses would, however, purchase medium-dated stocks and also equities in appropriate circumstances, for example favourable interest-rate expectations and 'thinness' in the short-dated market. Generally, however, operations were confined to shorts because bonds, like other assets, had to be sufficiently liquid to serve as collateral on loans, against which the Bank extended special transfer facilities and last-resort lending facilities. The largest holders of medium, long and undated gilts were 'the institutions' (for example insurance companies and pension funds). Banks generally preferred gilt-edged within about seven years of maturity.

6 E. Chalmers, *The Gilt-Edged Market* (London, 1967) p. 51. Probably 80 per cent of the turnover in gilt-edged was, in the later 1960s, handled by a dozen firms with specialist departments in this field: Hamilton, *Stockbroking Today*.

7 Hollom, *Journal of the Institute of Bankers*, 171–2.

8 Ibid., 175.

9 When calculating earnings from a stock or comparing two stocks account must be taken of the effects of taxation.

10 When 'minimum lending rate' was substituted for Bank rate.

11 A generic term for fixed-interest securities displaying the characteristics described above.

12 It was generally acknowledged that on a Bank rate increase the houses would lose money on their *bill* dealings for at least five or six weeks. The effect on bond holdings would be much more severe, the severity increasing with the average life to maturity of the bonds. Goodson, 'Functioning of the London Discount Houses', p. 43.

13 The change in interest rates may not have been uniform over the whole market. In practice, short-term yields would tend to fluctuate more than long-term yields. In periods of very high interest rates, short-term yields may even have risen above long-term yields. As a result, when interest rates began a downward movement, stimulated by reductions in Bank rate, yields may have fallen faster and to a greater extent at the short end than at the long end. Initially, yields at the long end may hardly have reacted at all to downward movements in short-term rates.

14 Sayers, *Gilletts*, pp. 143–6.

15 Because so much importance was attached to the liquidity of bonds, it is worthy of mention that bonds with optional maturity dates were classified according to their *last* date of maturity except in circumstances in which yields obtaining on comparable securities were significantly below the coupon on the bonds in question, when the expectation would be that the bonds would be redeemed at the *earliest* possible date.

16 *First Report,* Session 1969–70: Bank of England (H.M.S.O., 1970) Q. 1310.

17 Outside demand for Treasury bills was at its peak at this time. See Chapter 8.

18 The analysis relates to the period 1951–67 during which 'traditional' assets entirely dominated the portfolio. The growth of new instruments in portfolio during the 1960s is dealt with in the next chapter.

19 In contrast to the Radcliffe Committee view and that of J. C. R. Dow, *Management of the British Economy*, p. 252, J. H. Kareken, 'Monetary Policy', in laves *et al.*, *Britain's Economic Prospects* (London, 1968) p. 79, found evidence of the 'bunching' of measures in the expansionary phase as well as the restrictive phase of the cycle.

20 *BEQB* (June 1967) 151.

21 For a view by the largest house, contrary to that of the Bank, see the Union Discount Co. of London Ltd, *Report of the Directors and Accounts* (31 Dec 1969) p. 14.

22 Higher even than in 1950 when houses' holdings of Treasury bills had been over £250m higher.

23 See Sayers, *Gilletts*, p. 148.

24 *BEQB* (June 1967) 151.

25 The year 1955 produced circumstances beyond the experience of both the market dealers and the Bank of England.

26 As noted in the previous chapter, commercial-bill holdings did not continue to grow after the Bank rate rise in 1957 because of the exchange control regulations.

27 The growth in the discount houses' holdings of commercial bills was resumed after February 1959 as the restrictions on their use for financing trade between overseas residents were removed.

28 Sayers, *Gilletts*, p. 150.

Chapter 11

1　The new banking system, which co-existed with the old, was composed of banks both of long establishment and of new foundation. See the authoritative account of secondary banking in J. R. S. Revell, *The British Financial System* (London, 1973) ch. 9.

2　*BEQB* (June 1969) 181. The Bank also described the remarkable growth of their foreign currency deposits – mainly Euro-dollars and, after 1966, dollar negotiable certificates of deposit – mostly owned by non-residents. Because the dollars were largely re-lent to non-residents, much of the business represented purely financial intermediation between foreigners: 'an entrepôt business that raises the United Kingdom's invisible earnings in the balance of payments, but otherwise has a negligible impact on domestic financial conditions.'

3　Ibid., 188.

4　Discount houses' total borrowed funds – excluding capital and reserves – stood at £2259m in 1970 and £2961m in 1971 (see Table 3), compared with totals outstanding of parallel market claims of £12,297m for 1970 and £14,928m for 1971.

5　Revell, *British Financial System*, p. 297.

6　Commercial paper is a long-established money market instrument in the United States, consisting of short term unsecured notes placed on the market by leading corporations (companies) through brokers. 'Finance paper' is a similar instrument, usually placed direct by the big finance companies. See J. S. G. Wilson, *Monetary Policy and the Development of Money Markets* (London, 1966) pp. 138, 163.

7　See P. Einzig, *Parallel Money Markets*, vol. 1: *The New Markets in London* (London, 1971) pp. 41–2.

8　Ibid., pp. 38–9.

9　Though, of course, prudent houses would maintain uncommitted security ready in portfolio to guard against any sudden withdrawal.

10　The relaxation, for C.D.s, of the rule that income tax had to be deducted at source in respect of securities with a maturity of more than one year, meant that overseas residents could be attracted as holders.

11　With a term deposit, withdrawal would often cause the depositor to incur heavy penalties.

12　Revell, *British Financial System*, p. 277.

13　The amount of unsecured borrowing in both dollars and sterling on this score was about £200m in December 1970 and about £277m in December 1971.

14　Although secondary banks sought dealing profits in this way, they held C.D.s largely on account of the matching requirement, as noted earlier.

15　R. J. Clark, "The Evolution of Monetary and Financial Institutions', *Money in Britain 1959–1969*, ed. D. R. Croome and H. G. Johnson (London, 1970) p. 143.

16　For a good coverage of detail of the market see Einzig, *New Markets in London*, pp. 106–20.

17　The intensity of demand for funds was exacerbated by the participation as borrowers of the hire-purchase finance houses, which because of the nature of their business and the profitable times they had enjoyed, had always been prepared to bid up to get the sums they required.

18　The so-called 'yearlings', the tenor of which could nevertheless be from one to five years.

L

19 'Continued Expansion in "Complementary" Markets', *Midland Bank Review* (Nov 1969) 3.
20 See, for example, E. R. Shaw, *The London Money Market* (London, 1975).
21 In September 1970 finance houses introduced their own 'base rate', which reflected movements in the rate for three months' inter-bank deposits.
22 It would be greater for 'non-standard' and longer maturities.
23 Revell, *British Financial System*, p. 275.
24 The question of control in a situation in which deposits are tiered is dealt with in the following chapters.
25 A further means of control would be to influence the inflow of funds to complementary markets by regulating the conditions on which foreign funds swapped into sterling could be 'covered forward' against exchange risk.

Chapter 12
1 More precisely, after 1890 when systematic lending through discount accounts was reinstated after the suspension of 1858. See above, Chapters 1 and 2.
2 H. G. Johnson's comment on the 'long and frequently confused debate' which he omitted from his survey of monetary theory 'as not lending itself to generalisation'. See 'Recent Developments in Monetary Theory', *Money in Britain 1959–1969*, op. cit., pp. 113–14.
3 The dominant constituent of the money supply in Britain.
4 Following W. T. Newlyn, *Theory of Money*, 2nd ed. (Oxford, 1971) pp. 20–1. As a caveat, attention could be drawn to the marginal conditions which limit the expansion of banking firms, a qualification made familiar by J. Tobin, 'Commercial Banks as Creators of "Money"', *Banking and Monetary Studies*, ed. Deane Carson (Homewood, Ill., 1963) pp. 408–19.
5 Committee on Finance and Industry, *Report*, Cmd. 3897 (H.M.S.O., 1931) para. 222.
6 It has not, however, been accepted in official circles for use as an instrument of policy, as will be shown below.
7 J. M. Parkin, 'The Supply of Money', *Readings in British Monetary Economics*, ed. H. G. Johnson *et al.* (Oxford, 1972) p. 204.
8 Because of the unreliability of the bank deposit multiplier this gives a direct reduction of bank deposits at the first stage. Consequently it is more efficacious than sales to banks or to discount houses. See A. B. Cramp, 'Control of the Money Supply', *Economic Journal* (1966) 278–87.
9 For a rigorous analysis of the logical possibilities of the sequence see A. B. Cramp, 'The Control of Bank Deposits', *Lloyds Bank Review* (1967) 16–35.
10 Against this, however, it has been argued that the houses would not thereby be put into disequilibrium because penal borrowing at the Bank would not in itself affect the marginal conditions but would merely reduce the level of profits. See appendix to this chapter.
11 Houses would be 'locked in' to their bond holdings by the rise in interest rates.
12 Note that as the liquidity ratio fell towards the minimum the banks would be forced to adjust cash and liquidity ratios by reducing their earning assets, i.e. investments and advances.

13 Macmillan Committee, *Report*, p. 274.
14 In addition, neither sales of bills to non-bank holders nor borrowing from outside sources were viewed as viable routes by which a contraction could take place.
15 Radcliffe Committee, *Memoranda of Evidence* (1960) vol. 1, pt 1, paras 8, 24.
16 *Radcliffe Report* (1959) para. 376.
17 Therefore, of the two versions of New Orthodoxy, the first, associated with, for example, W. M. Dacey ('The Floating Debt Problem', *Lloyds Bank Review* (Apr 1956) 24–38) objected to Old Orthodoxy on the grounds of the changed nature of the bill market; the second, associated with R. S. Sayers ('The Determination of Bank Deposits in England 1955–56', *Central Banking After Bagehot*, Oxford, 1957), on the grounds of the authorities' policy towards short-term rates. In either case, in the context of the 'orderly markets' policy the implications obviously had drawbacks in that it was thought to be both dangerous and difficult to sell stock on a market possibly severely weakened by the effects of a restrictive credit policy involving rising interest rates.
18 Cramp, *Lloyds Bank Review*, 24–6. For the second stage of the linkage Cramp compared total liquid assets of the clearing banks with their Treasury bill holdings.
19 Radcliffe, *Minutes* (1960). Although the views expressed obviously related to the year in which the evidence was given (1957) and those immediately preceding, nothing that was said in evidence to the Select Committee on Nationalised Industries, *First Report*, Session 1969–70: Bank of England (H.M.S.O., 1970) contradicted them. Furthermore, the publication of the Radcliffe Report coincided with the peak of outside demand for Treasury bills.
20 'The Treasury Bill', *BEQB* (Sep 1964) 188.
21 *First Report,* Session 1969–70: Bank of England, Minutes of Evidence.
22 It was generally acknowledged that the Bank always obtained the bills it wanted. In the changed conditions after 1971, however, this was not always to be the case.
23 *First Report,* Session 1969–70: Bank of England, Minutes, Q. 497.
24 R. L. Crouch, 'The Inadequacy of "New Orthodox" Methods of Monetary Control', *Economic Journal* (1964) 916–34.
25 The assumption implicit in Neo (Old) Orthodox theory.
26 A. D. Bain, 'The Treasury Bill Tender in the United Kingdom', *Journal of Economic Studies* (1965) 62–71.
27 In this regard it was Bain's contention that the syndicate would choose to supply their outside customers (public corporations and large business enterprises) even at the expense of failing to maintain their own desired portfolios – with a consequent reduction in supply to the banks. On the other hand banks could always buy in bills from brokers.
28 Bain, *JES*, 69.
29 B. Griffiths, 'The Determination of the Treasury Bill Tender Rate', *Economica* (1971) 180–91.
30 As in Crouch's model the outside tenderers' demand for Treasury bills is seen as being represented by a stable demand curve, with rates of return on alternative financial assets held constant.
31 An aspect given significance by Bain's empirical findings. It could be argued that this was not Griffiths' prime objective: he was, however,

challenging Bain's 'conventional view' with an alternative methodology.

32　To the enterprising treasurer the Treasury bill tender offered the possibility of his being able to obtain bills more cheaply and therefore more profitably than if he purchased them subsequently, from an authorised agent. He would, of course, make his own bid through an authorised agent. For those authorised agents who bought on their own behalf bills for subsequent resale to potential customers, it was obviously important to obtain the bills at the lowest possible price so as to maximise profits in the competitive conditions of the bill market of the following week.

33　*Radcliffe Report* (1959) para. 590.

34　Cramp, *Lloyds Bank Review*, 28–9. This view is in accord with that of the Bank (Radcliffe, *Minutes*, Q. 2621). It was suggested by J. H. Kareken, 'Monetary Policy', *Britain's Economic Prospects*, ed. R. E. Caves *et al.* (London, 1968) p. 98, footnote, that the pattern of outside demand at the tender was strongly shaped by the knowledge that the syndicate tendered for the whole issue at an agreed price, and thus those who would otherwise come in at prices lower than the expected syndicate bid drop out so that demand appears less than it would otherwise be.

35　Cramp, *Monetary Management*, pp. 51–3. Note that Griffiths, *Economica*, 189–90, argues: 'At an *a priori* level one can postulate exactly the opposite of Cramp, which is that given the existence of speculation in financial markets one would expect the observed variation in rates to be very small.'

36　This example is of course taken from a time after Competition and Credit Control, which had been introduced with the explicit intention of encouraging greater flexibility of short-and longer-term interest rates.

37　It is Cramp's contribution to have made this clear.

38　For example in October 1963 and March 1965 (roughly the period of the Neo (Old) Orthodox revival) the discount houses were forced to borrow heavily at Bank rate until they reversed an unwelcome shift in the rate.

39　That this was the Bank's view is confirmed by statements made officially, for example to the Radcliffe Committee, *Minutes* (1960) Q. 421, and in *BEQB* (Mar 1963) 15–16.

40　R. F. G. Alford, 'Bank Rate, Money Rates and the Treasury-Bill Rate', *Essays in Money and Banking in Honour of R. S. Sayers*, ed. C. R. Whittlesey and J. S. G. Wilson (Oxford, 1968) pp. 1–25.

41　Griffiths, *Economica*, 189–91.

42　Ibid.

PART THREE

Chapter 13

1　See *BEQB* (June, Sep and Dec 1971; Mar 1973). 'Competition and Credit Control' was reprinted in the June 1971 issue.

2　Published in July 1971, by which time the proposals were being discussed with the L.D.M.A. See 'Competition and Credit Control: the Discount Market' (press memo, July 1971) reprinted in *BEQB* (Sep 1971) 314–15.

3　The public sector debt ratio was applied to the discount brokers and the money trading banks but not to the money brokers or gilt-edged jobbers.

4　Following discussions with interested parties, details of the new arrangements were set out in 'Reserve Ratios and Special Deposits', *BEQB* (Sep
1971) supplement.

5　B. Griffiths, 'Development of Restrictive Practices in the U.K. Monetary
System', *Manchester School* (Mar 1973) 4.

6　See H. G. Johnson, 'Report on Bank Charges', *Bankers Magazine* (Aug
1967); and 'Harking Back to Radcliffe', *Bankers Magazine* (Sep 1971).
Also B. Griffiths, *Competition in Banking* (London, 1970).

7　D. C. Rowan, 'The Monetary System in the Fifties and Sixties', *Manchester School* (Mar 1973) 31.

8　*The Times*, 17 Nov 1970.

9　For example, see the Governor of the Bank of England, 'Key Issues in
Monetary and Credit Policy', *BEQB* (June 1971).

10　Ibid.

11　The banking system's sterling deposit liabilities of less than two years'
original maturity, plus resources obtained by switching foreign currencies
into sterling and including inter-bank transactions and sterling certificates
of deposit (both held and issued) on a net basis irrespective of term.

12　Full details of the new scheme were set out in 'Reserve Ratios and
Special Deposits', *BEQB* (Sep 1971) supplement.

13　Ibid.

14　Deposits made would bear interest at a rate equivalent to the Treasury
bill rate. Provision was made for the possibility of different rates of call
relating to overseas deposits.

15　Plus purchases of bills direct from the banks in the normal course of
money market management and any facilities which other members of
the discount market enjoyed at the Bank.

16　'Sykes Memorial Lecture', reprinted in *Competition and credit control*
(Bank of England, 1972) p. 19.

17　Initially, all base rates were set at the same level as Bank rate.

18　See 'Reserve ratios: further definitions', reprinted in *Competition and
credit control*, op. cit., p. 25; also 'Competition and Credit Control:
Further Developments', *BEQB* (Mar 1973) 54.

19　That is, non-call-money reserve assets and non-reserve asset outlets.

20　In one discount house it was said that a clearing banker, when tackled
on this point in the early days of the new conditions, had assured them
that for his own part he had always regarded his fixtures as callable!

21　In the same way, houses that had wholly-owned subsidiaries dealing as
brokers in the local authority market might have felt that the goodwill
they got from taking the bills at very fine rates would stand them in good
stead as far as the other side of their business was concerned.

22　This, of course, occurred prior to 1971 but under the new interest-rate
regime it was possible that the houses could find themselves 'locked in' to
heavier carrying losses.

23　Chief Cashier, Bank of England, in *Competition and credit control*, pp.
17–18.

24　By retaining the right to make outright purchases of stock of any maturity
at their own initiative the Bank could, on the other hand, implement an
easy money policy by means of expansionary open-market operations.

25　Chief Cashier, in *Competition and credit control*, p. 18.

26　'Reserve ratios: further definitions', reprinted in *Competition and credit
control*, p. 25.

27 See P. J. Lee, 'Implications for the discount market', *Competition and Credit Control: A Banking Revolution* (report of a one-day seminar organised by Gillett Brothers Discount Co. Ltd, Nov 1971) pp. 31–2. The report covers reactions to the new system given from a variety of viewpoints.

28 Apart from public-sector ratio requirements the amount of houses' business in C.D.s was limited by the extent of their conventional obligation to discount bills of exchange.

Chapter 14

1 The downward trend came to a halt in January as monetary conditions tightened with the inflow of revenue to the Exchequer.

2 With the introduction of Competition and Credit Control, banks lost interest in Treasury bills fairly rapidly, though the real decline seems to have begun in 1972.

3 Other business included an increase over the same period of dollar C.D.s from £39m to £108m. The total outstanding in the market rose from £1650m (equivalent) at the end of 1970 to £1856m (equivalent) at the end of 1971. Dollar C.D. issues by London clearing banks began in February 1972.

4 The special arrangements made by the authorities to meet the banks' liquidity crisis are dealt with below.

5 These would be made with the approval of the Chancellor and announced at midday on a Thursday. Only when market rates had adjusted would the minimum lending rate formula be reapplied. In fact the Bank used its powers on Tuesday 13 November 1973 when the rate was increased from $11\frac{1}{4}$ per cent to 13 per cent.

6 A paradoxical result was produced in that the shorter money became, the more the houses had to bid up for bills to replace the ones that had been bought off them as part of the Bank of England 'help' operations. This in turn reduced the rate on Treasury bills and, consequently, the minimum lending rate. In other words, the Bank had produced a scheme under which the shorter money became, the lower minimum lending rate fell!

7 Induced by official policy pronouncements.

8 Banks were encouraged to keep base rates strictly in line with parallel market rates so as to minimise the recycling of overdraft funds.

9 This enabled them to make their deposit rates more competitive.

10 Following substantial growth in the previous year.

11 Loans from the London and Scottish clearing banks rose from 36 per cent to 50 per cent while those from other deposit banks, accepting houses, overseas banks, other banks and other sources, fell from 64 per cent to about 50 per cent.

12 Offers were as low as £60m.

13 P. J. Lee (Union Discount Co. of London Ltd), 'What has happened to the money market?', *Competition and Credit Control . . . one year on* (report of a one-day seminar arranged by Gillett Brothers Discount Co. Ltd, 5 Dec 1972) pp. 30–1. *Note:* when he refers to the 'Government broker' in the quotation, P. J. Lee means the 'Bank of England's broker', or the 'special buyer' as he has been termed throughout this book.

14 It should, of course, be borne in mind that discount houses deal only at the short end of the maturity spectrum.

15 The falls took place right across the maturity spectrum and apart from the very short-dated, shorts sometimes fell faster than longs. See N. F. Althaus, 'The gilt edge market: where is the market now?', *Competition and Credit Control ... one year on*, op. cit., pp. 13–14.

16 For details, see *BEQB* (June 1972) 169; (Sep 1972) 309–12.

17 The technique employed by the Bank to give aid to the gilt-edged market, the 'sale and repurchase agreement', was one long familiar in the United States. In Britain it would be called a 'loan against securities', although at the time the equivalence of the two devices was not appreciated in London.

18 There were also four very small firms.

19 The ratio was well above the minimum until mid-June but came under pressure during the currency crisis and fell to 53 per cent in July. Subsequently it recovered, to nearly 60 per cent in September, but was only 52 per cent in February 1973.

20 Lee, *Competition and Credit Control ... one year on*, op. cit., p. 32. As a result of the June 1972 crisis, the premium for ineligible bills over eligible bills increased and some of the old-established overseas banks in London were beginning to consider the possibility of giving up their acceptance business because of the cost involved in getting their bills discounted. In the case of some large American banks there had been a complete switch from acceptance business into direct lending to customers.

21 In fact, some nationalised industries' trade bills could count as public-sector paper, in the unlikely event of their being used to finance exports.

22 Holdings of dollar C.D.s lost £1m over the year, from £113m at 19 April 1972 to £112m at 18 April 1973, although they fluctuated slightly and reached a peak of £147m at 17 January.

23 *BEQB* (Dec 1972, June 1973) Table 11.

24 See D. C. Rowan, 'The Monetary System in the Fifties and Sixties', *Manchester School* (Mar 1973), for a cogent analysis of this question.

25 Text of an address by the Governor of the Bank of England to the International Banking Conference in Munich, May 1971, reprinted in *BEQB* (June 1971).

26 The 'New View' can be traced back to J. G. Gurley and E. S. Shaw's 'Financial Aspects of Economic Development', *American Economic Review* (1955). It was developed in their *Money in a Theory of Finance* (Washington, D.C., 1960) and by J. Tobin, 'Commercial Banks as Creators of Money', *Banking and Monetary Studies*, ed. Deane Carson (Homewood, Ill., 1963).

27 J. H. Gutentag and R. Lindsay, 'The Uniqueness of Commercial Banks', *Journal of Political Economy* (1968).

28 The growth of financial intermediaries outside the scope of official controls in the 1950s and 1960s was dealt with in Chapter 11, above.

29 See R. L. Harrington, 'The Importance of Competition for Credit Control', *Issues in Monetary Economics*, ed. H. G. Johnson and A. R. Nobay (Oxford, 1974) pp. 548–66.

30 A minimum proportion of collateral was to be in the form of Treasury bills. Normal 'smoothing' purchases of bills from the houses and banks would continue to be made.

31 The loans would normally be for one week and rates would take into account the cost of the houses' borrowing and yields on their assets: they

would give the houses a limited time in which they might respond more flexibly to temporary shortages of money in the market.

32 *BEQB* (Sep 1972) 322.

33 It is assumed that available public-sector and reserve ratio assets would have been switched between discount houses and banks until optimally placed.

34 That is, if the funds were attracted out of the public sector the government would be forced to create reserve assets by borrowing more from the banking system. Similarly, if the deposits came from overseas residents (i.e. foreign currency reserves rose), the government would have to increase the supply of market Treasury bills to compensate for the loss of sterling funds.

35 Using published monthly data, it can be shown that over the half year from April 1972, when pressures on the banking system began, the banks' reserve ratio showed great stability compared with the instability of the discount houses' public-sector ratio. The inference would be that the discount houses played a buffer role. When the monthly change in the total of the banks' reserve assets was compared with the change in their call money and the difference compared with the change in the public-sector ratio of the discount houses, it was found that on all five occasions when the banks increased call money to the discount market relative to total reserve assets, the houses' public-sector ratio suffered a corresponding decline. See G. T. Pepper, 'Credit Control and the Pattern of Short Term Interest Rates' (London, Nov 1972), mimeo, for an exhaustive analysis of the processes sketched in these paragraphs.

36 See also M. Parkin, 'The Discount Houses' Role in the Money Supply Process under the "Competition and Credit Control" Regime', *Manchester School* (Mar 1973) 89–105, which provides an empirically based analysis of the role of call money in frustrating the authorities' attempts to exercise control over the supply of credit.

Chapter 15

1 *BEQB* (Sep 1973) 306–7. Comparable changes were made in respect of operators in the discount market outside the L.D.M.A.

2 The differentials acted as an inducement to houses to increase their holdings of the higher-yielding assets and so extend more credit to the private sector at times when they were not under immediate pressure from their ratios.

3 The figure for resources to be calculated as a three-year moving average.

4 'Usually to the extent that there will not be room within their overall limits for them to hold other assets amounting to twenty times their resources.'

5 Because of low offers at the weekly tender, attempts to maintain public-sector ratios by bidding up for Treasury bills brought downward pressure on the Treasury bill rate, at a time when the authorities were looking for an increase.

6 At 20 November 1974 holdings had fallen to only £9m.

7 The Bank's figures relate to the discount houses, discount brokers and the money trading departments of certain banks.

8 Also, operations in support of over-committed secondary banks could be seen as a very peripheral infringement.

9 Explained in *BEQB* (Mar 1974) 37–9.
10 For an excess of 1 per cent or less the rate would be 5 per cent of the excess; between 1 per cent and 3 per cent it would be 25 per cent and thereafter 50 per cent.
11 *BEQB* (Mar 1974) 38.
12 For a more detailed treatment of these points, see *Midland Bank Review* (Aug 1974) 11–18.
13 From Table 3 it can be seen that the shift in relative importance of sources of borrowed funds away from the London clearers (see previous chapter) was maintained down to December 1974.
14 The effect of using radio communication, in addition to the high-speed telephone systems and closed-circuit television, should be to make markets more perfect, more competitive and therefore more efficient.
15 When quoting a buying rate for a C.D. a house will take into account, apart from the usual dealing criteria, its credit limit for the issuing bank – a C.D. being an unsecured debt bearing a single name. Quotations for purchases and sales are made on a yield-to-maturity basis.
16 More than 140 banks held the specific authorisation of the Bank.
17 Alexanders, Allen, Harvey and Ross, Cater Ryder, Clive Discount, Gilletts, Jessel Toynbee, King and Shaxson, Smith St Aubyn, Union Discount.
18 R. J. Truptil, *British Banks and the London Money Market* (London, 1936) pp. 112–13. There were also eight firms of running brokers.
19 Clive Discount had merged with a firm of running brokers, Burn and Peace, in 1958.
20 Later in the same year a number of houses obtained exchange control permission to act as principals in the secondary market in dollar C.D.s.
21 See for example the *Radcliffe Report*, paras 163, 180; W. T. C. King, 'The Market's Changing Role', *The London Discount Market Today* (London, 1969) pp. 12–18; W. M. Scammell, *The London Discount Market* (London, 1968) pp. 108–12; E. R. Shaw, *The London Money Market* (London, 1975) pp. 167–9.

Index

References to sources and suggestions for further reading can be found in the Notes. Authorities referred to in the Index are those which are discussed in the text.